T0006364

ALSO BY ALEC ROSS

The Industries of the Future

THE RAGING 2020s

THE RAGING 2020s

COMPANIES, COUNTRIES, PEOPLE—AND THE FIGHT FOR OUR FUTURE

ALEC ROSS

Henry Holt and Company
New York

Henry Holt and Company
Publishers since 1866
120 Broadway
New York, NY 10271
www.henryholt.com

Henry Holt® and Ⓗ® are registered trademarks of
Macmillan Publishing Group, LLC.

Distributed in Canada by Raincoast Book Distribution Limited

Library of Congress Cataloging-in-Publication Data

Names: Ross, Alec, 1971– author.
Title: The raging 2020s : companies, countries, people—and the fight for our future / Alec Ross.
Description: First edition. | New York : Henry Holt and Company, 2021. | Includes bibliographical references and index.
Identifiers: LCCN 2021021336 (print) | LCCN 2021021337 (ebook) | ISBN 9781250770929 (hardcover) | ISBN 9781250770936 (ebook)
Subjects: LCSH: Corporate power—United States. | Business and politics—United States. | Corporations—Political activity—United States. | United States—Economic conditions—2009–
Classification: LCC HD2785 .R59 2021 (print) | LCC HD2785 (ebook) | DDC 322/.30973—dc23
LC record available at https://lccn.loc.gov/2021021336
LC ebook record available at https://lccn.loc.gov/2021021337

Our books may be purchased in bulk for promotional, educational, or business use. Please contact your local bookseller or the Macmillan Corporate and Premium Sales Department at (800) 221-7945, extension 5442, or by e-mail at MacmillanSpecialMarkets@macmillan.com.

First Edition 2021

Designed by Kelly S. Too

Printed in the United States of America

1 3 5 7 9 10 8 6 4 2

To my children Colton, Tehle, and Sawyer,
whose adulthoods will be shaped by the choices
we make during the raging 2020s

CONTENTS

THE RAGING 2020s

INTRODUCTION

The first thing I do this morning is make coffee. I roll out of bed, brew a pot, and make breakfast for the kids. I'm leaving for a business trip today, so I pack my overnight bag and book a rideshare to the airport. My wife, Felicity, and I wrangle the kids into the car and Felicity drops them off at school on her way to the elementary school where she teaches. As everyone starts their day, I'm passing through security. "Now boarding," "fasten your seat belts," and "prepare for takeoff." By 9 a.m., I'm in the air.

It is an uneventful morning. But when you peel back its layers and examine the invention and ingenuity that power our daily lives, it can boggle the mind. In less than three hours, I went from sleeping in my bed to flying across the country—soaring thousands of feet in the air in an insulated metal tube. It is a feat of science, technology, engineering, and mathematics that humans in most previous eras would have considered something like sorcery. Yet I sit here unfazed, scrolling through emails.

We hardly notice it, but our lives are built atop a webwork of collaboration and exchange between individuals, governments, and businesses. When it all works in concert, we end up with a kind of everyday magic: life made easier by a thousand tricks just outside our vision.

Rewind to that coffeepot, for example. Or even to the water. The drinking water that pours out of my faucet and into my coffeepot is provided by a public water system built all the way back in the 1920s that ensures it is safe. The coffee I bought from Zeke's, my local roastery, costs me less than thirty cents a cup to make. The fact that I can have what was once a luxury at a favorable price every day is the result of centuries of agricultural progress, topped by free trade agreements with the Central American countries that produce the beans.

Or consider all the factors that go into a simple commute. When my wife steps out the door, she drives our kids to school in a Honda designed in Japan and manufactured in Alabama, on roads built by government, using rules that have been refined over decades to keep everybody from driving into each other. If they do get in an accident, we can trust in the government-mandated airbags that Honda installed.

Meanwhile, as I use a rideshare app for the drive to the airport, the driver finds me and navigates us using government-created GPS. And at the airport, I am as cool as the other side of the pillow because I know the Transportation Safety Administration (TSA) will ensure that no guns or knives will be brought on the plane. The barcode technology used by the TSA on my boarding pass and driver's license was developed by government-funded university research.

I board a plane that is Boeing's state of the art, managed by one of America's four remaining major airlines, and flown by a pilot who the Federal Aviation Administration ensures is rigorously trained. That pilot will fly through traffic-controlled skies monitored by government radar, navigating away from storms monitored by the US weather system.

Before we take off, I text Felicity using a mobile phone made by Apple over a network managed by AT&T over cellular frequencies administered by the Federal Communications Commission. The touchscreen technology that allows me to use LinkedIn, Instagram, Otter, and half a dozen other apps on my phone before we take off was developed thanks to the CIA and America's National Science Foundation. And, when I check the time—now 9:15 a.m.—I know that it's accurate due to time standards set by an international body with 164 country members.

This invisible, silent interplay between government, business, and citizens continues to take place all day, every day. It's a quiet equilibrium. We do not consciously sit there and think of all that goes into the delicate balance by which the government builds systems and sets standards, which enable businesses to build and sell goods, and which allow everyday individuals to chart easier and better lives. At least, ideally that's how it should work.

But in the last twenty years, the equilibrium has been thrown off.

Look closer at that coffeepot. The same free trade agreements that benefit me, my local coffee roaster, and billions of workers in the developing world have provided shocks to the working class in Western developed economies. The result has been political unrest on both ends of the political spectrum in the United States and Europe.

The water system built in the 1920s is crumbling. Somehow, we were able to commit to huge public works programs one hundred years ago, but we do not build bridges, rail lines, or new utility systems anymore. We work them until they crumble, and then we patch them up again. The number of new infrastructure projects in the US is at a historic low, not for lack of need but because the political process has ground to a halt.

Felicity's car was built in Alabama because of the state's tax giveaways and anti-union laws. The workers ended up losing out while the benefits accrue only to shareholders. Meanwhile, the car's airbags had to be replaced after a defect was found to have led to at least sixteen deaths.

My children's public schools are overcrowded and underresourced. My son wears a winter coat in class because the school's heating system does not work. Racial tensions smolder and flare.

The rideshare app I used on the drive to the airport was founded on the crest of a glistening new wave of American innovation. But its founder proved to be the very caricature of the brotastic boy billionaire, kicked out of his own company for its misogynistic culture. And the driver is working on terms that seem more 19th century than 21st—she makes near minimum wage, with zero worker protections or benefits because her employment status classifies her as an independent contractor.

Boeing and the airline I'm flying recently received massive government bailouts despite the airlines having generated more than $49 billion in free cash flow during the previous decade. The reason they were not able to tap that $49 billion once trouble hit was not because they had been in investing in new planes, better service, or better salaries for their workers. No, they had spent $47 billion of that $49 billion on stock buybacks. Boeing spent $43 billion of its $58 billion in free cash flow during that period on stock repurchases, despite the need for investment to make its planes safer. These stock repurchases did nothing for passengers or employees; they just fluffed up the stock for investors, and as soon as trouble hit, taxpayers bailed them out. This is corporate socialism for the 2020s: we socialize costs to taxpayers and privatize gains to shareholders.

This interplay goes on all day, every day. There is something fundamentally off, a disequilibrium in the relationships between business, the governing, and the governed.

Our social contract is broken and needs to be repaired.

WHAT MAKES SOCIETY WORK

The social contract is one of the most basic features of human civilization. In every society across the world, people have worked for thousands of years to balance the rights and responsibilities of individuals with those of larger powers like states and corporations. The social contract is the accord that sets the balance. It defines the rights of citizens, governments, and businesses, as well as the duties they owe to one another.

The exact terms of the social contract are never set in stone, because it encompasses both the laws of a society and its unwritten rules. But the basic idea is simple: when humanity can come together and live and work as part of a society, we are vastly better than the sum of our parts.

The prospects of ancient humans skyrocketed when they learned to work together to hunt a mammoth or settle down to plant a field of grain. But when people gather en masse, it also presents an opening to our species' crueler impulses. Those bands of early humans could only ever live and thrive in close quarters if they agreed that certain behaviors—like murder and theft—were unacceptable. They had to figure out a basic code of conduct and draw a line between what people *could* do and what they *should* do.

That moral code is the kernel of a social contract—and it is the glue for any functioning society, past or present. It is what summons up humanity at its best, while leaving our worst at the door.

With simple versions of that code in place, humanity developed. Scattered villages grew into city-states and modern nations. Governments emerged. Churches and academies put down roots. Guilds and businesses sprang up. These were entirely new and powerful ways of organizing humanity's efforts—but they too could channel either our angels or our demons. So, as life grew more complex, the underlying code of conduct had to adapt. It had to enfold not just individuals but also all the newly established powers of society.

Every social contract is also constantly being tested and renegotiated by its various parties. Often, this change is slow and steady, nearly invisible and almost self-correcting. When a society-shaking technology emerges, governments and businesses adapt. But sometimes corrections are too few and far between. Sometimes there is a long pause, where the equilibrium tips and groans with nothing to right it. Until it topples, and the world flips upside down. That then produces rage—rage that can divide families, communities, and countries against each other; rage that can produce body counts until systems and governments change for those brought to rage by the disequilibrium. The absence or presence of rage is a product of a well-managed or a broken social contract.

The choices about what to do in moments of inflection and often revolution can take societies in totally different directions. This was the case in the 1930s when the United States rewrote its social contract with Franklin Roosevelt's New Deal, while Germany and Italy were overtaken by fascism.

THE ORIGINS OF OUR OWN CONTRACT

Social contracts tend to be rewritten amid the moments of greatest change. During the 1800s, vast technological changes swept through much of the world, drastically altering the structure of society. It was this shift that sparked the social contract that still, in one form or another, predominates in the world's developed nations.

In 1800, nearly 75 percent of Americans worked on farms, but then the Industrial Revolution hit. By 1900, this figure was cut in half. During that same period, the portion of American manufacturing workers increased more than sevenfold. In 1801, about 17 percent of the population in England and Wales lived in urban areas. By 1891, the figure had more than tripled. French and German cities also saw their populations explode during the 19th century. This period saw Western economies transform from predominantly agricultural to industrial, and labor moved from farm to factory.

It was a messy transition, particularly in the early years of industrialization, before the social contract had adapted at all. This period, known as Engels' Pause (named after Marxist philosopher Friedrich Engels), introduced the industrialization, inequality, and squalor you see in Charles Dickens novels. It was a period of stagnant living standards in the face of rapid technological change. Its by-products included ideological movements like Marxism and the largest wave of revolutions in Europe's history.

The only thing that made industrialization work was that, over a period of decades, industrial societies completely rewrote their social contracts. Ask anyone to name the great innovations in human history and the answers will likely be technologies like the wheel, clock, steam engine, or microprocessor. But just as significant as the technologies that reshaped the economy are the innovations that reshaped our humanity. These include worker pensions, free public education, and the minimum wage. All of these emerged from the tumult of industrialization in the 19th century. Workers and citizens mobilized to ensure that governments and rapidly expanding industrial businesses rewrote the social contract to allow industrialization to benefit more than just the owners of industry. As the 19th century ticked into the 20th, new checks and balances continued to emerge—antitrust protections, income tax, child-labor prevention, a social safety net, environmental standards. These revisions to the social contract allowed societies to harness rapid industrial innovation so that it could enable citizens to rise together.

A NEW SOCIAL CONTRACT

Out of the tumult of the Industrial Revolution, we developed a basic equilibrium among governments, people, and corporations. Companies now held the power to shape our daily lives in ways both positive and negative, while the state held the power to make them fall in line, and the people held the power to choose their leaders.

But in the 21st century, that balance has shaken loose through much of the Western world, and the damage is seeping into Asian and developing-world economies. A dizzying combination of factors has risen in recent decades to rattle the world—the digital revolution, globalization, deregulation, populism, the arrival of a global climate crisis. These have fundamentally reshaped the relationships between government, citizens, and business—within every country around the world and on the international playing field. But too many of our societies have not yet developed new social contracts to account for these massive changes.

The power of the state was the creeping concern of the original social contract theorists, but the chief power creep in our present day is the growing power of business. Today's global companies are as big as countries, and they act the part. This trend has already disrupted geopolitics, and it is set to continue. Meanwhile, on the home front, we are governed more by companies than by governments on a wide range of issues—from privacy to sustainability to equity and workers' rights.

Over the last fifty years, the United States and other developed governments have failed to make strides in these realms, and companies have filled the void. Meanwhile, anti-monopoly measures and checks on corporate power have fallen away. The results have been weaker labor movements, weaker democratic governments, and a cratering of economic prospects for hundreds of millions of workers. Over the last thirty years, just in the United States, the top 1 percent have grown $21 trillion richer, while the bottom 50 percent have grown $900 billion poorer and the middle class has stagnated. This trend is playing out across much of the Western world while the developing world is watching and taking notes.

If the level of inequality in the United States had stayed at a constant level over the last forty years instead of widening to its current *Mad Max*–like state, it would have meant that $50 trillion would have gone to workers earning below the 90th percentile. That is an additional $1,100 every single month for every single worker.

We are now in a sort of Engels' Pause for the information age. The social contract that had been successfully revised and rebalanced has fallen out of balance. And the future of the world now hinges on how that contract between business, government, and citizens is redrawn during the 2020s.

The goal of this book is to map out what went wrong, and then work out how to fix it. We will look back at what happened over the last half century to companies, governments, labor, and citizens around the world. We will look at how these changes have affected the global landscape and outcomes for everyone, rich and poor, in developing and developed countries. And we will then look forward, pinpointing the shifts that are necessary to return to balance.

For the past twenty-five years, I have worked intensively at the intersection of business and geopolitics, moving between the US Department of State, political campaigns, academia, and entrepreneurship. Over those decades I have worked all over the map and from top to bottom of each of these overlapping spheres. For this book, I spoke with many of the world's most prominent leaders in business and government, seeking to understand their unique perspectives on our past and future, and to compile them all into one larger story. The book will gallop from a board of directors in Arkansas that set environmental standards for the entire country to tax havens in the Caribbean, and from Zimbabwe's implementation of a Chinese-designed surveillance apparatus to the hills of my native West Virginia, where people are dying because they can't buy insulin. We will see how decisions in Beijing are roiling the political landscape in the heartlands of the Americas and Europe, and how all these issues that seem to have nothing to do with one another are inextricably linked, as are the solutions to make it all work better.

I'll bring forward different perspectives from a range of public thinkers and figures; my hope is that you agree with some and disagree with others—but that they help you think beyond our current crisis. I think that when two people agree about everything, only one person is doing the thinking.

For the first three chapters, I will dig into what has happened over the last fifty years to each of the three key pillars of the social contract—government, business, and citizens.

The first chapter looks at the rise in corporate power since the 1970s. Since then, the most destructive aspects of capitalism have been given free rein, as businesses embraced the dogma that shareholder value was the only metric that mattered. Five decades have revealed the brutal cost of that trend: even as companies have risen in power, those gains have not been felt by the vast majority of employees, communities, or other stakeholders. This chapter maps out the past half century's errors, examines their broader effects—both expected and unexpected—and suggests how we can change course. I'll connect the dots to show how we can avoid the worst excesses of capitalism and allow the world's largest companies to do what they are best at while actually benefiting the world.

The second chapter turns its attention to the state, and looks at how government power in developed countries has slumped as business has boomed in the last fifty years. I spoke with politicians and political scientists alike to offer a deep dive into the US government and ask why it has stopped functioning effectively. We weigh the impact of various factors—from polarization to brain drain to lobbying—and explore the changes that will need to happen within and without government to restore some sense of balance. The chapter ends with a spin of the globe, examining which factors are unique to America and which are common to other nations. We will also look at why authoritarian models are gaining ground on liberal democracies throughout the world, and what to do about it.

Chapter 3 takes up the third pillar of our traditional social contract—citizens and their labor. Just as the power of government has sagged in the 21st century, so has the power of organized labor and workers. This chapter maps out the recent history of labor's decline and explores why unions are at such a weak point in some places—including the United States and United Kingdom—and comparatively strong elsewhere. The same forces of shareholder capitalism that led to record profits also undermined labor, but this shift is compounded by the stagnancy of organized labor. I interviewed some of the world's biggest union leaders as well as founders of upstart labor movements to understand a single, simple question: What does the labor movement of the 21st century look like?

Companies, governments, and citizens make up the three core parties of our social contract and the first three chapters of the book. Each tells the broader story of why these pillars have started to buckle, and how each will need to adapt to meet the needs of the 2020s and 2030s. But these three chapters stay largely within the confines of national borders, asking how each of the world's 196 countries can build a better social contract for themselves. However, the reality of our world is that many of its biggest concerns are now global; they do not stick within national borders, and instead tend to metastasize in the gaps between countries. Climate change, human rights abuses, tax evasion, cyber war, economic crises, pandemics—all of these are issues that affect people the world over and demand international responses. Any social contract for our new world needs to include means for addressing these issues and reaching beyond borders in a way that the industrial-age contract did not need to.

So the second half of the book turns to the nature of these international issues. Chapter 4 zeroes in on the subject of taxes. It is a skeleton key for understanding the limits of our global politics and economy, and the problems that emerge out of using a 20th-century set of policies to solve 21st-century problems. Of the people reading this book, 99 percent would pay less in taxes, and our governments would have more to spend, if we fixed a system where trillions of dollars in tax goes missing each year and entire nations have been captured by outside interests. Tax serves as a microcosm for many of the global issues whereby governments are divided and conquered. I talked with experts on tax havens, government officials, and bankers—all of whom have seen the ins and outs of this shadow system. We will look at what governments need to do on the global stage to solve not just the problem of tax avoidance, but also other global coordination problems such as climate change.

Chapter 5 offers a category of problem that might well be new to the 21st century. While tax avoidance serves as an example of an international problem that only governments can fix, there are other issues on the global stage on which governments are hopelessly divided or stagnant and where we will need to see companies and citizens lead. This is a controversial idea, and we will unpack that in this chapter. But there are some hotly contested issues—on subjects including data, artificial intelligence, privacy, and cyber war—where it is dangerous to give too much power to governments alone. When it comes to the weaponization of code, the private sector in the 21st century is capable of leading and providing a stabilizing force in the global social contract. Chapter 5 focuses on the race for technology dominance between China and the United States, and the two drastically different models they present for how data should be used in society. China has completely aligned its corporate sector and government, channeling both toward a stifling surveillance state. But for the sake of citizens' privacy, and as a check on government overreach, it is possible for companies to provide an important buffer between government and citizens. For this to work out, a range of checks and balances is needed—but one of the new aspects of the social contract of the 2020s and beyond is that we are unlikely to solve some of the most contested issues in the world without leadership from the corporate sector.

In chapter 6 and the conclusion, we will begin to bring all the pieces of a working social contract together. We will have seen all the gaps and tears in that fabric, and we will look at the ways in which they can be rewoven to create a more balanced system. Chapter 6 offers a tour of the many styles of safety nets that exist across the globe. It picks out the most useful features and innovations that the world's 196 countries have to offer, while also identifying some of the most worrying or fragile developments in social policy. By looking all around the world, we can start to get a sense of what an ideal social contract for our future looks like.

There have been many books devoted to each of the trends described in this book individually, but it is still hard to wrap one's head around the biggest of them and see how they are all interconnected. It is harder still to imagine solutions that would begin to right the balance. But that is the goal of this book. In order for government to deliver more effectively for its citizens, we need to fill the resource gap created by tax avoidance; for tax systems to work effectively, we need to kill off the worst practices of shareholder capitalism; to improve our capitalism, we need labor to have much more power than it does today; and on and on. It is all interconnected.

The aim is simple: the 2020s have begun with citizens and systems raging, and to start the world spinning smoothly again we need acts of creation greater than the acts of destruction taking place around us.

1

SHAREHOLDER AND STAKEHOLDER CAPITALISM

Gabriella Corley was seven years old when the family pediatrician diagnosed her with Type 1 diabetes. Like 1.6 million Americans, her body did not produce enough insulin, the hormone responsible for maintaining proper glucose levels in our blood. For most of human history, the condition has been a death sentence—sooner or later an unregulated spike in blood sugar would have sent her into ketoacidosis, which would have led to a coma and eventually death. But luckily, Gabriella's diagnosis came in 2014.

Nearly a century earlier, a trio of scientists at the University of Toronto discovered a method for extracting insulin from the pancreases of cows. In 1922, a fourteen-year-old boy named Leonard Thompson became their first patient. As Leonard lay dying in a bed at Toronto General Hospital, the scientists injected him with their insulin solution. Within hours, his blood sugar levels had returned to normal. Soon after, the trio visited one of the large wards where the hospitals kept children dying from ketoacidosis. They went from bed to bed injecting patients with insulin. By the time they reached the final patients, the first few had already started to wake from their comas, their families rejoicing around them. As a parent, I imagine it felt like witnessing a miracle.

Back then, most people with Type 1 diabetes died within two years of their diagnosis. Insulin gave them a new lease on life. Realizing the implications of their discovery, the three scientists—Frederick Banting, Charles Best, and James Collip—sold the patent for insulin to the University of Toronto. The price of their miracle drug: three Canadian dollars (roughly thirty-two 2020 US dollars), split three ways. As a reward for discovering insulin, Banting, Best, and Collip got to treat themselves to lunch.

Even their small sale was controversial—at the time, many considered it inappropriate for scientists and universities to patent medical innovations at all. The University of Toronto ultimately let pharmaceutical companies start manufacturing insulin royalty-free. In 1950, George W. Merck, president of Merck at the time, delivered a speech in which he famously said, "We try never to forget that medicine is for the people. It is not for the profits." A century later, this mindset and approach is largely nonexistent.

Today, three different pharmaceutical companies sell insulin, which comes in the form of fast-acting or slow-acting formulas, through pumps or pens. Instead of using their market power to make the drug more affordable for diabetics, the companies have leveraged their clout to increase their profit margins.

Andrea Corley, Gabriella's mom, works as an administrative assistant and her husband as a janitor, both for the public school district in Elkins, West Virginia, not far from where I grew up. Together, they make approximately $60,000 a year. Their health insurance is provided by the West Virginia Public Employees Insurance Agency. When Gabriella first got her diagnosis, the Corleys' health plan covered all her supplies, Andrea told me. But after the first year, co-payments for Gabriella's insulin prescription increased to around twenty-five dollars a month. The family joined a program that covered the payments as long as Gabriella regularly met with a pharmacist, but their insurance company capped the coverage at two years. As Andrea noted, Type 1 diabetes does not go away after two years. "It's not something that she can fix. It's not something she can reverse. She's stuck with it the rest of her life."

Then the Corleys discovered that Gabriella was allergic to an ingredient in her medication. She switched to a different brand of insulin, but the insurance provider informed the family that it would cover only 20 percent of the cost. That left the Corleys paying $300 per month out of their pocket, not including the cost of pumps and other supplies. Their doctor also recommended they keep an EpiPen at the house just in case Gabriella developed another serious allergic reaction. That added another $200 to the cost of keeping their daughter alive.

This scenario would be unimaginable in many parts of the world. Dozens of countries provide universal health care to their citizens. The quality of care varies widely, but everyone can get it. Among the world's most developed countries, the vast majority of governments provide universal or near-universal health coverage to their citizens. Two countries—Switzerland and the Netherlands—offer universal coverage through a heavily regulated and subsidized market of non-profit providers. In others, like Germany and Chile, a small portion of the population pays for private insurance while the rest are covered by government plans.

The US government provides health insurance for the elderly and the poor through the Medicare and Medicaid programs. The 2010 Affordable Care Act expanded Medicaid, but enrollees still needed to pay hundreds of dollars per year. While the developed world embraces health care as a human right, the United States instead relies on the market to care for many of its citizens. Approximately three in five Americans receive their health care through private insurance companies. As we will see, when decisions of life and death are left to the market, people do not always get the best results.

Eventually, the Corley family was able to secure affordable insulin and EpiPens only through a special program at their pharmacy, a program that kicked in after the family's insurance dropped its coverage of the drugs. This gave them a narrow window of affordability within a convoluted system, but it could still close at any time. And even with the savings program, even with insurance, the Corley family still spends between $14,000 and $18,000 on health care every year. Andrea Corley said that even as they struggle to keep up, she fears for the future. Insulin prices are rising rapidly, and Gabriella, now twelve years old, may not be able to afford the medication when she grows up.

"I'm afraid that by the time she gets old enough to get her own, that she won't even be able to," Andrea said. Her fear is not unfounded. When adults lose coverage and cannot afford their own diabetes medication, they discover just how brutal the American health care system can get.

In 2017, Alec Smith decided to move out of his childhood home in Minneapolis and get his own apartment. He was almost twenty-six years old, the age when young adults in the US can no longer be covered by their parents' health insurance. This transition would be complicated, considering he had been diagnosed with Type 1 diabetes two years earlier.

Alec had planned to become a paramedic, but with his disease, that was not an option. He took a job managing a restaurant—his new plan was to open his own sports bar. In the meantime, however, his job did not provide insurance. When Alec's mother, Nicole Smith-Holt, started to research different health care plans available to her son, she was stunned. He would need to pay more than $400 per month, and insurance would kick in only after he had paid $8,000 out of his own pocket. Alec made less than $40,000 per year, meaning more than a third of his income would go to health care. Ultimately, Alec decided to forgo insurance and pay for his insulin out of pocket. Neither he nor his mother realized the cost of that choice.

More than 90 percent of the insulin market is controlled by three companies: Denmark's Novo Nordisk, France's Sanofi-Aventis, and Eli Lilly and Company in the United States. Despite the appearance of competition, numerous lawsuits have alleged that the trio operate as a cartel to keep the price of insulin artificially high. On more than a dozen occasions, the companies raised the price of their drugs in near lockstep. In 2001, a vial of insulin cost an average of $14. In 2019, that same vial cost $275. Across the United States, the scarcity of affordable insulin has had dramatic effects. Insulin thefts—from pharmacies or even people's doorsteps—have been on the rise in recent years. And nearly a century after insulin's inventors brought children back from the brink of death, data suggests that people are once again dying because they cannot access the drug. A Yale University study found that a quarter of diabetics in the United States used less insulin than they were prescribed due to its cost. Between 2017 and 2019, researchers found, thirteen people died after rationing their insulin.

One of them was Alec Smith. After talking with Alec's girlfriend, the coroner, and the detective, his mother Nicole realized he had been holding out on buying his medication until his next paycheck. Initially, Nicole said she was angry at Alec for not asking his parents for help. She was also angry at herself for failing to recognize the warning signs. It was not until she went public with her story that she realized Alec's experience was not unique. Other people began to write to her, describing loved ones in their midtwenties managing diabetes diagnoses, trying to support themselves for the first time as young adults and paying for their newfound independence with their lives.

Like Alec, Jesy Boyd was living in an apartment on his own for the first time while managing his Type 1 diabetes. Since Jesy was only twenty years old when he moved out, he was able to stay on his family's insurance. Still, he paid for the cost of the medication with his own job as a restaurant manager. "He was trying to manage everything on his own," said Jesy's mother, Cindy Scherer Boyd.

Cindy realized Jesy was struggling to pay for his insulin in the spring of 2019. He had asked his parents to pick up his insulin prescription and bring it to his apartment. When they got there, they found Jesy incoherent. They took him to the hospital, where he was treated for a blood sugar spike and released. Jesy assured his parents that he would never let his supply get so low again.

But the following month, Cindy heard that Jesy had called in sick to work. She tried calling him, but he did not answer. Cindy hurried to his apartment with a friend, where they found Jesy dead. In his backpack was an application for an electrician job. In the obituary, the family wrote that Jesy had died from complications from Type 1 diabetes. Not long after, Cindy received a message from Nicole Smith-Holt, asking if Jesy had been rationing his insulin.

Nicole, whose previous political activism had been limited to voting, became an outspoken advocate following her son's death, and she recruited other parents to join the fight. In 2019, she helped organize a demonstration outside Eli Lilly's Indianapolis headquarters, protesting the high cost of insulin. Nicole stood in the middle of the street, blocking traffic and reading off the names of people who had died after rationing their insulin. Among them were her son and Jesy. She was eventually arrested.

Nicole and her husband, James, worked to get the Minnesota legislature to pass a law that limited insulin co-pays to thirty-five dollars if an uninsured patient's supply was running low. The Alec Smith Emergency Insulin Act was passed in April 2020. It was a victory, but Nicole knows that state-level reforms will not fix the underlying system that lets medicine like insulin and EpiPens get so expensive.

"Pharmaceutical companies can get away with it because we don't have any laws in place that restrict them or prohibit them from raising the price to whatever they feel the market will bear," Nicole said. "When you're presented with a pay-or-die situation, typically somebody is going to go with, 'I'm going to pay it, and I'm going to do whatever I have to do to pay for it.' Just because the companies can, they do."

This point is worth stressing. The state of the insulin industry is a far cry from the three-dollar patent sale a century ago, or even the postwar era when George Merck could say "medicine is for the people . . . not for the profits." The drastic contrast is representative of a broader change that swept through the entire business world in the last half century. The power and size of companies have skyrocketed since the mid-20th century, as has their influence on our everyday lives. This is true within the United States and the world as a whole. The world's major companies have grown larger, more concentrated, and more profit-motivated, while governments and individuals have seen their power fade. The balance has been shaken so thoroughly that in recent years even business leaders, who are benefiting massively from the state of affairs, lament the power they have rapidly gained.

The last fifty years have witnessed a quiet reimagining of what companies are for and how they operate. But what brought us to this point?

THE HISTORY OF the social contract is a story of power and how it redistributes over time. Throughout history, the rights and responsibilities of capital, labor, and the state have been mostly determined by whichever group possesses the most power and is able to set the terms without overplaying its hand to the point of creating unrest or revolution. In the agricultural societies of the past, sovereign rulers exercised near-absolute authority over their lords and the peasantry and their economic lives. During the Industrial Revolution, the scales tipped toward the wealthy and politically connected owners of capital. In the early 20th century, American and European workers reined in the power of corporations through labor unions and the ballot box. Today, power has concentrated in the private sector yet again.

What caused this shift? How have corporations amassed so much size and power over the last half century? If you want to understand the trigger point, you can look to a single idea, a single sentence even.

After the calamities of the Great Depression and World War II, the economy began to boom throughout the United States and Europe. But strong checks were placed on it by both organized labor and government regulators, who were all too familiar with the cost of monopolies and stock-market crises. In this context, the vast majority of businesses saw themselves as fitting within a clear niche in society. Companies were expected to turn a profit while also working to improve the well-being of their employees, support the communities where they did business, and generally serve the public good.

Yet not everyone thought this model was sensible. In 1962, in his book *Capitalism and Freedom*, economist Milton Friedman wrote,

"There is one and only one social responsibility of business—to use its resources and engage in activities designed to increase its profits so long as it stays within the rules of the game."

This idea marked a dramatic departure from the existing social contract—a world where a lifesaving patent was sold for a few dollars and where George Merck could speak of profit as a secondary motive for doing business. But in Friedman's eyes, such decisions were inefficiencies, flaws in the market. And according to the theories of Friedman and his colleagues at the University of Chicago, the world would benefit several times over if every individual pursued maximum profit and then reinvested the gains. In Friedman's view, a company's only loyalty was to its shareholders, and any leadership decision that kept a dollar out of shareholders' pockets was mismanagement. In time, this profit-optimizing philosophy would come to be known as shareholder primacy.

The idea did not catch on right away. But it began resonating with a core group of supporters in the 1970s, when the booming postwar economy began to stagnate. Economists pointed to government regulation and inefficient management as the problems, and discontent opened the door for Friedman's ideas to circulate. Then, in the 1980s, his philosophy hit the mainstream. Shareholder primacy melded perfectly with the Reagan and Thatcher eras, providing an intellectual cornerstone for deregulation and trickle-down economics. Soon, clear opposition to the New Deal–era checks on corporate power emerged. These critics argued that government had kept a lid on business for too long: managers of big businesses had grown complacent and had stopped driving profits, and the whole economy was stagnating as a result. If companies were turbocharged to maximize profits, it would jolt the whole country and the whole world into growth. To get there, all you had to do was prioritize profit. A pithier version of Friedman's big idea soon swept through the culture, expressed by Gordon Gekko in Oliver Stone's *Wall Street*: "Greed is good."

The effect of shareholder primacy was to drive a stark line between a company's shareholders and its stakeholders, defined as every other party affected by its business and including its employees, its community, its country, its customers, and the environment. Under the new model, shareholder profits came first and foremost, and any significant investment in other stakeholders became a liability.

The mid-1980s saw the rise of hostile takeovers and corporate raiders, who were in many respects the vanguard of shareholder primacy. They would identify distressed or stagnant companies and buy up equity until they gained control. Then they would reorganize every division toward maximizing returns to shareholders, rooting out any inefficiencies they could find. This often meant making job cuts, relocating headquarters, selling off real estate, and taking on loads of debt—using any tool in the arsenal for channeling assets toward generating a short-term return on investment. The prospect of a hostile takeover struck fear into the hearts of corporate leaders. And a series of legal decisions made it increasingly difficult to resist hostile takeovers, especially in cases where shareholders stood to turn a profit, which ultimately forced many companies to shift toward shareholder primacy just to avoid being a target for a sudden takeover bid.

Throughout the 1980s, mergers and acquisitions swept through the world's largest economies, aided by increasingly laissez-faire attitudes toward regulation and antitrust. The United States had been the world leader in antitrust, standing firmly against monopolies since the early 20th century, when it had launched hundreds of lawsuits against large corporations to break up Gilded Age monopolies like Standard Oil and U.S. Steel. In the aftermath of World War II, policy makers established a new wave of antitrust when the world saw how monopolies contributed to the rise of authoritarian regimes in Japan, Italy, and the Third Reich. During the drafting of new constitutions and laws around the world, the United States often encouraged (and, in the case of Japan, imposed) tough new antitrust laws. But in the 1970s, a new school of thought came to dominate the debate around monopoly and competition.

The newer theory, popularized by judge and legal scholar Robert Bork, held that economic concentration was a bad thing only if there was demonstrable harm in the form of higher prices to consumers. As long as monopolies charged fair prices, they were perfectly acceptable.

Bork's narrow interpretation of antitrust law aligned perfectly with the Friedman doctrine and the political atmosphere of the 1980s. Government watchdogs began to bring fewer suits against large companies, and Bork's theory became the prevailing basis for the government's approach to competition. All the while, the private sector grew steadily more consolidated through mergers and acquisitions. Like many people, I went through the experience of the local bank where I had an account being purchased by a larger regional bank, which was then purchased by a national bank, which then merged with another national bank. This happened across sectors of the economy.

In this same period, as we will explore further in the next chapter, companies also began to recognize the benefits of expanding their influence in Washington. Under Friedman's philosophy, businesses could maximize their profits as long as they followed the letter of the law. But through lobbying and unlimited political donations, companies could remake the boundaries by shaping the laws themselves, gaining outsized returns for relatively modest allocations of capital.

Each of these trends amplified the next, and the result has been a rapid expansion of corporate size and power since the 1970s. Shareholder primacy unleashed the ugliest face of capitalism. In theory, profit in the hands of shareholders would lead to the benefit of all, by increasing the overall efficiency of the economy and freeing up excess capital that would be reinvested in communities.

But in practice, it squeezed out other stakeholders like employees, local communities, and the environment. When the economy was booming in the decades after World War II, just about every medium-sized or larger city had a major corporate headquarters. Companies' executives sat on the local boards. They supported everything from after-school programs to local arts and sports programs. The children of the CEO went to the same schools as the children of middle managers. If a downturn hit, the company did not lay off employees as soon as a consultant or MBA determined it was balance-sheet optimal; they waited until the last possible moment because the company and community were inextricably tied, and each felt a responsibility to the other for the long term. This is how the social contract worked in a hyper-local context.

But once shareholder primacy emerged, the thinking changed. The 1980s wave of mergers and acquisitions led to widespread layoffs in smaller cities, the uprooting of corporate headquarters to tax-optimized locations, and whole local economies spiraling into freefall. I saw this where I grew up in Charleston, West Virginia, when all its banks, mining companies, and chemical companies were swallowed up by companies on the coasts. Shareholder capitalism meant that if an economic benefit was projected by moving the company's headquarters, a company that had spent decades growing alongside its community would now up and leave, or at least change where it was nominally headquartered and paying taxes. In the United States, this resulted in two-thirds of all job growth taking place in just twenty-five cities and counties; the same pattern took place in Europe.

FAST FORWARD TO the present, and we have seen the first part of Friedman's vision pan out: the world's largest companies have posted remarkable profits, and shareholders have seen enormous returns. But the second part—the promise that these profits would come back around and benefit everyone—never arrived. We have seen all the growth in the last few decades go to senior executives and shareholders, not to workers. We have seen money drain out of individual communities where robust local economies had existed, routing instead to financial hubs and shareholders. We have seen major centralization and—instead of the healthy competition promised—a new age of monopoly.

In 2019, the five hundred largest companies in the United States generated a combined $14.2 trillion in revenue, with nearly half coming from the country's fifty biggest firms. That year, the gross domestic product of the United States was $21.7 trillion. That means the five hundred largest firms in the country represented two-thirds of the country's total economic output. The top fifty accounted for a full third of national GDP. When the Fortune 500 list was first published in 1955, the fifty largest companies generated less than 16 percent of the country's economic output. At no time since the Great Depression have so few firms controlled so much of the wealth in the United States.

There are certain benefits that big companies bring to the table. Large firms can take advantage of economies of scale—the cost savings that come from doing commerce in bulk—which theoretically lead to lower prices for consumers. But more often than not, large companies tend to use their clout to entrench their own dominance. Thanks to their wealth and global distribution, these companies have access to resources that remain out of reach for their smaller competitors. Large firms can use the offshore financial system to optimize their tax bills. They can leverage global supply chains and labor markets to lower costs. They can wage effective influence campaigns to win over policy makers. They can weather price wars, raise barriers to entry, and buy out would-be rivals before they get off the ground. They have access to larger data sets that they can use to optimize against smaller rivals. They can create a feedback loop in which economic power begets more economic power. The rise of shareholder capitalism has incentivized firms toward larger and larger size. And by reinforcing their own dominance, large companies can make it almost impossible for other firms to compete.

The lifeblood of capitalism is competition. In the effort to outperform one another, firms are forced to respond to consumer demands, pursue more efficient operations, and pioneer new products. In a competitive market, consumers pay fair prices and companies earn fair profits. New firms strive to unseat the old guard or break into uncharted markets, and established companies aim to fend off rivals by investing in innovation. One of the reasons that socialist and communist economies stagnate and fail is the lack of dynamism in economies without competition. The notion that an ingenious entrepreneur or scrappy start-up can succeed by merit of their inspiration, perspiration, and persistence relies on the existence of competition.

If companies become too entrenched to topple, innovation and entrepreneurship stagnate. That is exactly what we are seeing today.

Not every multinational firm engages in anticompetitive practices, but when given the opportunity, shareholder capitalism compels them to. And the consequences can be severe. As we saw in the pharmaceutical industry, the lack of competition can end up costing lives. Author and activist Matt Stoller told me that this amounts to a "crime spree."

The concentration that we see in the insulin market is now the new normal for many other sectors of the economy as well. Four airlines—American, Delta, Southwest, and United—control the vast majority of domestic air travel in the United States. This consolidation has reduced service and increased ticket prices in small- and medium-sized cities and created de facto monopolies in hubs, where one airline dominates. Two telecommunications companies—AT&T and Verizon—provide cell service to nearly 70 percent of American mobile phone users. Charter Communications and the Comcast Corporation service four in five American cable subscribers. AB InBev and Molson Coors are responsible for more than 70 percent of beer sales in the United States. Google handles more than 90 percent of worldwide internet searches.

Matt Stoller's research has shown that market consolidation is also in niche industries like portable toilets, prison phone services, mixed martial arts leagues, board games, and cheerleading equipment. He told me that "it's simply a corrupt way to run a society. If you believe in corruption, which a lot of people seem to, subverting the public interest for private gain, then that's fine, works well. If you don't, then you should make sure that people are not subject to market power and it's all just structured by the state. Corporations are just grants of state power."

As the United States becomes a country of conglomerates, the effects of mass mergers and acquisitions on customers, employees, communities, and more can be seen vividly in a vast range of industries. One of the most striking places to look is where the American dream once rang loudest: the family farm.

Less than a ninety-minute drive from my home in Baltimore is the Delmarva Peninsula. A 170-mile-long comma separating the Chesapeake Bay and the Atlantic Ocean, the peninsula feels a world away from the knowledge-industry mania of the metropolitan East Coast. The landscape is flat and swampy, bordered by sleepy fishing villages and beach towns. Aside from tourism, the main driver of the Delmarva Peninsula's economy is agriculture, specifically poultry farming. In Delaware—one of the three states that claim part of the peninsula—there are more than two hundred chickens for every human being. Drive around the peninsula and you will see countless rows of stout, six-hundred-foot-long by sixty-foot-wide aluminum buildings, inside of which live tens of thousands of chickens. You will also see a growing number of chicken houses sitting rusted and abandoned. They are the detritus of a decades-long battle to raise the most birds at the lowest possible cost.

In the aftermath of massive farm failures during the Great Depression, the Roosevelt administration adopted policies that allowed small farmers to survive the sudden swings of food markets. If the price of meat, dairy, grain, or other crops suddenly fell, as happened in the Depression, farmers would need to produce more to cover their debts and living expenses. But as a result, the increasing supply only drove the prices down further. This chain reaction helped force one out of every nine farms in the United States into foreclosure and bankruptcy in just five years. The Roosevelt administration responded by creating a series of taxes, quotas, and subsidies to sustain farmers and stabilize the country's food supply, offering security to a wide range of smaller farm operations in the decades that followed.

However, in the 1970s, the government started stripping away these controls on price and supply. The world's appetite for meat was growing, and the United States wanted to feed it. It would take a lot of grain to raise cows, pigs, and poultry, and the New Deal policies kept farmers from producing enough corn and soybeans to meet the demand. Earl Butz, a food industry executive who served as the US secretary of agriculture from 1971 to 1976, went on speaking tours to encourage American farmers to meet the growing global demand for grain. Conservation techniques like rotating crops and soil management started to go out the window as Butz encouraged farmers to maximize their grain output. "Get big or get out," he liked to say. "Adapt or die."

Early on, many farmers were suspicious of the government's push for large-scale monocropping, as well as the food companies that stood to benefit from the subsequent trade deals. At the time, Wisconsin senator Gaylord Nelson warned that "corporate farming threatens an ultimate shift in power in rural America." Many bought into Butz's vision. Farmers took out loans to buy bigger plots of land, and the country's food exports rose. But Butz's vision for free-market farming quickly began to fall apart. In 1979, the US placed a grain embargo on the Soviet Union after it invaded Afghanistan. Overnight, American farmers lost one of their biggest international customers and were left sitting on grain they could not sell. By 1984, the total debt held by the nation's farms hit $215 billion, double the level of just six years earlier. Thousands of small farmers went under. The ones who survived bought up foreclosed farms on the cheap and rolled them into larger operations. The consolidation continued for decades, and by 2011, 11 percent of US farms controlled more than 70 percent of the country's cropland.

That trend is consistent across all sectors of the agriculture industry. The family farms that sustained rural America for generations have been replaced by corporate agriculture. As food production has become more concentrated in the hands of a few large companies, rural communities have suffered heavily.

One can argue that consolidation is simply the invisible hand of the market working its magic—the more efficient the farm, the better. But as farms optimized for efficiency, the animals, the environment, and even farmers ended up worse off. Large-scale operations pack as many animals into as small a space as possible and maximize the production of each animal. The result is a facility that looks more like a factory than a farm. The government does not even refer to these large-scale facilities as farms. Instead, they are known as concentrated animal feeding operations, or CAFOs. The vast majority of the beef, pork, poultry, milk, and eggs that Americans consume today come from CAFOs. Instead of grazing on a pasture, animals are stuck in cages eating corn and soy from a trough. And even factory farms are having a difficult time keeping up with the demands of the market.

Over the last sixty years, the United States' growing appetite for meat has been fueled almost single-handedly by chicken. The average American's consumption of beef and pork actually fell between 1960 and 2012, while the consumption of chicken meat more than tripled.

Dave Layfield's family has been farming on the Delmarva Peninsula since the late 17th century. For generations his forefathers grew grain and produce, but his parents—Dave Sr. and Patricia—got into the chicken business in the 1970s, soon after the modern poultry model took flight.

As chicken production concentrated after World War II, farmers began signing contracts with so-called poultry "integrators." These companies handled the vast majority of the chicken production process: hatching chicks, delivering them to farmers, supplying feed and other supplies, picking up full-grown chickens, slaughtering them, packaging the meat, and selling it to commercial vendors. All farmers needed to provide was the labor, land, and facilities to grow the birds. Before the integrator model, only a small number of farmers had the infrastructure, relationships, and capital to turn a profit from raising "broiler" chickens rather than raising chickens for eggs. But with integrators taking on the costs of hatching, feeding, transportation, and processing, the barrier to entry fell and the broiler business became more accessible. As more farmers on the Delmarva Peninsula and elsewhere started raising broilers, supermarkets across the country were flooded with low-cost chicken meat and Americans adjusted their diets accordingly.

The Layfield family operated small-scale poultry farms for decades, growing between thirty thousand and sixty thousand birds at any given time. Until late 2019, they operated a small farm with two older houses, each with a sixteen-thousand-bird capacity. Though technically labeled a CAFO by the government, their operation was small by modern poultry farming standards. Some of the largest farms on Delmarva can raise more than a million chickens at a time.

As a child, Dave spent his Saturdays "cleaning the drinkers," scrubbing feed and debris out of the chickens' long metal watering troughs. It was not easy work. Thousands of birds would be clucking around him while he scrubbed away, the smell of ammonia burning his nose and dust clouding the air. Once while cleaning the troughs, Dave, who had always been tall for his age and today stands six foot six, inadvertently stuck his whole head into a wasp nest. He got stung twenty-six times on his scalp, chest, and back. It was around then, as a preteen, that Dave decided to pursue a different line of work. He eventually became a real estate developer, though he continued to help out around his parents' farm as needed. But as the poultry industry grew more consolidated, the Layfields found it harder and harder to stay afloat.

Among economists, a business arrangement where a single company controls multiple stages of production is known as vertical integration. The more of the supply chain the company controls, the more it can reduce its production costs. Lower production costs mean lower prices, and lower prices mean more customers. Vertical integration is what enabled Gilded Age monopolies to conquer their industries. Modern poultry integrators have used it to entrench their dominance over the chicken supply chain. With integrators leveraging economies of scale, it became almost impossible for independent feed mills, hatcheries, farmers, and processors to stay in business. The entire industry began to consolidate around the integrators. In 2018, three companies—Tyson Foods, Pilgrim's Pride, and Sanderson Farms—produced approximately half of the chicken in the United States. They own every part of the process except the CAFO facilities where the chickens are raised. And this is no mistake. One of the tried-and-true tactics of shareholder capitalism is to shift capital expenditures (like building and maintaining thousands of farm facilities, or paying for the benefit packages that come with full-time employment) onto other parties. This allows for lower liabilities and higher profits. So today, most commercial chicken farmers work as contractors for the big poultry integrators. The relationship between integrators and poultry farmers is similar to that between a rideshare company and its drivers who own and maintain their cars. Crucially, each individual farmer is responsible for building and maintaining the CAFOs and related equipment, often funding them via loans offered by the integrators. In that dynamic, the integrators have all the power.

Under this model, the integrators have wide latitude in determining the amount of money that farmers like the Layfields earn. The income that the Layfields and their fellow chicken farmers earn depends on their performance relative to other farms that "settled" that week. Every time a flock is harvested, companies rank farmers against one another based on a handful of variables—weight per bird, feed consumption, mortality rate, and so on—and then pay them out based on their relative efficiency. A farm that produced heavier birds with less food and energy consumption would earn more than a farm with a lower "conversion" rate. Dave Layfield said that his parents' earnings could swing from $150 per thousand chickens to $300 per thousand, based on how well they and other farms performed. The ranking calculation was often very opaque, Dave told me. "Sometimes it was absolutely luck of the draw. There were times when Mom and Dad came in first and didn't know why, and there were times they came in last and didn't know why. But the difference between first and last was huge. Like the difference between making the mortgage payment, electric bill, and putting food on the table—and having a little disposable cash."

By setting up competition between its chicken suppliers, the integrator is able to soak out as much profit as possible while also keeping its farmers racing against each other on a treadmill. The pay structure favors the farms with the most capital, as operations with modern feeding, watering, and ventilation systems can grow chickens more efficiently than older ones. Soon, older farms see their relative ranking (and therefore earnings) start to slide. To top it off, the integrators began, in the late 1980s, explicitly requiring older farms to upgrade their equipment. The cost of that investment fell mostly on the farmers themselves, which in many cases kept the farm stuck in debt. If a farmer could not keep up with the requirements, she risked having her contract dropped by the integrator. This typically happened to older farmers with older equipment. If they lost their contract, elderly farmers would be left with empty chicken houses, unable to sell the farm or obtain a new contract, Dave told me.

This is the situation that Dave's parents find themselves in today. When Dave was a child, his parents used to consistently rank near the top of every harvest, but as more modern farms started popping up, they slid toward the middle. Then in 2019, the Layfields' integrator, Mountaire Farms, told Dave's parents that they needed to invest $8,000 to upgrade their equipment. They did, and Mountaire sent them another flock. A few weeks later when the integrator picked up that batch of birds, the company said the Layfields needed to do another $80,000 worth of upgrades or they would lose their contract. The family was stuck. If they made the upgrades, Mountaire might just hit them with another costly upgrade requirement the following year. They could sell the farm, but then the new owner would need to make an even costlier capital improvement requirement. Either way, the Layfields would end up footing the bill. They had a third option—let the contract expire—but that would leave them with an inactive, unsellable farm. Ultimately, the Layfields chose option three. Patricia and Dave Layfield Sr. are both in their seventies, and their single most valuable asset has been rendered virtually worthless.

"The modernization of the poultry industry has just hung hundreds of older farmers and older farms out to dry," said Dave Jr. "Just go on Google Maps and pan around the Delmarva Peninsula. You'll see hundreds of long rusty rectangles. Those are old abandoned poultry houses and almost every one of them has an old farmer behind it who is out of luck. That's the cost of modernization and industrialization of farming."

The effect on communities can be just devastating. Local farmers end up taking on much of the risk, as they load up on debt to try to keep their CAFOs state of the art. Yet most of the profits leave the local economy, as they are realized further up the food chain by integrators and their shareholders in distant financial hubs. By way of illustration, Tyson Foods has a market capitalization of more than $40 billion and its largest shareholders are all asset managers clustered in the very small number of places—all urban—that have benefited from the last thirty years of wealth creation. Decades ago, in the era when independent farms had more stability, their profits would have been funneled back into local towns, communities, and other small businesses. But that local economy has dried up, and the cost has been borne by families like the Layfields.

All the incentives now drive farms toward scale and size, and this is true not just for livestock but also for farms that produce corn, soy, wheat, and other crops. Maximize plants, maximize output, minimize space. The consolidation of the agriculture industry has devastated America's rural communities. In the 1950s, for every dollar spent on food at the grocery store, fifty cents went to the farmer. Today it's fifteen cents. With family farms no longer offering a path to a viable economic life, more young people are leaving small towns for better-paying jobs in urban centers. Rural populations are shrinking, and the people who remain tend to be older and poorer. Nearly a quarter of the children in rural America grow up below the poverty line. Rural Americans are 45 percent more likely to commit suicide than their urban counterparts. In the United States and elsewhere, populist leaders have capitalized on the economic and political grievances of these communities. This is reflected in my native West Virginia, where the population has shrunk from 2.1 million to 1.8 million during my lifetime, with only a small percentage of my classmates choosing to stay. Politically, it has moved from being dominated by "union Democrats" to being radicalized, with the populist fringe now mainstream. Its politics have gone from union to nativist as it has grown poorer and sicker.

SHAREHOLDER CAPITALISM ACCELERATED during the 1990s after the Soviet Union fell and it was clear that capitalism had won. Companies doubled down on Friedman's ideas, leading to an increase in short-term planning. Senior executives saw their pay increasingly linked to equity rather than salary, meaning the higher a company's stock price, the richer the reward for the executive team. Private equity, activist investing, and mergers and acquisitions activity accelerated as antitrust protections weakened further.

Economists found that between 1997 and 2014, three-quarters of US industries became more concentrated and the largest firms in most industries increased their share of the market. There were 66,847 corporate mergers and acquisitions in the United States between 1970 and 1989—an average of 3,342 per year. Between 2000 and 2019, there were 236,895 total mergers and acquisitions, about 3.5 times as many per year. In 2019, the total value of those mergers hit $1.9 trillion. In nearly every industry, from construction to finance, start-ups make up a smaller share of the market than they did in 1979. Through mergers and other means, established firms are snuffing out potential competitors before they ever leave the cradle.

"Being a small economic unit—which has traditionally been the core of the American economic project—is a loser's game," said Columbia Law School professor Tim Wu. "Being a producer right now feels a little bit like a sucker's game. There are a lot of areas where the actual producers are squeezed."

This dynamic is especially concerning in western and central Europe, where small- and medium-sized businesses are more predominant than they are in the United States and more deeply embedded in local culture. Small businesses in countries including Italy, France, and Spain were not as impacted by the mall-ification and big box stores that wiped out America's main streets. Now, these smaller firms are having to hold out against digital platforms and against an overall economic tide accelerated by COVID-19 that puts them in a more tenuous position. Walking through the neighborhood in the university district of Bologna, Italy, where I lived during my time there as a professor, I am struck by the number and variety of locally owned bookstores, grocery stores, and myriad other specialty retailers that would never stand a chance in the United States. Germany, Switzerland, and Austria are home to millions of what are called the *Mittelstand*, family-owned businesses of small to moderate size that tend to measure their impact across generations rather than quarters and refuse to be acquired by larger firms.

As firms have gotten bigger, they have also taken a larger share of the profits generated in the economy. The companies on the original Fortune 500 list earned a combined $8.3 billion in profit in 1955 (approximately $79 billion in 2019 dollars). In 2019, the Fortune 500 came out $1.2 trillion in the black. But instead of raising wages for workers or lowering prices for consumers, modern companies direct more of their gains to shareholders.

If workers held equity—an ownership stake—in the companies where they work, then they would benefit from the appreciating value of their capital, but the numbers state plainly that workers tend not to be owners. In the United States, the top 1 percent owns $15.86 trillion in stocks, while the bottom 50 percent owns $0.18 trillion. A population group a tiny fraction the size of another owns eighty-eight times its stock market wealth.

This trend is global. The world's twenty-six richest people now hold more wealth than half of the globe's population. This is more medieval than progressive.

To continue to meet market expectation for profits quarter after quarter, businesses have also come to rely on short-term strategies to juice their share prices. The most common of these, and perhaps the least productive to society, is the stock buyback. Companies learned they could drive up their value by simply using revenues to repurchase their own stock rather than investing in innovation or workforce development. Doing so reduces the supply (or "float") of available shares and thereby pushes the share price higher. Such price manipulation is legal because of a Securities and Exchange Commission rule enacted during the surge in shareholder capitalism policies in the 1980s, immunizing executives and boards from prosecution for stock manipulation using stock buybacks. And since the 1990s, buybacks have become all but ubiquitous.

Stock buybacks are Exhibit A demonstrating that if share price is all that matters in shareholder capitalism, then it creates major incentives not to invest capital toward productive uses. A buyback is as productive to society as a bonfire of banknotes. When people scratch their heads and wonder how it can be that the stock market is booming and executive compensation is at an all-time high but the overall economy is less dynamic and workers are not benefiting, look no further than the trillions of dollars in stock buybacks.

S&P 500 companies spent $4.3 trillion on stock buybacks over the last decade. That is more than half of their net income, with another 39 percent ($3.3 trillion) going to dividends to shareholders. These are trillions of dollars that were not spent on research and development, employees' salaries or training, equipment, or anything else that increases the productive capacity of the company. At least with dividends, shareholders can reinvest or otherwise spend the money as they choose to, but with stock buybacks the money just disappears.

This $4.3 trillion produced nothing material. It increased the stock price, which is the sole marker to which most boards hold their senior executives to account.

And when over 50 percent of all profits are pumped into artificial buybacks, we have a major problem.

Some Friedman school purists justify this by saying "this is capitalism," but that obscures the fact that, in practice, whenever these companies hit a crisis they go to the government for a bailout. Because they spent all their free cash flow on stock buybacks, they do not have the money to rescue themselves, so they ask taxpayers to do it for them. Far from some pure form of capitalism, this is corporate socialism. When times are good, these companies are capitalist and privatize their gains. When times are bad, they are socialist and allow the taxes paid by teachers, plumbers, and nurses to get them back to solvency. We saw this with America's airlines in 2020. The airlines received massive government bailouts despite generating more than $49 billion in free cash flow during the previous decade. The reason they were not able to tap that $49 billion once trouble hit was not because they had been in investing in new planes, better service, or better salaries for their workers. No, they had spent $47 billion of that $49 billion on stock buybacks.

We saw an even more dramatic form of corporate socialism when the US central bank, the Federal Reserve, injected trillions of dollars of liquidity into corporate America during the 2020 crisis. As we will later explore, other nations prioritized keeping their citizens employed or their small businesses open, but the official policy of the United States (backed by trillions of dollars) was to aid its largest corporations, those that had spent more than 50 percent of their profits over the previous decade on share buybacks.

THE ABSURDITIES OF shareholder capitalism have become so clear and extreme in the last decade that the tide seems to be turning. Nobel Prize–winning economist Joseph Stiglitz has spoken repeatedly about the flaws of Milton Friedman's vision. To put it bluntly, "he was wrong," Stiglitz said at a World Economic Forum panel in 2018. Decades of the Friedman doctrine have not brought about a more efficient, effective economy for the many. Even business leaders have begun advocating against shareholder capitalism and for a return to stakeholder capitalism. In an interview with the *New York Times*, Salesforce CEO Marc Benioff said, "It influenced—I'd say brainwashed—a generation of C.E.O.s who believed that the only business of business is business. The headline said it all. Our sole responsibility to society? Make money. The communities beyond the corporate campus? Not our problem. I didn't agree with Friedman then, and the decades since have only exposed his myopia. Just look where the obsession with maximizing profits for shareholders has brought us: terrible economic, racial and health inequalities; the catastrophe of climate change. It's no wonder that so many young people now believe that capitalism can't deliver the equal, inclusive, sustainable future they want."

"Stakeholder capitalism" has become a buzz phrase of choice for a whole sea of top executives.

In August 2019, 181 members of the Business Roundtable—the trade association that decades ago helped bring shareholder capitalism into the mainstream—signed a letter committing their businesses to delivering value to stakeholders as well as shareholders. "While each of our individual companies serves its own corporate purpose, we share a fundamental commitment to all of our stakeholders," including employees, customers, and the communities in which businesses operate, the letter said. In effect, the statement called for a return to the more holistic approach to business that dominated the private sector during the mid-20th century.

In some instances, signatory companies have adopted more socially conscious policies. In January 2020, BlackRock committed to making environmental sustainability a central tenet of its investment strategy, and the following month JPMorgan Chase announced it would cut back financing for fossil-fuel companies. But absent any sort of broader tools of accountability, it is guesswork to determine how real the Business Roundtable pledge really is.

What is necessary is a set of very clear, transparent, industry-specific measures with goals and benchmarks that define who a company's stakeholders are and their performance against stakeholder goals. This would be the functional equivalent of the balance sheet tools we use to measure financial performance.

Hedge fund billionaire Daniel Loeb railed against the movement toward stakeholder capitalism when he said, "Stakeholder capitalism distorts the incentive that prompts investors to risk their capital: the promise of a profit on their investment. So, I share Friedman's concern that a movement toward prioritizing ill-defined 'stakeholders' might allow some executives to pursue personal agendas—or simply camouflage their own incompetence (until it is starkly revealed by poor shareholder returns)." In his polemic Loeb accurately captured what now needs to happen: we need to define who the stakeholders are and provide the kind of measures of performance and accountability for those stakeholders that we provide for shareholders.

For example, right now publicly traded companies in most countries are required to disclose the compensation for the CEO and other top executives. It would be productive to also produce a sort of "Gini coefficient" measure across the company to show the distance between top and bottom earners and to demonstrate where people fall in the averages (including mean and median).

The assumption here is not that equal pay is the ultimate good, any more than zero pay would be an ideal measure for CEO compensation.

But publicizing CEO compensation makes CEOs publicly accountable to shareholders, and to anyone else who would critique their earnings. Similarly, while it is unrealistic to expect that the janitor of a company will make anywhere near the same wage as the CEO, it is reasonable to have a measure and judge the company based on whether the difference in that compensation is ten times or one hundred times or ten thousand times.

I remember being at a party in Davos during the World Economic Forum, held in the chalet of a billionaire. Stakeholder capitalism critic Dan Loeb was talking to a fellow billionaire, Sean Parker, discussing the costs of private jets relative to the altitudes they can reach.

"I won't pay $10 million for another five thousand feet of altitude," Parker said to Loeb.

"I will," Loeb responded with a shit-eating grin.

I don't detest Loeb for his wealth or private jet ownership. I don't believe every billionaire is a policy failure. But I do believe that Loeb's critique of stakeholder capitalism has to be placed in the context of an economy that has become comically unequal and, in turn, is producing the rage all around us.

"In some companies' minds, there is a tug-of-war between the profit motive and social responsibility," Mohamed El-Erian, the legendary asset manager and president of Queens' College, Cambridge, told me. "These companies will slowly be reminded that you cannot be a good house if you don't care about the neighborhood. . . . But left on their own, they're not gonna move fast enough."

Indeed, many executives feel like they are caught in a bind. All the incentives continue to push CEOs toward exclusively serving shareholders. To resist them can be incredibly risky and costly, even when the decision to do so is perfectly justified. For instance, Amazon announced in the midst of the 2020 COVID-19 pandemic that it would spend $4 billion to increase safety for its nearly six hundred thousand workers. The stock market swung against the company, which saw its share values immediately drop 7.6 percent in response to the decision. Because of a $4 billion investment in the well-being of its workers, $83 billion of shareholder value was lost. Why? Because in the eyes of traders, Amazon's decision took profits away from shareholders and posed a threat to the bottom line. The absurdity of this form of shareholder capitalism pits the interests of workers and shareholders directly against each other, and it belies both the real health and the real value of the company. Two months later, Amazon regained $400 billion in market cap as its businesses spiked in growth, increasing share value by more than 30 percent.

A system that is amoral and imbecilic enough to compel selling Amazon's stock because it invested in protecting its workers during a pandemic is not one that we should trust to steward the overall health and well-being of our economy. And it is worth noting that many other companies might well have hesitated to invest in workers' safety, knowing all too well that it would bring the ire of shareholders. The vast majority of CEOs are working on smaller time scales than Amazon's Jeff Bezos and are more vulnerable to the whims of their boards. So, instead of protecting workers, that rival CEO could take an easier route by opting for a stock buyback instead.

What makes this even more obvious is that it is not just Wall Street analysts overthinking the short-term effects of a CEO's actions; it's a bunch of dumb algorithms.

CEOs are now speaking differently on quarterly earnings phone calls to account for all the AIs listening in. The algorithms measure the tone of the CEO's language and weigh certain words more optimistically and favorably (therefore producing more favorable reporting, pushing to buy more stock) and others more pessimistically (producing more stock sale signals). The CEOs are using language developed by their staffs to optimize for what the algorithms want to hear. It's not just bad human judgment propelling the inanity of shareholder capitalism, it's bad algorithms.

The calls for a turn to stakeholder capitalism are well justified. The track record for stakeholder capitalism demonstrated more inclusive growth, which meant stronger communities, and stronger long-term growth, which meant better returns for stakeholders and shareholders alike over time. Shareholders may well have seen their returns soar under shareholder capitalism, but one can make the case that the model has failed even them. This may come as a surprise, but companies that are more rooted in stakeholder capitalism—that take responsibility for their impact on the environment and for the well-being of their employees, customers, and communities alike—make more money than their equivalents that espouse shareholder capitalism. Shareholder primacy has failed both shareholders and stakeholders. And now, as our society stands at a crossroads, stakeholder capitalism offers the only potential path to relief. Our biggest unsolved problems are interconnected across issues of economics, race, climate change, and health; and they require an interconnected response that includes business. Business cannot solve every big problem, but no big problem can be solved without the participation of business. And under the shareholder model, many CEOs are unable to act in meaningful ways.

Consider the issue of minimum wage. If the US minimum wage had increased at the rate of productivity since 1960, it would now be $22.50. Instead, it's $7.25, and it has been stagnant since 2009, which has led to a game of chicken among many businesses. One of the strangest points came recently when Doug McMillon, the CEO of Walmart, called on Congress to raise the minimum wage. Why would he make a request that could cut into his margins? McMillon started his career at Walmart making minimum wage as a teenager unloading trucks, but the answer is not rooted in his experience on the trucks or in the born-again Christianity that he says animates his choices as a father and leader. After all, he can just raise wages at Walmart as high as his board of directors will allow without concerning himself with Congress. The answer is shareholder capitalism. If Walmart unilaterally raises wages at a time when its competitors do not, it will take a walloping in the market for sacrificing potential profits. But if the company is forced to make a change by Congress, and if that change hits all of Walmart's competitors at once, then there is less risk.

It also was not lost on McMillon that if people making the minimum wage were earning more, they would have more to spend at Walmart. This ostensibly would help both Walmart and its competitors, but the short-term punishment doled out by Wall Street analysts reducing stock prices for any unilateral action makes it tricky for McMillon and his competitors to rationalize bets on the long-term benefit of having financially better-off customers or, for that matter, just paying hardworking employees more than a poverty wage because it is the right thing to do.

There is a steady current pulling all sizable companies toward shareholder value, which makes change difficult to come by.

"I see very little evidence that absent either effective internal negotiation or external pressure, companies will move towards a fairer and more equitable distribution of profits towards their stakeholders," said Douglas Alexander, a former British Labour Party politician and cabinet member.

Still, it is possible to swim against the current. And the companies that do so offer glimpses of new models.

ONE OF THE chief stakeholders that gets short shrift in shareholder capitalism is the environment. As the shift toward share price encourages companies to minimize employee benefits, community investment, and long-term research and development, it also incentivizes businesses to disregard pollution and environmental damage. Every dollar not spent to reduce environmental impact is a dollar that goes to the bottom line. If pollution costs can be shrugged off onto the broader public or future generations, then profits have more room to grow. As a result, corporations generally don't make environmentally responsible decisions unless the law compels them to do so. The examples of businesses chasing profits at the expense of the planet are too numerous to count. From energy to transportation to manufacturing to agriculture, every industry leaves the environment worse than they found it.

The effects are now despairingly obvious, and increasingly hard to reverse. In 2019, the global average temperature was approximately 1.1° Celsius (2° Fahrenheit) higher than levels in the late 19th century. Absent "drastic action," the United Nations expects global temperatures to rise as much as 3.2° Celsius (5.8° Fahrenheit) by the year 2100. Climate change will rock the foundations of society: droughts and famines will become more frequent, natural disasters will grow more devastating, and seven hundred thousand square miles of land (an area larger than Alaska) will sink beneath the ocean, displacing hundreds of millions of people.

Environmental causes have become a staple of corporate responsibility efforts. But on balance, such efforts tend to be public relations stunts or otherwise minor efforts that fail to offset companies' real impact on the environment.

The original sin of industrialization was environmental destruction. Our planet now needs to be a key part of our social contract for the first time in history. Businesses need to embrace sustainability across their full enterprises even when they are not legally required to do so. Governments need to reduce pollution and carbon emissions, protect natural spaces, and promote the development of green technology even at the expense of short-term economic output. Citizens need to examine the impact of our consumption choices. Yet the incentives of the current shareholder-dominated economy stand in the way of real change.

Despite the challenge, a small segment of companies has already started moving in that direction, even creating a special corporate structure in the United States to cut against shareholder primacy. These firms prove it is possible to turn a profit while minimizing their environmental impact. We have even seen a few such companies pop up in the sectors of the economy most in need of reform.

Take the fashion industry. It is not the first sector that comes to mind when most people think of environmental impact. But fashion is responsible for 10 percent of the world's carbon emissions and 20 percent of the world's wastewater, more than all international flights and maritime shipping combined. Most people do not realize the wastefulness of their wardrobes, but at its current growth rate, the fashion industry will produce a quarter of the world's carbon emissions by the year 2050. Some brands do not mind cashing in on humanity's shopping sprees, but others have pioneered a more sustainable approach to clothing their customers. Prominent among them is Patagonia.

Patagonia is a *benefit corporation*, a relatively new class of company that aims to serve the public good as well as turn a profit. It was the first "B Corp" in California. The legal purpose of a benefit corporation designation is to provide cover for board members and executives to make decisions that may not maximize shareholder value over the short term, but create public benefit and sustainable value in addition to generating profits. It might sound ridiculous to have to establish that kind of legal cover, but after my friend Craig Newmark sold his website Craigslist to eBay, eBay actually sued him—and won—with a finding in court that any nonfinancial mission that "seeks not to maximize the economic value of a for-profit" for its shareholders is inconsistent with directors' duties, and therefore against the law. As sad as it is that it's necessary, a benefit corporation designation allows a company to serve stakeholders without fear of a similar ruling—and to go further by establishing an obligation to stakeholders within the company's mission.

The environment has been a stakeholder in Patagonia's business model for decades. The company's founder, American rock climber Yvon Chouinard, is an icon among outdoors enthusiasts and environmentalists. He came of age in the climbing scene that emerged in California's Yosemite Valley in the 1950s. Chouinard and his comrades—known affectionately as "dirtbags"—lived off the grid, forgoing careers and general hygiene to spend time scaling the valley's towering granite walls.

After teaching himself to use a forge and anvil, Chouinard started fashioning handmade steel pitons (the spikes climbers drive into walls to hold their rope) and selling them to fellow climbers from the back of his car for $1.50 apiece. His equipment became the gold standard for "big wall" climbing, but Chouinard did not let success change his lifestyle. He lived out of his car, sustained by cat food, dumpster diving, and small game he could kill with his climbing tools. Any profits he made went primarily to climbing and surfing trips. By the 1960s, Chouinard Equipment Ltd., then headquartered in the chicken coop in his parents' backyard, expanded to other climbing equipment and apparel. When the clothing business took off in 1973, Chouinard and his wife Malinda spun it into a new company, Patagonia.

That was about the time Vincent Stanley joined the company. Tired of working at a car wash, Stanley asked his uncle Yvon for a job. He planned to stay for a few months, but nearly fifty years later his fingerprints are all over the company.

Today, Stanley's official title is director of philosophy, a role that lets him serve as the de facto caretaker of the Patagonia ethos ("we didn't know what else to call me," he said). He trains employees on the company's history and values, advises student entrepreneurs at Yale, and evangelizes for benefit corporations. A soft-spoken poet with high cheekbones and a grandfatherly demeanor, Stanley puts you at ease the minute he introduces himself.

Though Patagonia was born in the outdoors, the company did not always see itself as a protagonist in the effort to protect the environment. "In the early seventies, I think our conception was that anything to do with environmental protection was the business of the government," Stanley said. "Because we were such a small, tiny company, we didn't see that we had any agency . . . to look at the environmental implications of what we did."

Within its own lane, however, the company worked to reduce the mark it left on the environment. In the early 1970s, Chouinard discontinued his trademark pitons and began selling chocks, aluminum wedges that climbers could remove without scarring the rock. It was a risky move, considering piton sales accounted for 70 percent of the company's business, but in a 1972 catalog Chouinard published a twelve-page article explaining the decision to customers. Within months, the company was selling chocks faster than it could make them.

The company took an even bigger leap in 1996 when it switched 100 percent of its clothing line to organic cotton. A few years earlier, Patagonia had opened a store in Boston. Within three days, it was shut down after multiple employees called in sick. The company soon discovered the cause: the cotton clothes stored in the basement were emitting formaldehyde into the ventilation system.

This prompted Patagonia to investigate its supply chain. The company did not like what it discovered: not only were cotton clothes finished with formaldehyde resin, but the pesticides and fertilizers used to grow cotton left the surrounding area devoid of life. "When they cleared the fields to plant, they used chemicals that had been originally developed as nerve gases," Stanley told me.

As it researched the problem, the company realized the only solution was to go organic. Again, the decision was risky—making the switch would require retooling Patagonia's whole supply chain, and it would raise production costs of each item of clothing by three to five dollars. Many people thought it would make the company less competitive. But Chouinard issued an ultimatum: "If we can't figure out how to go organic, I'm getting out of sportswear."

To bring the rest of its employees on board with the decision, Patagonia showed them the reality on the ground. In groups of forty, employees loaded onto buses and ventured to the San Joaquin Valley in central California. They first stopped at conventional cotton farms. Before they even got off the bus, they could smell the pesticides hanging in the air. "It smells like the inside of a poorly vented laboratory," Stanley said. When people stuck their hands in the soil, they found it barren. "There's no life in [the soil] because it takes three years for the worms to come back after you stop spraying."

The employees then ventured up to the organic farms where Patagonia planned to source its cotton. The difference was stark.

"People would see birds landing in the fields—there was life in the soil," Stanley said. "People would come back from that and say, 'Okay, this isn't abstract anymore. This isn't reading some kind of paper about chemicals. The company's made the right decision, and we're going to help make it happen.' That I think was the big turning point."

After it switched to organic cotton, Patagonia was forced to cut one-third of its clothing line. It took years to return to its original sales level, Stanley said, "but when we did, the company had a new identity. We had the basis of a new relationship with customers. We had employees who were committed to this and they were willing to do the next thing because they had this cultural confidence that you could pull this off."

As of June 2020, Patagonia was still the only major apparel company that relied exclusively on organic cotton. Over the last decade, the company has made it a mission to fight against "fast fashion," a practice of quickly translating every season and every moment's movement in high fashion to mass production. On Black Friday in 2011, Patagonia took out a full-page ad in the *New York Times* that alerted consumers to the environmental impact of its clothes and called on them to think twice before buying something they did not need. The ad, which depicted one of the company's popular fleece jackets, was titled in all caps "DON'T BUY THIS JACKET."

In 2015, Patagonia launched the "Worn Wear Wagon," a mobile truck that repaired damaged Patagonia clothes. During an interview around the launch, Chouinard said, "I hardly own any new Patagonia stuff—I just don't have a need for it." He proudly announced the shirt he was wearing was ten years old. Two years later, the company expanded the program, creating an online platform where customers could trade, sell, or buy Patagonia clothes secondhand.

Patagonia became more aggressive in its activism when it sued the federal government in 2017, joining a lawsuit filed by Native American and grassroots groups over plans to reduce the size of two national monuments in Utah. The company announced the lawsuit on its website with the caption "The President Stole Your Land." While other businesses might have wrung their hands about such a decision, Patagonia employees were fully on board, said Corley Kenna, my former State Department colleague who now runs the company's global communications team. At the end of the day, customers were on board too.

"Our community rewarded us, and we attracted a lot of new people who didn't know about us before, because people thought, 'Wow, that's really great that this company is willing to do this,'" she told me. "It's not something that a Harvard MBA marketing class . . . would recommend as a great way to sell jackets. That's not why we did it. But at the end of the day it was good for the business in all ways."

After Congress passed the Tax Cuts and Jobs Act in 2017, Patagonia donated its $10 million return to environmental groups. In a LinkedIn post, CEO Rose Marcario called the tax cut "irresponsible." In a profile, Chouinard criticized his wealthy Wyoming neighbors who took advantage of the state's lax tax laws. "I happily pay my taxes," he said.

Patagonia's business model allows it to cast economics to the wind in a way that most companies cannot. For one, Patagonia is privately owned, which means there are very few shareholders to answer to. Secondly, it can afford to invest in organic cotton and other eco-friendly policies because its clothes are more expensive than most. As of June 2020, the fleece jacket that Patagonia told consumers "not to buy" cost $169 before taxes. There is a reason that the company is sometimes labeled "fratagonia" among college students and "Patagucci" among outdoorsy types. That is not to disparage its strategy: Patagonia has proven that many people are willing to pay higher prices for more sustainable, high-quality products that last longer.

The effort to bring more responsible and sustainable practices to fashion has found an intriguing foothold in China, the capital of cheap manufacturing. China is the world's largest garment manufacturer and has reaped the economic rewards of the explosion of fast fashion. But the same boom has devastated the environment in China. A detailed investigation by Greenpeace International found that international brands like Abercrombie & Fitch, Adidas, Calvin Klein, and H&M obtained their supplies from factories in China that regularly dumped toxic dyes from textiles into waterways. The following year, the influential Chinese environmentalist Ma Jun published a report stating that he had found six thousand environmental violations committed by apparel factories, including illegally dumping toxic wastewater into rivers and streams that supplied drinking water.

Ye Shouzeng and Shawna Tao are strong examples to the contrary. They founded a luxury clothing brand in Shanghai and named it

Icicle in 1997. Their slogan, "Made in Earth," represents an aesthetic of clothing that is contemporary and minimalist, with sweaters and jackets in neutral tones. Rather than use tissue paper, Icicle wrapped newly sold clothes in reusable cloth bags. Price tags were made from corn fiber rather than plastic, and buttons from natural materials like shells. In the production process, Icicle committed to using only environmentally friendly materials, including natural dyes and only organic cotton when it used cotton at all. Icicle also works only with suppliers that own their production facilities, rather than outsourcing the work. Icicle, along with its suppliers, says that it participates with various independent nongovernmental organizations to scrutinize and verify its sustainability claims. Perhaps most importantly, the clothes are intended to be kept for years and to survive and outlast short-term trends.

While the Western fashion industry has embraced Chinese apparel factories for their ability to produce fast fashion, Icicle bucked the trend with Chinese-made slow fashion. And like Patagonia, it has proven a success. Since its founding in the 1990s, Icicle has opened more than two hundred storefronts in China, but for most of its existence, the brand was largely unknown outside the country. That changed in 2019, when Icicle purchased the French couture brand Carven, which was facing bankruptcy. Since then, Icicle has recruited European fashion executives to help introduce it to a wider audience and create a new "Made in China" ethos that wears sustainability on its sleeve.

A new wave of the fashion industry, focusing on eco-friendly clothing, has caught up with Icicle and Patagonia in recent years. According to a January 2020 report by Barclays bank, sustainable fashion has the potential to grow into a €100 billion industry. A 2017 study on consumer trends in China found that 58 percent of consumers were willing to pay more for responsibly made clothing.

Companies like Patagonia and Icicle increasingly have loyal customers who are interested not just in the products but also in the mission. Patagonia has repeatedly taken political stands and made real-world contributions to the environment through its status as a benefit corporation. And its customers have stood behind it every time, to the point where brand loyalty to a company like Patagonia is something of a political statement.

ALL TOO MANY corporate responsibility efforts are just fluff, a hand wave at citizenship that distracts from more significant harms elsewhere in the corporate food chain. But there are also clear examples of positive initiatives from some of the largest companies in the world, which start to reveal how they can operate meaningfully as leaders while prioritizing the breadth of their stakeholders rather than just shareholders. One fascinating story comes from none other than Walmart.

Walmart is the largest company on the planet, measured by both revenues and number of employees. With 2.1 million workers, it is the world's third-largest employer behind the US and Chinese militaries. The company operates more than forty square miles of retail space across the globe, an area almost twice the size of Manhattan. If it were a country, Walmart would have the world's twenty-fifth largest economy, just ahead of Thailand. Given its size, Walmart's decisions can transform entire sectors of the economy. Where many intellectuals hold Walmart up as a caricature of the worst of capitalism and consumption culture, Walmart is so big and so very good at what it does that there is now a transgressive movement of leftist intellectuals who think that Walmart and its (very few) peers are laying the groundwork for socialism. As Cory Doctorow wrote, "We are now *surrounded* by companies and organisations that within the same order of magnitude as the Soviet economy at its apex, undertake breathtakingly efficient allocations of goods and resources, and all without markets, running as command economies." The idea is that the socialism that failed last century could emerge smarter and stronger if it learns from companies like Walmart and Amazon about how to allocate goods and resources.

Facing criticism for its shoddy labor practices and sizable environmental footprint in 2005, Walmart executives committed to using the company's clout to bring more eco-friendly products to consumers.

Under the Toxic Substances Control Act, the US government can halt production of a chemical if regulators can prove it poses an "unreasonable risk to health or to the environment." However, due to the cautious nature of environmental researchers and heavy lobbying from industry, proving that risk is a long and arduous process. It turns out major retailers can use their leverage to force a product off the shelves much faster than the government can. And over the last fifteen years, Walmart has used its size and power to drive the market toward greener products.

One of its first targets was the laundry room. In 2007, Walmart announced it would begin selling only concentrated liquid detergent, which used less water and smaller packaging than traditional detergent, at its US stores. It worked with suppliers like Unilever to ramp up production, and within the year Walmart had finished making the transition. Over the next three years, the company estimated that the switch saved 400 million gallons of water, 95 million pounds of plastic, and 125 million pounds of cardboard. This was good for both the environment and the bottom line. Suppliers saved money on production, packaging, and shipping costs, and Walmart itself freed up tracts of shelf space that could be put to more profitable use. Soon, the rest of the market fell in line. Concentrated detergent became the new normal.

Later, the company shifted its attention toward taking harmful chemicals off its shelves. In 2013, Walmart announced that it would phase out ten chemicals from all the cleaning and personal care products sold at its stores, requiring suppliers to rework their formulas if they wanted to continue being sold. In 2017, Walmart became the first retailer in the United States to agree to join the Chemical Footprint Project, a nonprofit, voluntary program that gives retailers a blunt assessment of how their suppliers use and dispose of potentially toxic chemicals. Walmart also asked its suppliers to voluntarily reformulate their cleaning, pet, baby, and personal care products, citing a growing consumer demand for "natural" products.

Walmart's commitment to removing harmful chemicals from its stores had a ripple effect down the supply chain and across the retail industry. The nonprofit group Safer Chemicals, Healthy Families, which releases an annual report "grading" retailers on their chemical policies, said that retailers averaged a B– in 2019, a dramatic increase from the D+ average just three years before. Walmart, Target, and Apple earned the top A ratings. The nonprofit thanked the retailers for filling what it described as a "growing regulatory void" in relation to chemical safety in the United States.

Today, Walmart is actively engaged in other efforts to build a more sustainable supply chain. It is working with suppliers to reduce greenhouse gas emissions and invest in renewable energy. Walmart has also made notable strides in diverting its own waste away from landfills, reducing food waste, shrinking the size of packaging, and improving the efficiency of its truck fleet.

If the world's largest company by revenue takes concrete steps to reduce its environmental footprint, the impact can be enormous—and made all the more necessary by governments not compelling companies to change their practices through law or regulation. By pressuring its supply chain to embrace sustainability and remove harmful chemicals from products, Walmart was more effective in bringing about change than any government regulator. In this way, Walmart should serve as a model for the rest of the private sector. If Macy's, Nordstrom, or Kohl's started carrying only brands that used organic cotton, Patagonia would no longer be an outlier. Leveraging their clout, large corporations can galvanize change across the market.

Just as Walmart was able to shape up its environmental record in recent years and refocus its power toward positive ends, sectors more commonly cast as capitalism's greatest villains have taken surprising acts of moral leadership.

There are few organizations that have had more ink spilled over their power and market influence than Goldman Sachs, arguably the most powerful investment bank in the world. Journalist Matt Taibbi famously characterized the bank as "a great vampire squid wrapped around the face of humanity, relentlessly jamming its blood funnel into anything that smells like money." Goldman Sachs has become the very caricature of Wall Street power, but perhaps to the surprise of its more radical critics the company is now wielding that power to push for more diversity at the highest levels of the private sector in industries the world over.

At the 2020 World Economic Forum, Goldman Sachs CEO and chairman David Solomon announced that the company would underwrite initial public offerings (IPOs) only for American and European companies that have at least one board member who is a woman or a person of color. In 2021, that minimum number rose to two. In other words, if your whole board is made up of white guys, Goldman will not take you public.

In 2018 and 2019, some sixty companies in the US and Europe went public with all-white, all-male boards. In the US, 40 percent of the companies that IPOed in the first eight months of 2019 had all-male boards. As the top underwriter of IPOs in the world, Goldman Sachs had a platform to push the very white, very male financial industry to prioritize diversity across the upper echelons of business.

"Venture capitalists really didn't feel like it was their job to worry about the construct of a board the minute a company goes public," Goldman CEO Solomon told me. "None of them would debate . . . that they need to have diverse boards, but they weren't focused on it. It was lower on the priority list. One of the things our policy did is it accelerated or brought forward the focus on certain communities in private equity, in venture capital. This shined a light on it and amplified it, and I think it has moved the conversation forward."

Solomon's thinking was shaped in part by his two daughters. "When they were in college, I started to really appreciate much more how I saw things through their eyes differently than I saw them as a white male in the workforce," he told me. "When I became CEO, I decided literally day one that diversity was something I really wanted to focus on during my tenure."

Solomon's support for diversity initiatives helped him land the top job in the first place. He was in a two-man competition with his colleague Harvey Schwartz to succeed Lloyd Blankfein as Goldman's CEO. Schwartz was closer to Blankfein and considered the front-runner. But in the run-up to Blankfein's retirement, the board of directors wanted a plan and presentation on diversity initiatives. This was considered "a tough fucking thing to present to the board," according to Gregg Lemkau, then the co-head of Goldman's investment banking. So Schwartz ceded to Solomon the responsibility of making the presentation ("to let him eat the shit sandwich," according to one Goldman leader). Solomon embraced the opportunity. He went big, outlining an aggressive diversity initiative that would reshape the composition of the bank. Solomon's plan and presentation so impressed the board that he moved in front of Schwartz as Blankfein's likely successor, a transition that happened not long thereafter.

Soon after taking over as CEO, Solomon fought to ensure that women made up half the bank's entry-level hires and set hiring minimums for African American and Latino applicants.

When Gregg Lemkau suggested setting a diversity threshold for IPOs, Solomon jumped at the idea. "Can we do that?" he asked Lemkau.

"We can do anything we want," Lemkau replied.

There was not much time to shop it around: it was December 2019, and Solomon wanted to announce the initiative the following month at the World Economic Forum in Davos. As Lemkau hammered out the details of the policy, he met some resistance. Certain energy companies and family-owned businesses asked for exceptions. Within Goldman Sachs, some people feared the decision would cost Goldman business. Emails between Solomon and Lemkau pegged the number of new US listings they had done since 2016 without female directors at approximately 20 percent. That is a big chunk of their business. Yet Solomon kept pushing, and Lemkau's message internally was that this was going to get done without any waivers or exceptions. The day before the announcement, Lemkau said some were suggesting limiting the policy to US companies. "This is not bold enough and I want to go further," Solomon responded in an email. Ultimately, they expanded the requirement to European companies and set a date for raising the threshold.

In addition to creating more-inclusive boardrooms, Solomon said the policy is good for business. He has the data to back up his statement. Among the US companies it has IPOed since 2016, Goldman Sachs found that firms with at least one woman on the board had a median return rate of 19 percent. The return rate for those with all-male boards was only 2 percent. "Differences create better performance," Solomon said.

Ensuring that women and people of color get seats in the boardroom is a step toward reducing inequality in the workplace. Women fill just 20 percent of the board seats in major US companies, and people of color hold approximately 10 percent. Meanwhile, pay gaps and discrimination still exist. However, for the dozens of Western companies that Goldman Sachs brings public every year, the policy will at least raise the floor for representation. Solomon acknowledges the policy is still a work in progress and said the company will continue to revise its scale and scope in the years ahead. "It's not perfect," he noted, "but it sends a very strong message."

The idea that Goldman "the great vampire squid" Sachs is using its power for good cuts against the grain of today's narrative and hashtag snark commentary. That makes it all the more consequential.

When companies like Walmart and Goldman Sachs take a stand on social issues, they usually justify it on the basis of values and social responsibility, but more often than not, those decisions boil down to a simple economic calculation: Do the long-term benefits outweigh the short-term costs? For Goldman Sachs, the answer was yes. Positioning itself on the right side of history was an investment in the long term.

"You get a handful of opportunities when you can try to move the needle," Solomon said of his thinking. "If you see one and you think you can make a difference, I think you have a responsibility to try to step forward and make a difference."

More and more business leaders are reaching this conclusion and trying to find ways to use their power for more than just the bottom line. In 2019, Robert Smith, the founder of the private equity firm Vista Equity Partners and the wealthiest African American person in the United States, committed to paying off the student loans of all 402 students in the graduating class of Morehouse College. In 2020, Jeff Bezos, Amazon's CEO and the richest man alive, committed to investing $10 billion toward combating climate change. For decades now, Bill Gates has committed his fortune to humanitarian causes through the Bill & Melinda Gates Foundation, with the couple's contributions rising to $50 billion since 1994.

All these acts—the philanthropy of our richest citizens, the corporate leadership of Goldman Sachs and Walmart—have a strange duality. They are inspiring, but they also highlight the scale of the problems that need solving and demonstrate where government is not doing the job it ought to be doing. It is nothing but admirable that David Solomon is trying to find ways to use his company's incredible power for good, and these stories show that when people with real power use it for the right reasons, we can get better outcomes. The social contract does not have to keep fraying.

But when it comes down to it, individual philanthropists and companies can accomplish only so much on their own. Their efforts tend to be piecemeal, and they're eclipsed by the magnitude of the tear in our social contract. It is notable that as Robert Smith was giving away millions, he was also entangled in a criminal tax inquiry for engaging in tax evasion using offshore accounts. And if you zoom out to look at the broader problem of student debt that his donations and foundations are addressing, you can see the limitations of individual action. In 2020, Americans collectively owed $1.6 *trillion* in student loan debt. This debt can utterly cripple students' long-term economic prospects, and Smith's program will be a lifesaver for thousands of students. But it is a drop in the bucket when seen within the scope of the whole debt. Some 43 million students and their families carry that $1.6 trillion in debt. It is completely out of reach for philanthropy. No individual can solve such a problem—not Gates, not Bezos—not if nearly every top billionaire put their whole fortune to the task.

"If you want to see big social and economic change, political change, you have to line up government leadership, business and NGO innovation, and mass mobilization," said David Miliband, a former British foreign secretary who now leads the International Rescue Committee. "Philanthropy is not anywhere near substituting of the government role. . . . When government leadership is absent then the middle-tier or even the mass-mobilization tier can step up, but you shouldn't kid yourself that you'll ever solve a problem unless government gets with the game."

RIGHT NOW OUR incentives pull us toward a more dystopian, *Mad Max* form of capitalism. The incentives drive companies toward share buybacks instead of investments in workers, equipment, and research and development. The incentives drive businesses to grow bigger through mergers and acquisitions, and then to fire rather than hire. And as we will read, the incentives encourage breaking up unions and sending headquarters to tax-optimized locales instead of to communities that are not in a race to the bottom on taxes. The incentives mean refusing to pay even a cent more for renewable energy than for fossil fuels.

The nightmare is that all this optimization for nonproductive uses of capital and for the short term ensures that the long term will be worse for all of us. The inequality and climate crises we are already suffering from are direct consequences of optimizing for the short-term shareholder gains decades ago. And the problems compound.

One of the criticisms of the old model of stakeholder capitalism is that it did not allow for a coherent set of guiding principles. One of the reasons shareholder capitalism exploded in popularity in the 1980s is that its goals were clear-cut. Shareholder capitalism asks businesses to optimize for a single variable: financial returns to the business (and thus the shareholders). By contrast, stakeholder capitalism forces companies to balance the interests of a number of different groups that often come to the table with competing priorities. The more variables you add, the harder the calculation becomes.

In an ideal world, a business would maximize certain variables—like shareholder value, social impact, and employee well-being—and minimize others, like carbon emissions. But in the real world, those decisions always involve trade-offs. Using offshore havens to lower taxes generates more revenue for the company but takes away funds from government programs that make us safer, healthier, and better educated.

There is no perfect formula for implementing stakeholder capitalism—striking the right balance between those competing interests will require thoughtful conversations with input from across a range of stakeholders. This itself is a shift. There needs to be meaningful communication and negotiation among stakeholders before the social contract will begin to return to any semblance of balance.

To make those discussions more productive, there are concrete steps we can take to map out a company's footprint. A good first step would be to quantify the impacts, both positive and negative, of a business's decisions on various stakeholders. Today, businesses have countless metrics for measuring shareholder value. There is return on assets, return on equity, price/earnings ratio, internal rate of return, gross and net margins, and on and on. An entire industry is built around accounting metrics for measuring shareholder value. We need similar standards for calculating stakeholder value. Douglas Alexander, a British Labour Party politician and cabinet member, suggests creating the equivalent of generally accepted accounting principles (GAAP) for corporate impact.

"To measure both the positive and the negative externalities of major corporations we need a common metric or common language by which to be able to undertake those comparisons," Alexander told me. The next generation "in survey after survey say that they want value aligned with values. They want to be confident that when they get up in the morning, they don't then go and work for a company or invest in a company through their pension plan that right now is at odds with their own values and their conception of how they would like the world to be. There's a significant opportunity for developing common standards that will allow a more transparent account of where businesses are having a negative impact and where businesses are having a positive impact."

One possibility is to use the tax code to drive behavior change. In the same way that GAAP provide a structure for determining a company's tax burden, structures could be created that implement a similar set of measures for stakeholder impact and then provide the data to adjust a company's taxes higher or lower. Companies respond to incentives, so we need to provide incentives for them to stop the race to the bottom on everything from environmental damage to workers' rights.

Former Bank of England governor Mark Carney has suggested that this approach be extended to executive compensation as well, saying that banks should link executive pay to climate risk management. The more a company does to contribute to goals set out in the Paris climate accord, the more its executives get paid.

Economic inequality and environmental destruction are concrete problems, and addressing them this decade and beyond will require equally concrete strategies. For a company to actually understand the positive and negative impacts of its decisions, it needs data. Without metrics, stakeholder capitalism will remain a squishy phrase that companies will use in public relations campaigns but not pursue in the boardroom. But it is fully within these businesses' power, and society's power in the digital era, to log and report and respond to such data on a broad scale.

To that point, however, we cannot expect companies to enact such reforms all on their own, especially when incentives remain misaligned. Many business leaders will relish the opportunity to pursue more sustainable, socially responsible business models, but many will not. And we must recognize that there are limits to what business will accomplish of its own accord. Capitalism is a system driven by incentives rooted in compensation, taxation, and share price, and the way to enlist our most powerful capitalists and their companies to act in the interests of citizens and governments is to rewire their incentives. Make it in the financial interests of executives, their boards, and their shareholders to be better to their stakeholders.

We must use public policy to compel data collection and transparency on social impact and then have rules to force the re-internalization of those costs into the business. In some cases (such as with Walmart), that will bring long-term economic benefits to the company. In others, it definitely won't, but it will shift the market with new incentives that are more in balance with the social contract.

Real change also requires that the other key signatories in the social contract—governments and everyday citizens—actually have enough power to help drive the choices and actions of business. Governments and labor need greater force and effect. But right now they are floundering. How did they get that way? And what is the route back?

2

THE GOVERNMENT: BILLIONS OF PEOPLE ARE GOVERNED MORE BY COMPANIES THAN BY COUNTRIES

At the crack of dawn on Wednesday, September 20, 2017, Hurricane Maria made landfall in southeast Puerto Rico. With 150-mile-per-hour winds, it was the strongest hurricane to hit the island in nearly a century. Within twenty-four hours, the storm had deluged some parts of Puerto Rico with more than thirty inches of rain. The island's power grid and communication networks, which were already in poor condition before the storm, were knocked off-line. More than half of Puerto Ricans—some 1.9 million American citizens—were left without access to drinkable water. Some towns saw 80–90 percent of their buildings leveled by the storm.

There is no time that people need their government more than after a natural disaster strikes. It takes an incredible amount of resources and coordination to rescue victims, distribute food and water, clear debris, and bring critical infrastructure back online. Only the government has the mission, resources, and capabilities to do this work. In the wake of Hurricane Maria, Puerto Rico needed exactly this kind of rapid, all-hands response. But the United States government failed to deliver—and it failed spectacularly, resulting in thousands of avoidable deaths.

The government's response to Hurricane Maria was a disaster from the start. It took four days for the first shipments of food, water, and equipment to arrive on the island. Senior government officials did not visit Puerto Rico until five days after Maria made landfall, and the president did not attend a meeting on the federal response to the disaster until day six. It took eight days for the White House to waive a decades-old shipping regulation that limited which vessels could transport supplies to the island, and it took thirteen days for the USNS *Comfort*—one of the navy's two hospital ships—to reach Puerto Rico. The ship was equipped to care for 250 patients at any one time, but it admitted an average of only six people per day. By the two-week mark, the Pentagon had deployed nine thousand troops to the island, approximately half as many personnel as it sent to Haiti in the first week after that country's 2010 earthquake. The government was slow to clear roads, distribute food and water, and bring remote parts of the island back online.

All the while, Puerto Ricans were struggling to survive. Weeks after the storm, more than half the population still lacked electricity and cell service, and hospitals were triaging victims amid power outages, evacuations, and dwindling supplies. One cardiovascular surgeon in San Juan put the situation bluntly: "If you are sick in Puerto Rico, the best thing is to get on a plane and abandon the island." The island's power grid would not be fully restored for eleven months, and two years later, tens of thousands of Puerto Ricans were still living under tarps. At that point, the US government had still not funded a single permanent road reconstruction project.

Several key factors contributed to the government's poor response to Hurricane Maria. One was straight-up bad luck. Maria came on the heels of two similarly powerful hurricanes—Harvey and Irma—that had devastated the US Gulf Coast. Hurricane Irma had brushed Puerto Rico, leaving its power grid damaged. The Federal Emergency Management Agency (FEMA), the branch of the US government responsible for disaster response, found its resources stretched thin by the time Maria bore down on the island.

Another factor was Puerto Rico's colonial history. Officially, the island is a territory, not a state. Some 3.2 million people live in Puerto Rico—a population larger than that of Iowa, Nevada, Arkansas, or seventeen other US states—but they cannot participate in presidential elections, and their sole representative in Congress is not allowed to vote. Even though the people of Puerto Rico are Americans, many on the mainland do not see them that way. A poll taken days after Hurricane Maria made landfall found that almost half of all Americans did not know Puerto Ricans were citizens of the United States. Had Maria hit the mainland—like Harvey and Irma—the American public and federal officials would no doubt have clamored for a stronger response.

The island was also in poor financial condition before the storm made landfall. Beginning in the 1950s, the US government attempted to stimulate the Puerto Rican economy by offering tax breaks to companies that set up shop on the island. One provision eliminated corporate taxes on profits made in US territories, which brought pharmaceutical companies and other manufacturers to the island, jolting the local economy into overdrive. However, after the tax break was repealed in 1996, businesses fled as quickly as they had arrived. The Puerto Rican government started borrowing money from Wall Street. As the island's economy ground to a halt amid mass emigration and the financial crisis of 2007 to 2008, the banks encouraged officials in San Juan to borrow more and more. Eventually, the debt became crippling. The government ran out of money to maintain roads and pay out pensions. Hospitals closed, and the power grid fell into disrepair. On the eve of Hurricane Maria, the Puerto Rican government had barely enough money to keep itself up and running, much less bring an entire island back to life.

Regardless of Puerto Rico's precarious finances and shoddy infrastructure, the responsibility for responding to Hurricane Maria ultimately fell on the federal government. It failed. FEMA's recovery plan for the hurricane was a logistical catastrophe. Officials did not account for the scale of the storm's destruction, and they were slow to adapt to the reality on the ground. They did not have enough personnel; they underestimated the amount of food, water, and equipment survivors needed; and they did not anticipate how hard it would be to get those supplies to the people who needed them.

Large, established organizations like FEMA and the Red Cross have the mission and resources to respond to a disaster the size of Hurricane Maria. At the same time, there are numerous parties to coordinate. The response to Hurricane Maria involved not only FEMA, but also the Defense Department, the Puerto Rican government, the Red Cross, the National Guard, and countless other agencies and private-sector groups, each performing its own set of functions. When you deploy such a complex system in a large-scale disaster zone, important things are bound to slip through the cracks. One of the many issues neglected in Puerto Rico was food relief.

Three weeks into the recovery effort, FEMA estimated that it needed to provide the people of Puerto Rico with 2.2 million meals per day. But it was distributing only two hundred thousand per day at the time. Two-thirds of those were MREs, or "meals ready-to-eat," the prepackaged, built-to-last rations that troops eat on the battlefield. The remaining third, the only hot meals that FEMA was able to distribute, came from an outside nonprofit called World Central Kitchen, led by chef José Andrés.

Andrés had landed in Puerto Rico five days after Hurricane Maria hit the island. His plane was only the second commercial flight to San Juan following the storm, and he arrived the same day that senior US government officials first visited the island. But while the officials flew back to Washington that night, Andrés booked a hotel room. He had an island to feed.

I first got to know Andrés in 2009 when I worked at the State Department and recruited him to get involved in our effort to help bring clean cookstoves to poor communities where people burn dung, wood, and charcoal in open fires to heat their living spaces and cook their food. Some of our initial work focused on Haiti, which was hit by a massive earthquake right around the launch of the cookstove initiative.

José Andrés is a force of nature. When he first came to the State Department to visit with me, he was wearing dirty chef's whites and sweating profusely. He seemed like a crazy man with blazing blue eyes, manically thumbing a Blackberry phone and talking about his excitement about the naturalization process (a native of Spain, he would become an American citizen four years later). He threw himself into the clean cookstove work in Haiti and made an emotional connection to the people there. After an earthquake hit the island a handful of months later, he began an effort to bring nutritious food to a starving island. This evolved into World Central Kitchen, his nonprofit that sought to heal disaster-stricken communities one hot meal at a time. Seven years later, the organization had only three full-time staff. But it would not stay that way for long.

After Hurricane Maria hit Puerto Rico, Andrés called up Nate Mook, a documentary filmmaker who had produced a TV special on his work in Haiti. Soon, the two were in San Juan brainstorming a plan to bring hot meals to the people of Puerto Rico. The next morning, they secured fuel and ingredients from a local supplier, assembled a group of local chefs and restaurateurs, and churned out 2,500 meals in a restaurant parking lot. The next day, they prepared 4,000 meals. More volunteers and nearby restaurants quickly joined the effort, which Andrés had started calling "#ChefsForPuertoRico." Within a week, he and his team were cooking 20,000 meals per day. The group tapped into the local economy, using food trucks as mobile kitchens to deliver hot meals to remote parts of the island. They secured a government contract but it soon ran out. When Andrés tried to get a longer contract that allowed the group to expand its efforts, FEMA turned him down. The agency later admitted that bureaucratic red tape kept officials from extending the offer. Even so, Andrés found another way. Within a few weeks of the disaster, World Central Kitchen transformed the kitchen of San Juan's *Choliseo*—Puerto Rico's largest indoor arena—into its base of operations. A month in, the group was churning out more than 146,000 meals per day, using sixteen different kitchens spread across the island.

World Central Kitchen was able to quickly scale up its efforts and deliver real food, tapping into the island's preexisting networks and businesses. Meanwhile, FEMA was floundering and failing to distribute even the MREs it had at its disposal.

In the past, the US government ran the most effective logistics network on the planet. Today, that is simply not the case. The very idea that a nonprofit led by a chef would outperform a federal agency with a $20 billion budget and fourteen thousand employees is just bizarre. But in the case of Maria that is what we saw.

Credit goes to Andrés, Mook, and World Central Kitchen; they represent social entrepreneurship at its scrappiest and most effective. But the contrast also shows government at its most bumbling and ineffective. The consequences of its failure—at all levels of government, from Washington to San Juan—were deadly. For nearly a year after Hurricane Maria, the Puerto Rican government maintained that 64 people died in the storm, but in August 2018 it raised the official death toll to 2,975. The actual number may be even higher: researchers at Harvard estimated as many as 8,000 people may have died. Even so, the official figure cements Hurricane Maria as one of the deadliest disasters in US history, on par with the 9/11 terrorist attacks and the 1906 San Francisco earthquake in terms of body count. The vast majority of those deaths resulted not from the storm itself, but from the inadequate access to health care, electricity, and clean water in the months that followed. Had the government acted faster and more effectively, countless lives would have been saved.

In the aftermath of the 2017 hurricane season, FEMA officials acknowledged that they dropped the ball in their response to Maria. They made recommendations to improve their future response plans. But they also set a worrying precedent. They urged people to lower their expectations for the federal government.

José Andrés and his World Central Kitchen stepped up, but they could do only so much. They were never going to be enough to fill the void left if a government agency with a $20 billion budget, fourteen thousand employees, and the actual responsibility for emergency response decides to step back.

Yet the weakening of FEMA is part of a worrying decades-long trend, a steady decline in the effectiveness of governmental power in the United States and around much of the rest of the world. Just as shareholder capitalism boomed, the effectiveness of the governments of too many nations slumped. And we need to understand that downslope in clear detail. Where inspiration and leadership came from the United States after World War II, we should now also look to additional countries whose models of governance are outperforming the American model.

TODAY'S REALITY IS that, on issues ranging from privacy and sustainability to workers' rights and diversity, billions of people around the world are now governed more by companies than by governments.

We are guided through our days by the noiseless algorithms of technology giants that have gathered more data points on individuals around the world than any government. Forty years of efforts to address global warming have been more thoroughly defined by a handful of oil companies than by the 196 sovereign nation states and masses of citizens advocating for action. Our tax, trade, and labor laws are more likely to be drafted by the government affairs department of a multinational corporation than in the offices of a democratically elected legislature. As of this writing, the choices made by the twenty biggest CEOs on the global stage have more impact on my family's life than the decisions made by the twenty world leaders at the G-20.

As the private sector has grown in power, we have seen it expand into domains where once the government would have taken the reins. We have seen that in the stories of Walmart and Patagonia in relation to the environment, Jeff Bezos's $10 billion commitment to battling climate change, and Bill Gates's work on public health. But the examples we have covered so far do not just shine a light on the rise of corporate power throughout the last half century; they also cast a shadow on the corresponding fall in the power of governments to enact real change. Even for something as basic as minimum wage, where government has been a crucial regulator for over a century, there's now a power vacuum. In the United States, the federal minimum wage has not risen from $7.25 since 2009. Activists and employees who directly petitioned Amazon to raise its minimum wage to $15.00—a bar the company met—put change into motion faster than years' worth of appeals to Congress. Private actors are filling a perplexing void—doing what they can in an era where government seems to have lost the ability to act.

Yet there is a danger in relegating such responsibilities solely to the largesse of individual or corporate actors. It is not just that their efforts come piecemeal, and not just that they are beholden to their shareholders. The danger cuts to the very question of what government is for.

The social contract that allowed stable democracies to emerge was a historic innovation. It cracked an ever-present problem—that those who gained power were likely to abuse it. Through democracy, it became possible for individuals to come together and use their collective power to make life better for the whole, while guarding against the rampant abuse that is always possible when power ends up in the hands of a small number of people or those merely anointed at birth. Representative governments, particularly democracies, are some of the most remarkable creations that humans have ever invented.

On the one hand, this is very basic. But on the other, it has been too easily forgotten over the years. From the Reagan era to the present, one of the prevailing ideas in Western governments has been that governments should know when to get out of the way: governments were too big, too clunky, too poorly run—and whenever possible, responsibility should be handed over to the private sector, where market forces would make it run more efficiently. This idea spread like wildfire in the 1980s and 1990s—fueled by the Friedman doctrine and then the fall of the Soviet Union. And there are certainly scenarios where market forces can work wonders. Among the many examples is the creation of the consumer internet, which transitioned from a military project to a multi-stakeholder system with business at its core.

But the triumph of capitalism over communism led to it becoming accepted wisdom that all problems were best left to the market to solve. The result was that many functions of government were either gutted or handed over to the private sector in the name of "efficiency." Yet while there are distinct ways in which checks and balances can become inefficient, there was a clear loss in all of this, and that loss created a kind of self-fulfilling prophecy. If you constantly batter government as ineffective, defund its institutions, and cripple its impact, people lose confidence in these institutions and vote for less of them, even though they are what the people need most.

There are simply some realms where there is no better tool for the job than government. When it comes to developing public infrastructure and transportation, or ensuring that all citizens have access to affordable health care, the public sector is able to lead in ways that businesses cannot. The market can come up with solutions to these problems, but it cannot fix them without excluding the hundreds of millions of people who are not "attractive" to the market (usually meaning they are low-income). Yet these are the people who need access to services like public transportation and health care the most. So when government steps up, it can provide the rare solution that helps the people as a whole.

On top of that, once government power starts to fade and corporations or wealthy individuals fill the void, you start to lose democracy's most hard-won victory: the ability of people to influence their own fates. You end up with corporate autocracy. You end up losing meaningful accountability, and with it the egalitarian ideal of democracy. A good government is beholden to all citizens, not just customers or shareholders. It rules by law, not by a product's terms of service. This is what makes effective disaster relief or universal health care or universal mail service so deeply powerful when they are put into action. They provide a foundation—a set of standards and opportunities available to all. Unlike business, the charge of government is to serve those it might be profitable to ignore.

In this respect, government is not just important in the 21st century as a check on corporate power. It is, crucially, the social backstop that remains when other parties vanish. In a world of chaotic shifts and global risks, this is the bedrock for a life that's livable and enjoyable, rather than a step away from ruin at all times.

But what has happened to this idea? Why is an organization like FEMA stepping back instead of stepping up as disasters grow more prevalent? Why are national bodies, in developed and developing countries around the world, so gridlocked and immobile?

What happened to government?

Representative democracy is inefficient by design. Political leaders move in and out of power. Policy goals change. Public opinion ebbs and flows. Checks and balances are designed to keep any one branch of government from moving too quickly. If you wanted to optimize the government for agility, it would not be elected every few years by citizens. However, if the goal is to execute the will of the people, democracy is the best option. Policy makers work to steer the country in the direction that best serves the common good. If not, they are voted out of office. Through the democratic process, countries move slowly and deliberately toward a future defined by their citizens.

Of course, this is much messier in reality. Throughout history, we have seen racial, ethnic, and socioeconomic groups co-opt the democratic system to serve their own interests. Democratically elected leaders have enacted authoritarian policies to undermine the democratic system. Other times, the wheels of government stop turning altogether. Adolf Hitler and Benito Mussolini were both democratically elected before destroying their countries' systems of democracy. In countries across the continent of Africa, democratic elections have too often resulted in the de facto election of autocrats.

Today, many Western governments—perhaps none more noticeably than the United States—are in a moment of stagnation and inflection. Governments are growing larger, but they seem less equipped to take on the grand challenges we face in the 2020s and beyond.

If we delve into much of the US government's paralysis, we can see several key factors at play—from polarization, kludgeocracy, and weakened institutions, to brain drain and the capture of government by industry.

Let's start with political polarization and its by-product vetocracy.

The divisions between the two major American political parties are deeper today than they have been at any point in the last hundred years. Some experts think we need to look back to the Civil War to find examples of similar division in America. This political division has made governing the country a nearly impossible task.

Political parties have been a feature of American government since the birth of the nation. However, for most of our history the ideological lines between parties were blurrier than they are today. There were conservative Democrats, liberal Republicans, and moderates of many shades in both parties. This ideological overlap allowed lawmakers to negotiate and legislate across party lines. As recently as the early 1990s, it was not uncommon for Democrats and Republicans to vote with the other side, especially on foreign policy issues. Most voters today may look down on this sort of political horse trading, but it kept the wheels of democracy turning for decades.

That changed with the end of the Cold War. The United States lost the existential challenge that forced it to unify, and in the aftermath, a variety of geographic, demographic, and ideological trends drew the parties further apart. Voters now tend to judge lawmakers more on their ideological purity than their bargaining skills. At the same time, both parties have become more evenly matched in congressional seats and public support. In the past, a single party more frequently had governing majorities across the executive and legislative branches, but in recent years Democrats and Republicans have won their majorities by small margins. This makes it easier for the minority party to stonewall legislation. And with each election hotly contested, the costs of working across the aisle began to outweigh the benefits.

Given the US government's complex system of checks and balances, this "us-versus-them" mentality makes it difficult to get anything done. For the federal government to enact a policy that lasts, the House of Representatives, the Senate, and the president must all sign off. It must also hold up to challenges in the courts. These numerous "veto points" bias the US government toward inaction—it requires a significant amount of buy-in and momentum to get anything done. Unless the same political party controls the White House and both chambers of Congress, the opposition can stop the legislative process in its tracks.

Between 2010 and 2020, that was the case for only two years—2017 and 2018—and Republicans used their control to enact what amounted to a $2 trillion tax cut for mostly large corporations and wealthy individuals. Not one of the 237 Democrats in Congress voted for the bill. Today, Democrats and Republicans disagree not just on taxes, but also on climate change, health care, immigration, foreign policy, economic regulation, and nearly every issue in between. Over the last decade, we have seen each party obstruct the other, preventing meaningful legislation on these issues from passing.

To describe this reality, where obstruction becomes the dominant mode of governance, political scientist Francis Fukuyama coined the term *vetocracy*.

"The delegation of powers to different political actors enables them to block action by the whole body. The U.S. political system has far more of these checks and balances, or what political scientists call 'veto points,' than other contemporary democracies, raising the costs of collective action and in some cases make it impossible altogether," Fukuyama wrote. "In earlier periods of U.S. history, when one party or another was dominant, this system served to moderate the will of the majority and force it to pay greater attention to minorities than it otherwise might have. But in the more evenly balanced, highly competitive party system that has arisen since the 1980s, it has become a formula for gridlock."

Vetocracy not only prevents Congress from passing effective legislation, it also makes it harder to get rid of redundant or out-of-date regulations and government programs. Eliminating an old policy becomes just as hard as enacting a new one. As a result, new laws often get glommed onto old ones. This leads to a second problem: kludgeocracy.

As policies overlap and intertwine, they become more difficult for government agencies to administer. Political scientist Steven Teles coined the term *kludgeocracy*, likening the legal clutter to "kludge," the clumsy patches that programmers use to temporarily fix a piece of software.

An example can be seen in America's inability to undertake major infrastructure problems like the municipal system that provides the water for my coffeepot. It is not that we know less now about how to build and manage a water system than we did a hundred years ago, it is that the process for doing so has become so overburdened by a thousand administrative layers and expenses that doing so has become near-impossible.

"For any particular problem we have arrived at the most gerry-rigged, opaque, and complicated response," Teles wrote of US public policy. "From the mind-numbing complexity of the health care system . . . our Byzantine system of funding higher education, and our bewildering federal-state system of governing everything from the welfare state to environmental regulation, America has chosen more indirect and incoherent policy mechanisms than any comparable country."

The Internal Revenue Service, for instance, needs to constantly update its efforts to reflect the tax policies of each new administration, while also studying increasingly complex transactions across the world's 196 countries to track the maneuverings of the world's largest companies and wealthiest people. It's dealing with the kludge of every nation, and it is also operating with fewer resources than it needs to administer the law.

The US government's tax collection agency is just one of several departments that have been weakened in recent years. Between 2010 and 2020, Congress cut the IRS budget by 21 percent. Today, the IRS employs fewer auditors than it did in 1953, and in 2019 the agency audited less than half as many tax returns as it did a decade prior. Audit rates for individuals making more than $10 million—the top 0.1 percent of income earners—fell from 14.5 percent in 2017 to 6.7 percent in 2018. In 2018, people making less than $20,000 per year were about as likely to face an audit as those making more than $500,000 per year. Ten years ago, the IRS performed annual audits for every US company with more than $20 billion in assets. In 2018, less than half of those companies came under the agency's magnifying glass. When auditing major companies, the agency also finds itself frequently outgunned by corporate lawyers. Untangling the tax schemes of big businesses and billionaires requires a substantial amount of expertise, personnel, and money. Right now at the IRS, all three are in short supply.

We have seen similar trends in other government agencies charged with keeping the private sector in check. The Environmental Protection Agency employed fewer people in 2020 than it did in 1988. After adjusting for inflation, its current budget is lower as well. The Federal Trade Commission, the US consumer protection agency, has also seen its real budget and staff reduced over the past decade. To address major public problems, government institutions will need more money and people, not less.

Political polarization and kludgy, weakened institutions have rendered the US government unable to address too many of today's challenges. We can see the effects of this stagnation in the country's soaring health care costs; its unequal and expensive education system; its crumbling infrastructure; its urban housing shortages; its growing economic inequality; its inaction toward climate change; its failure to lead in advanced manufacturing and other emerging technologies. We saw them in the US government's inability to prepare for and respond to the COVID-19 pandemic, a failure that cost hundreds of thousands of Americans their lives. We saw how FEMA's kludgeocracy led to the loss of lives in Puerto Rico.

Addressing these challenges requires big ideas and bold actions. In the past, federal, state, and local governments transformed the national landscape with infrastructure projects. The Erie Canal linked the Atlantic Ocean to the Great Lakes in 1825, the Illinois and Michigan Canal connected the Great Lakes to the Mississippi River a generation later, and the First Transcontinental Railroad connected the eastern United States to the West Coast a generation after that. For the thirteen years that I commuted from Baltimore to Washington, DC, my train traveled through a 1.4-mile-long tunnel built in the 1890s by 2,400 workers. In the 20th century, the federal government helped build the Lincoln Tunnel, the interstate highway system, a national air traffic control system, and the internet. Through programs like Social

Security, Medicare, and Medicaid, it also constructed a safety net for its most vulnerable citizens. Today it is difficult to imagine the state undertaking such large projects. It is frozen by kludgeocracy, vetocracy, and a lack of imagination and will.

The government needs fresh thinkers to break its stagnation, but it is also suffering from a fourth causal factor in its decline: brain drain. The loss of talent is not the chief cause of government's woes—we will get to that shortly—but real consequences add up when government is an unattractive choice for a nation's graduates. Few of today's best and brightest want to spend their careers fighting bureaucracy and resetting a derailed political system.

Throughout the Cold War, many talented, driven graduates from universities across both the Western world and the Soviet bloc were driven to work for their governments by a sense of mission and purpose. In the sciences, this could mean going to work for NASA or one of the national laboratories. For a student of business or economics, this meant going to work for the Treasury Department. The best and brightest students in the humanities often joined the Foreign Service, the CIA, or their non-US equivalents. The State Department and CIA were stacked with fresh graduates from America's top universities. The Foreign Office and MI6 were chock-a-block with Cambridge and Oxford alumni. But the popularity of government jobs began to decline as society started deifying captains of industry. Oliver Stone's movie *Wall Street* served more as an inspiration than as the harsh critique the filmmaker intended. The lifestyle of Gordon Gekko and his real-life equivalents drew more young men (and it was overwhelmingly men) to the world of business and finance. Beginning in the 1990s, it became rare for graduates of the most prestigious universities to view government service as an attractive career. More often than not, they chose an investment bank, an elite consultancy, or a technology company. Those with a real bent for public service gravitated toward Teach for America or large development NGOs.

Tom Fletcher is the principal of Hertford College, University of Oxford, which has roots dating back to 1280 and alumni that include John Donne, Thomas Hobbes, and Jonathan Swift. Before returning to lead his alma mater, Tom was the hottest of young hotshots in the UK Foreign Office. He served at Number 10 Downing Street as foreign policy adviser to three prime ministers—Tony Blair, Gordon Brown, and David Cameron—and went on to become the British ambassador to Lebanon, all before the age of forty. Today, however, fewer young people are trying to follow in his footsteps.

"The problem for government is that they're just outgunned, and not just in that they are lacking the resources and the energy and the tech to keep up," Tom told me. "If there's an arms race for talent the government's gonna lose it. . . . You look at the UK now, the best people are not going off to join the fast-stream civil service."

Some countries have taken innovative approaches to recruiting and retaining the very best people to serve in government. One notable example is Singapore. When I served in government, the White House held a monthly meeting for the innovation leads from each federal agency. The only time a foreign government was ever invited to participate was when representatives from the Singaporean government presented their government's long-term planning strategies (ours looked pathetic by comparison). The presentation was led by Aaron Maniam, a career civil servant with economics, politics, and philosophy degrees from Oxford and Yale, and a side hobby writing award-winning poetry. The impression Maniam and his colleagues made was unforgettable.

Singapore is able to recruit and retain Maniam and other dazzling talents in significant part because they are compensated like their private-sector peers. The formula includes pay for a "thirteenth month" and includes bonuses linked to the country's economic performance. Job stability for career civil servants is known as the Iron Rice Bowl. At the minister level, a compensation formula ensures an annual salary of more than $1 million a year, much like a top executive in business. Taking away the financial incentive to leave government allows real expertise to gather and grow in the civil service. It also increases the prestige of serving in government.

Unfortunately, that dynamic does not exist in the West. There are amazing people who devote their careers to public service, and

I worked alongside many of them during my four years of service at the State Department. But today, too few remain in government. The appeal of better pay, more independence, and sometimes even more power drew many of my colleagues to the private sector while they still had decades left in their careers. They have gone on to take roles at companies like JPMorgan Chase, Visa, BlackRock, Google, Twitter, Stripe, and Qualcomm. Several started companies of their own. I frequently receive emails from the career officials who have not yet left, asking for a cup of coffee and counsel about how to navigate the transition out of government.

Thanks to brain drain, much of the expertise in how to develop and implement policy—the skills needed to actually govern—exists outside of the government. And the private sector is more than happy to scoop up these former officials. The skills they developed in government transfer well to business, and so do their relationships with their former employer. Ex–government employees are a valuable asset to companies that want access to decision makers in Washington, Brussels, London, and other capitals.

This dynamic is especially pronounced in the legislative branch, where low pay and long hours (which average between sixty and seventy hours a week) push the majority of congressional staffers to leave before their thirty-second birthday. Once in the private sector, former congressional staffers can help their new employers build relationships with policy makers and navigate the machinations of Washington. The same goes for former White House staffers, agency officials, and foreign policy hands. In a city that runs on interpersonal relationships, your Rolodex can be just as important as your résumé.

This phenomenon is not unique to the United States. When I spoke with Tom Fletcher, he alluded to a similar revolving door between the British government and the financial services industry.

"HSBC has this guy Sherard Cowper-Coles who's a fairly notorious ex–UK ambassador," Tom remarked. "He styles himself as HSBC's foreign minister and will walk up to places and will expect to see the top people because he sees himself as at that level. He doesn't quite call himself 'His Excellency the Foreign Minister of HSBC,' but he kind of behaves like that."

WE HAVE EXAMINED the role of politicians and policy makers in the government's current dysfunction, but the most important factor to consider comes from the outside. The private sector has played a striking role in sterilizing the state. Rather than having a government of, by, and for the people, the United States and other countries around the world now have a government of, by, and for the businesses that purchase the governments they want.

Government policy affects virtually every corner of the economy, which gives all manner of companies incentives and vested interests to sway those decisions in their favor. Milton Friedman's famous position states that a business's purpose is to maximize its profits "so long as it stays within the rules of the game." But over the last four decades, mirroring the time period of the rise of shareholder capitalism, private companies have been remarkably successful at reshaping the rules of the game. They have attained a level of influence in Washington unrivaled since the Gilded Age.

The term—and practice of—*lobbying* dates back to the 1640s, when the British public would gather in a lobby outside the House of Commons to speak with members of Parliament. In the United States, citizens have lobbied lawmakers since the birth of the republic. But the industry grew more prominent and professionalized—and despised—in the late 19th century. In this era, the monopolies of the Gilded Age were deeply invested in currying favor with lawmakers and defending economic policies that sustained their monopolies. Lobbying boomed as a result, roping in a raft of retired congressmen to make the monopolists' case to their old colleagues. The industry came under increased scrutiny in the early 20th century, however, as Congress launched frequent investigations into corporate influence efforts and started requiring lobbyists to file quarterly activity reports with both the House and Senate. After the Great Depression and World War II, the lobbying industry hit a lull—and so did the private sector's influence in Washington. During the mid-20th century, the private sector and Washington had a mostly distant but cordial relationship, with each preferring to stay out of the other's day-to-day business. But as public support for stronger labor laws, consumer protections, and general business regulation grew during the tumult of the late 1960s, companies felt they needed to start playing stronger defense.

In 1971, just before that wave hit, future Supreme Court justice Lewis Powell Jr. noted that "few elements of American society today have as little influence in government as the American businessman, the corporation, or even the millions of corporate stockholders. If one doubts this, let him undertake the role of 'lobbyist' for the business point of view before Congressional committees." Today, there are zero elements of American society with *more* influence in government than corporations.

The rebirth of lobbying followed the same trajectory as the explosion of shareholder capitalism, and the two were intimately connected. In 1972, two anti-labor groups and a loose organization of corporate executives joined together to form the Business Roundtable. The group worked alongside a growing army of corporate lobbyists to reduce regulations, cut taxes, and kill labor reform. Instead of organized labor, this was organized capital. The business community's investment in government lobbying during the 1970s had something of a snowball effect. After logging a few early victories, companies saw the huge returns that a relatively small investment in influence operations brought to their bottom line. Instead of hiring lobbyists as one-off hit men to fight a new regulation or law, companies brought them on as full-time guards. As issues arose, new firms would enter the influence game, and if their interests clashed with existing players, the old guard hired even more lobbyists. It became a loop, with lobbyists creating the need for more lobbyists.

In 1975, federal lobbyists collectively drew less than $100 million in revenue. In 2019, lobbyists brought in $3.5 billion, thirty-five times what they had made forty-five years earlier. And that is just what is publicly reported. As in the Gilded Age, former members of Congress are flocking to the profession. Approximately a quarter of the lawmakers who left Congress between 2009 and 2019 went to work for lobbying firms. Still others work as private consultants, advisers, and government relations specialists without having to file as lobbyists.

Though most people associate it with corruption, lobbying is one of the few professions protected under the US Constitution. The First Amendment guarantees citizens the right to petition the government, and lobbying is one way for them to do so. In practice, lobbyists are something like mercenaries of the democratic process. Any special interest group can hire a lobbyist to advocate on behalf of virtually any policy. An oil company might hire a lobbyist to advocate on behalf of a new pipeline, and an environmental advocacy group might hire a lobbyist to fight against it. Lobbyists also play an important role in helping overworked policy makers make sense of complex topics. But, inevitably, lobbyists tilt the democratic process in favor of the interest groups with the ability to hire the most and the best lobbyists. Good lobbyists are expensive. While the advocacy group might be able to afford a single lobbyist to fight against a proposed pipeline, the oil company can afford to hire dozens. For every dollar that public interest groups and labor unions spent on lobbying in 2019, companies and business associations spent fifteen. Lobbyists give voice to competing points of view and priorities, but wealthy companies can raise the decibel level and drown out the competition.

In many cases, their roles are alarmingly hands-on. In 2013, the House passed a bill that would roll back a portion of the Dodd-Frank Act, a financial reform bill enacted in the aftermath of the 2008 financial crisis. Reporters found that seventy of the eighty-five lines in the measure were pulled directly from a draft bill written by Citigroup lobbyists. This is a common practice now. A separate investigation found that more than 2,100 state laws enacted between 2011 and 2019 were copied nearly verbatim from lobbyist proposals.

One leading lobbyist, Bruce Mehlman, walked me through the latest developments in the industry. Mehlman has moved between business and government his whole life. He began his career on Capitol Hill, moved to Cisco Systems, returned to government as a senior

Commerce Department official, and left the government again to start his own lobbying firm. Today, he helps companies including Walmart, IBM, Lyft, Procter & Gamble, and Twitter make their case to policy makers. Mehlman is lean, loquacious, and bursting with energy. While your typical workplace go-getter is content sitting or standing at a desk, Bruce outfitted his with a treadmill platform. He spends the first two hours of his workday, from 6:30 a.m. to 8:30 a.m., doing his reading for the day while walking the equivalent of five miles at his desk. With more than eighty clients, he is among the most prolific lobbyists in Washington. If you are a member of Congress who wants to understand a given piece of legislation, Mehlman can give you a level of analysis you could not get from even your most capable staffer.

Mehlman told me that the nature of the influence business has changed in the last few years. Registered lobbyists used to do much of the heavy lifting, but today the industry is becoming less overt. Instead of hiring an official lobbyist, many companies are now recruiting former government officials to serve as consultants or strategists. Unlike registered lobbyists like Mehlman, these "shadow lobbyists" do not disclose their list of clients nor the amount of money they receive. While such informal influence channels are not necessarily pernicious, they certainly have the potential to be. "I am a fan of disclosure," Mehlman said.

"Ideally, the more transparency there can be into who's investing in educating policy makers the better," he told me. Indeed, the number of registered lobbyists in Washington has declined over the last decade, while the money spent on lobbying remained relatively constant, an indication that even professional influence peddlers are retreating into the shadows.

Social media is also enabling more subtle, data-driven influence campaigns than would ever have been possible in the past. "The paths by which organizations engage government as a stakeholder are now surround sound—they're now 5-, 6-, 7-cushion bank shots," Mehlman said. "To influence policy makers, you want to influence what they read. You can now [through] big data have a far better understanding of who they find persuasive—who do they follow, who are they most likely to tweet or retweet, who have they posted on their Facebook pages, who do they quote in floor speeches—all of which is machine-searchable. That leads to the most sophisticated players thinking six steps removed."

By way of illustration, Mehlman told me a story about a pharmaceutical company hoping to influence the thinking of a specific United States senator. This senator and her staff are "especially" wary of corporate lobbyists, according to Mehlman, so the company turned to advanced artificial intelligence tools developed by ex–NSA employees. Based on the senator's use of Twitter, the AI program can determine whom the senator was reading and therefore who was influencing her. They determined that she was a close follower of the journalist Ezra Klein. Mehlman noted that "Ezra Klein is a pretty sophisticated fellow and you can't just bring a PR slick or executive to schmooze Ezra Klein and get Ezra Klein to do what you want. But then they went through a ton of Ezra Klein's writings and found a professor at Boston University that Ezra Klein clearly followed." Mehlman said the AI program identified that the professor was "not a famous guy" but Klein referred to his writing with unexpected frequency, and he was therefore persuasive. What did the pharmaceutical company do with this information? They commissioned an analysis from this professor, which they anticipated would be noted by Klein, who in turn would write about it and therefore influence the senator.

Will that work? It seems unlikely, but not impossible. That's the frightening level of forethought that now goes into lobbying. But, of course, it does not always take that level of sophistication.

In the United States, the last decade has opened the door for companies to add a blunter tool to their arsenal for influencing Washington: campaign finance. In 2010, the Supreme Court ruled that limiting "independent political spending" by corporations, wealthy donors, and other groups violates their right to free speech. Since then, money has poured into American elections. Outside groups spent a total of $680 million during the five national election cycles preceding the *Citizens United* decision. In the five cycles after the ruling, they spent $4.4

billion. The total spending on congressional and presidential elections has grown from $4 billion in 2000 to more than $14 billion in 2020.

Still, some companies hesitate to openly support one candidate over another—it could be bad for business if they back the wrong horse. But thanks to *Citizens United*, there are avenues for these cautious corporate donors to anonymously funnel money to their preferred candidates and causes. Under the ruling, political nonprofits can donate to super PACs and other outside groups without disclosing the origin of their money. Using these "dark money" groups, wealthy individuals and companies can support candidates without the public ever knowing. Dark money groups spent nearly $1 billion on elections in the decade after *Citizens United*. None of that would have been possible before the *Citizens United* decision.

Such a laissez-faire approach to campaign finance lets companies and wealthy individuals play outsized roles in shaping the government and its legislative agenda. Richard Trumka, president of the AFL-CIO, put the situation vividly when I spoke with him.

> If you go back to the time of the signing of the Constitution, there was an argument between Thomas Jefferson and Hamilton. Hamilton wanted to create corporations, and Jefferson said these are very dangerous creatures. To allow them to accumulate wealth and power could negate all the benefits of the revolution we fought. And Hamilton said, "But Tom we will give them a few prescribed rights, and that's how we'll control them." Corporations currently have more rights than the three humans sitting in this room. They have more rights, not equal rights, more rights. And then the Supreme Court decides that money equals free speech. Now, I don't think Jefferson and Hamilton and Washington fought for revolution so that Hamilton could say to Jefferson, "You know, Tom, I have more money than you, therefore, I will have more free speech than you." But that's what we have.

Donations do not guarantee a victory at the ballot box, but evidence shows that they certainly help. In 2018, 83 percent of Senate races and 89 percent of House races were won by the candidate who spent the most money. The result is that candidates are beholden to their donors, first to get elected and then once they take office. It is difficult to link a politician's stance on a specific issue to a specific donor, but the impact of campaign finance becomes more evident at the macro level. Candidates need donations to win elections, and to get donations, they must craft their platforms to appeal to donors, especially the ones with the deepest pockets. In 2018, just 225,000 people—less than one-tenth of 1 percent of American adults—contributed a combined $3.1 billion to political campaigns, PACs, parties, and outside groups. Collectively, that small fraction of the population provided 55 percent of the money spent in the 2018 race. Candidates who do not appeal to the concerns of this elite donor class—and shape their platforms accordingly—are unlikely to win.

Once politicians are in office, evidence shows that they continue to prioritize issues that are relevant to donors above those of everyday people. In 2014, a pair of political scientists studied how closely government policy correlated to the preferences of voters in different income brackets. After comparing public opinion and public policy on nearly 1,800 different issues, they drew a stark conclusion: "Economic elites and organized groups representing business interests have substantial independent impacts on U.S. government policy, while average citizens and mass-based interest groups have little or no independent influence."

Thanks to the influence industry and lax campaign finance laws, the US government has effectively been captured by the interests of corporations and a very small number of wealthy elites. It would be unfair to blame the government's current dysfunction entirely on the private sector, but a weak state certainly increases the relative power of industry.

At best, the private sector is complicit in the stagnation of American democracy. At worst, it plays an active role in promoting corporate autocracy and enabling corporate socialism, where the costs of bailouts are paid by taxpayers while gains are captured by shareholders.

When it comes to the influence game, many business leaders respond to criticism by saying that they did not break the law. This is also a common response when companies are criticized for optimizing the short term over the long term, or for catering to shareholders over employees, the environment, and customers. But there is a snag in this logic.

According to Columbia Law School professor Tim Wu, it downplays both the private sector's responsibilities and the consequences of its actions. "It'd be one thing if the rules were completely made external to your business. But if you help influence how those rules are made . . . you're playing by your own rules," Wu told me. "I think the older modeled corporation . . . had an idea of ethical duty that went beyond what was legal."

But since the rise of shareholder capitalism, the private sector has tended to favor legal soundness over moral correctness. And in doing so, it has fundamentally undermined the social contract in the United States, said Stanford University historian Niall Ferguson.

"There are three kinds of countries in the world," Ferguson told me. "There are countries where there really isn't that much corruption and there is a fairly high level of probity in both business and political life. There are countries where there is the exact opposite: corruption is endemic . . . private interests treat the state as a gravy train. And then there's the third category of countries, where corruption is legal and institutionalized and transparent. You know who's giving money to the campaign and you basically know who's in the room where it happens. The social contract says, 'we hold these truths to be self-evident, but cash counts.'"

Ferguson's case in point for that last category: the United States.

Every nation in the world is navigating some combination of factors that interfere with government's ability to meet the needs of its people; this is the reality of any complex society. But the confluence of forces in the United States puts it in unique territory. The US has seen more power shift from the government to capital than just about any other developed country. The United States is the wealthiest nation in the world—it boasts the world's largest companies, the world's richest individuals, the world's highest GDP, and the world's highest government budget. Yet many Americans of working age find themselves operating without an effective safety net.

This is a break in the social contract that emerged from the Industrial Revolution. In industrialized societies, where citizens' well-being can rise and fall with the forces of the market, the earliest decades of industrialization and instability known as Engels' Pause came to a close only when governments began taking on responsibility for citizens' economic security. Developed countries enacted policies to promote economic growth and to ensure that citizens shared in those gains. They also created social programs meant to prevent society's most vulnerable members from falling into poverty, a *safety net* that keeps people from hitting the ground when fortunes rise and fall.

Safety net programs have existed in various forms for millennia. The Roman Empire ran a pension program for retired soldiers, paying out veterans in land and lump sums of cash. During the Tang dynasty, the Chinese government distributed tax-free land to families with senior citizens, provided professional servants to people over the age of eighty, and distributed allowances to widows. Social welfare was similarly baked into the laws of the early Islamic caliphates. Citing Muslims' obligation to provide for the poor (a concept known as *zakat*), governments would redistribute a portion of the taxes they collected to the needy. These programs were so successful that in the 8th century officials struggled to find anyone poor enough to receive welfare.

Modern safety net programs tend to be more targeted than these general cash transfers. They can include retirement benefits, health insurance, unemployment insurance, housing allowances, childcare benefits, food assistance, and other initiatives meant to keep the country's most vulnerable members out of poverty. Some countries also provide cash welfare in the form of tax breaks and other transfers. While it is not a safety net program in the traditional sense, public education serves as a social good by offering children of every race, ethnicity, and class a path to economic stability.

The United States has always had a more limited social safety net than other Western democracies. American culture places a premium on individualism and self-sufficiency, and it tends to look down on those who receive support from the government. Unlike many other developed countries, the US does not provide free health care or higher education. Instead of relying on the state to provide a safety net, most Americans receive benefits like health care and retirement savings through their employer.

The private model emerged out of a quirk of World War II–era policy—whereby companies could use benefit packages, like health insurance, to compete for new employees while complying with a wartime wage freeze. The model stuck around as the postwar economy boomed, and it worked reasonably well when employees worked for the same company their entire career and benefit levels were high. Today, these are less often the case. Even those companies that offer long-term employment have seen benefits shrink over decades of shareholder capitalism.

Meanwhile, the costs of basic necessities like housing, education, and health care have skyrocketed. Between 2002 and 2018, Americans saw the cost of housing rise 26 percent, the cost of health care rise 35 percent, and the cost of education rise 70 percent. These growing expenses disproportionately affect low-income families, who already spend a larger chunk of their earnings on basic necessities than wealthier households.

In 2019, researchers found that 40 percent of American households were one paycheck away from falling into poverty. The figure rose to 57 percent for nonwhite families, and that was before COVID hit. Today, millions of Americans belong to the working poor, living right around the poverty line despite holding a job.

Private benefits also only work when people have jobs. As unemployment soared in the early days of the COVID-19 pandemic, millions of people lost health coverage at the time they needed it most. As people filed for unemployment, food stamps, and other benefits, US government safety net programs became overwhelmed. Some people found themselves waiting months to receive unemployment payments. Workers who received welfare payments found they covered only a small portion of the income they had lost due to the pandemic.

The pandemic revealed an inconvenient truth about the industry-driven social contract in the United States: it no longer works. Young people exiting school now seem more likely to have thirty jobs in thirty years than they are to have one job and one employer. Giving the private sector outsized influence over the country's economic, political, and social health has not led to better outcomes for Americans, and companies would be delighted to not be the principal source of benefits. Companies are driven by the demands of the market, and those do not always align with the demands of a fair and just society. It is in those moments when the market does not deliver that the government is supposed to step in.

THIS DEEP DIVE into the American system shows us how a combination of internal governmental issues and external influences of business and private wealth can ultimately warp the social contract. The whole picture looks grim when laid out in brief, but it is by no means unfixable or inevitable. In a sense, the United States went on a bender after its chief rival, the USSR, sputtered and fell. It took the guardrails off its economic system, massively decreased taxes for corporations and high earners, and now is realizing how the social contract becomes skewed when government leaves the market unchecked.

But there are numerous examples of effective social contracts and safety nets that we can look to in trying to right the balance. As you will read in greater depth later in the book, a number of European nations, as well as South Korea, Australia, and New Zealand, have found ways to balance commerce and innovation with robust protections for workers who get caught up in the ebbs and flows of the market. While each model has its strengths and weaknesses, they are all instructive.

The Nordics, Canada, Australia, and New Zealand have used

democracy to build some of the world's strongest social safety nets. Under their social contracts, the state and its institutions guarantee citizens a high quality of life from the cradle to the grave.

The political and economic systems of the United States seek to provide Americans with equality of opportunity, knowing there will be inequality of outcome. In Japan, it is the opposite: everyone can expect a near-equal outcome.

Countries as distant geographically and culturally as South Korea and Israel have embraced the unregulated freedom of American-style capitalism but pair it with a stronger safety net.

In contrast, the world's second leading power, China, has followed a completely different model. Over the last three decades, the Chinese Communist Party successfully implemented a social contract that combines the top-down control of authoritarianism with the efficiency and profitability of capitalism. This mix of political control and economic freedom—considered impossible decades ago—has transformed China from an agrarian state with two-thirds of its population living in extreme poverty into a formidable geopolitical player, though that requires consistently steep levels of continual growth in the absence of much in the way of formal state safety net programs.

The reality around the world is that developing nations are now choosing what social contract they will adopt as they come into their own in the 2020s and beyond. And the two leading models are the world's greatest powers, the United States and China. The United States has long been the gold standard among developed nations, and if it rights the rifts in its social contract, then it will continue to be the nation that other nations aspire toward. From its founding, the US government was designed to be flexible enough to meet the needs of its people but inefficient enough, with layers of checks and balances, to avoid governmental overreach. The result was a framework that could foster both human liberty and security—goals that any individual around the world can appreciate. But the United States' recent woes have invited doubts around the world about its future and its framework—even about the very compatibility of basic democracy with high-octane capitalism.

The growing interest among developing nations in China's model rests on exactly these doubts. China's model is rigid; it is founded on fast growth and firm executive action, which has kept companies and citizens alike in line with the party's goals. But China's social contract is ripe for the abuse of power. It is a throwback to social contracts from centuries past, where the people have little to no say in the direction taken by their governments. China has made it work so far, while it has been on a decades-long economic growth streak: Chinese citizens have seen their quality of life improve dramatically as the economy has opened up. Meanwhile, the iron hand of the Chinese government has offered shelter from the economic volatility that shook many other countries in the 2000s and 2010s. But if ever China's growth stalls or reverses, then the tacit social contract could be challenged. The Chinese people have given up major freedoms in exchange for growth and well-being. If the latter stalls, the deal will start to look very bad for hundreds of millions of people—at which point, authoritarianism and force are what would hold the government-dominated social contract in place.

The pressure is now on for the United States to both innovate and draw from fellow Western democracies to right its model. If it does not, much of the world will shift toward a more authoritarian approach that continues to take power out of the hands of everyday people.

3

THE WORKERS

The golden age of the American worker emerged out of a cloud of tear gas and bullets inside Fisher Body plant #2.

Thirteen days earlier, General Motors (GM) automotive laborers and their fellow employees had brought the company's sprawling Flint, Michigan, production facilities to a standstill. The workers wanted to unionize, and GM had fought their efforts every step of the way. On Wednesday, December 30, 1936, workers learned that the company planned to move the production of its dies—the equipment used to shape the bodies of cars—from Flint to factories with less union presence elsewhere in the state. That night, the Flint workers locked themselves inside the factory and refused to leave. The dies in Flint were one of just two sets used to stamp each of GM's 1937 cars. By taking over the plant, workers brought the company's production to a halt. Within days, the "sit-down strike" spread to other GM facilities in the area. The strikers' demands were straightforward: they wanted a minimum wage, improved working conditions, and bargaining rights for the newly formed United Auto Workers (UAW) union.

As the strike wore on, the workers made their home on the factory floors. Surrounded by the half-built bodies of Buick sedans, they read, gambled, sang, played table tennis, and lounged on floor mats and car seats. Supporters delivered food and supplies to the occupying workers while leading their own protests outside the plant. GM got a court order to break the strike, but it feared there would be backlash if workers were evicted by force. Instead, the company cut the heat to Fisher Body plant #2, hoping the cold Michigan winter would freeze out the men inside.

The heat shuddered off on January 11, but the strikers stayed put. That night, when the workers opened the factory gate for a food delivery, Flint police made their move. They stormed the facility, firing tear gas and buckshot at the strikers. The workers fought back by hurling car parts and spraying the police with fire hoses. The brawl, dubbed the "Battle of the Running Bulls," left twenty-eight people injured.

After the clash, Michigan's governor deployed 1,200 national guardsmen to the scene to protect the strikers and support negotiations between workers and management. At a time when labor disputes were often settled with violence, the decision proved critical to the workers' cause. The strike continued for another month. After some 136,000 GM employees at forty-four plants joined the strike in solidarity, the company reached an agreement with the UAW: the union would represent workers at seventeen plants, and employees were given a wage increase.

The GM sit-down strike was called "the most significant American labor conflict in the twentieth century" by labor historian Sidney Fine. The UAW's success in Flint galvanized union activity across the automotive industry. Within two weeks, workers in Detroit launched eighty-seven sit-down strikes, and within a year wages for auto workers increased nearly 300 percent and UAW membership shot up from thirty thousand to five hundred thousand. Workers in other industries began to unionize more aggressively as well. Between 1934 and 1943, the proportion of the US workforce that belonged to a union more than tripled, from 7.6 percent to 24.3 percent. By the early 1950s, one in three American workers was a card-carrying union member.

At the time of the GM strike, the United States was primed for an explosion in organized labor—the Flint workers simply lit the match.

The Great Depression had depressed wages and decreased job opportunities for working people, leaving much of the country feeling insecure and discontent. Unions promised economic security to workers at a time when they felt they had little to lose. The political atmosphere had also turned in their favor. The federal government guaranteed workers' right to unionize and participate in collective action in the 1935 Wagner Act, one of many pro-labor policies enacted under the New Deal. After signing the law, President Franklin D. Roosevelt summarized his administration's attitude toward labor: "If I went to work in a factory, the first thing I'd do is join a union."

It was at this same time and facing similar economic distress that Germany turned to Nazism and Italy to fascism. Those moments of the early 1930s are like those of the present: something dramatic is going to happen and it is not preordained what shape it will take. These are inflection points that can drive society to reshape its policies toward genocidal, nativist authoritarianism or toward liberalism.

After the crash of Wall Street and the Depression that followed, the US government and workers' unions effectively came together to revise the social contract so that it better fit the needs of workers. It was a move away from the boom-and-bust model of the "roaring '20s," which bears a heck of a strong resemblance to the 2010s in the United States. Coming out of the Depression there was a new sense of who the indispensable workers were—those building the cars, planes, trains, and skyscrapers that defined industrial America. A similar awakening came during the COVID pandemic, which brought about a new appreciation for frontline workers in health care, food, and services.

General Motors and the business community were forced to the table as signatories, and worker protections and benefits were systematically enshrined into law. A social contract is a living document of sorts that needs periodic renewal and revision, and the economic growth of the subsequent decades would benefit workers and executives alike.

But over the next half century, attitudes toward organized labor incrementally soured in the United States. Unions would come to be seen less as fierce advocates for working people and more as bloated, corrupt bureaucracies intent on maintaining their own power. Today, more people are familiar with the mob-affiliated Teamsters president Jimmy Hoffa than with Samuel Gompers, John L. Lewis, Sidney Hillman, or the other figures who built the modern labor movement.

In my personal and professional circles, few topics are more polarizing than labor unions. One camp holds them up as indispensable to achieving economic justice; another views them as inefficient, corrupt remnants of the past.

My first time working shoulder to shoulder with union members was a summer I spent working on a beer truck. Most of the truck drivers were Teamsters and those who were not were putting in the requisite years of work they needed to become eligible for membership.

The wheels of the truck rolled out of the warehouse at 6:00 a.m. That meant we had to be at the warehouse loading the truck up at 5:15 a.m. I am convinced that the men who worked in that warehouse were the strongest men on earth. I was nineteen years old and as strong as I have ever been in my life, but I could barely keep up with the fifty-five- and sixty-year-old men who worked on the beer trucks. These guys were tough. Most of them were from what we called the Hollows—the valleys that run down the edges of hills in West Virginia. Even though I had grown up and spent just about all my life living in West Virginia, some of the accents I heard in that beer warehouse were so thick I could barely understand them. It was a sing-songy accent derived from Old English that only lives on deep in the hills of Appalachia.

My job was to deliver the beer and guard the truck—a lot of these bars were in rough areas. We would show up at bars starting at 7 a.m., when many opened to serve workers coming off night shifts and chronic alcoholics who need a drink soon after they wake up. The bars would be completely full of men, each with exactly three things in front of them: a shot glass, a can of beer, and their pistol. In a lot of the really tough Hollows, we would not dare to enter a bar after noon.

These truck-driving Teamsters were successful. They made what was great money in the West Virginia of the 1990s. They bought new cars or pickups every two years. They owned boats and took vacations. They had the social cachet that accompanied their economic well-being and standing as Teamsters, and they worked hard as hell for it. It was a clear view into what happens when unionization works.

But in my first job after college, I caught a glimpse of what can go wrong when unions fail. I was hired as a public school teacher in Baltimore, and when it came time to check the box asking whether I'd join the union, I did not hesitate. My starting teaching salary was $22,459. The Baltimore Teachers Union withdrew $44 from my biweekly salary for membership fees, a noticeable amount for a guy who, after paying taxes, would end up with around $15,000 a year. If I had not joined the union, I would still have had to pay $39 every paycheck as an agency fee, meaning that although I would not have been a union member and would not have benefited from its protections, I was still mandated to pay the union for its service as the agent negotiating our salaries. Huh, I thought. This membership fee comes to almost $1,000 a year, and on top of paying student loans and the costs of starting a life on my own, it sure stings. But it's my union and it's here to help me and my fellow teachers.

Not so much. There was no evidence during my years in the classroom that the union did anything to increase the well-being of its members—except for protecting the teachers who probably did not belong in a classroom in the first place. We did not gain higher salaries, smaller class sizes, or access to increased resources for our students. The union's priority was to protect jobs, which in practice meant prioritizing the lowest-performing teachers and the teachers whose personal problems had seeped into the school. You haven't written a lesson plan in a year? No problem, we'll defend you. You smacked a student? You're addicted to heroin? Your students consistently demonstrate no evidence of having learned anything, year after year? These were the teachers the union went to bat for, and it fought against anything that might bring change into our school system, one of the lowest-performing districts in the United States. By the time I left, I saw it as an example of unions at their most ineffective: investing all its energy and power into maintaining the status quo, even when change would do a world of good.

The same dysfunction exists in America's police unions. Most police unions began as benevolent organizations raising money for the widows of officers killed in the line of duty. Today they are the single biggest impediment to reforms that would crack down on police misconduct. FBI statistics for the years 2017 through 2019 show that an average of fifty law enforcement officers a year were killed on duty. During that same period, the police killed an average of 996 people a year, a 20-to-1 ratio. Most police unions will not give an inch of ground for reform efforts. They bubble wrap their officers with protections like qualified immunity and secret peer reviews for misconduct.

It is another race to the bottom. A stagnant union ends up focusing on and protecting the behavior of the worst. This is true of both the police unions and the teachers unions, and it demeans the work of the good teachers and the good police officers who make up the vast majority of the membership. The losers in this are students and citizens, and the costs to society are substantial. It does not have to be this way. It isn't elsewhere.

When they were at their best, unions helped win workers a minimum wage, unemployment insurance, the forty-hour workweek, sick leave, antidiscrimination laws, child labor laws, and pensions. We can even thank them for weekends. The very basis for the European and American middle classes emerged out of the work of the labor movement. But what they delivered, they delivered in the too-distant past. Looking to the future, the United States, United Kingdom, Mediterranean Europe, and the comparatively nascent developing world labor movements need to look at models in central and northern Europe, as well as to innovative practices being developed inside some of the labor movement's own very small start-up world.

Organized labor in the United States peaked in 1954 when 35 percent of the workforce belonged to a union. By 2019, that number had fallen to 10.3 percent. Among employees in the private sector, only 6 percent belong to a union. Because unions derive their strength from numbers, this loss of members translates to a decline in power. Since the 1980s, many Americans have seen their wages stagnate even as corporate profits and market valuations continue to rise. Both trends are the direct result of workers losing their bargaining power (i.e., unions weakening). Even nonunion workers receive smaller paychecks when overall union membership goes down.

The demise of unions in the United States is a story of globalization, technology, shareholder capitalism, and social change. The economic and political forces that propelled organized labor to its heyday in the aftermath of World War II changed course in the last two decades of the 20th century. Industries that were historic union strongholds, like manufacturing, shrank as companies introduced automation and moved production to lower-cost labor markets overseas. The knowledge- and service-based jobs that took their place are more dispersed, mobile, and difficult to organize. Meanwhile, labor laws have been eroded around the country, which has in turn made any fledgling labor movements more fragile and easier to quash than in Franklin D. Roosevelt's day. When you add to this stew the mismanagement of existing unions—the incompetence and misplaced priorities I saw from my classroom—you end up with a situation in which the vast majority of workers have no real power.

Even so, most union leaders in the United States still cling to the same playbook that their predecessors used a hundred years ago. They favor tradition over innovation and factory-floor organization over strategies that could unite an increasingly decentralized and temporary workforce. They place their trust in politicians who relegate labor issues to the bottom of the to-do list and rub elbows with the elites they claim to oppose. Yet while they put all their efforts into maintaining the moment, the world spins on, and laborers see their wages shrivel.

In the United States there are a few examples to the contrary. Workers in new sectors of the economy are turning to technology to bring people together to advocate for their interests. Other groups are pioneering strategies to bring benefits to a mobile labor force. There is a growing awareness among workers that, whether in a traditional union or through a homespun, grassroots initiative, they need to find a way to mobilize so that their concerns are taken seriously. And even as the United States and United Kingdom offer few positive examples, nations of northern and central Europe offer viable routes toward balancing workers' well-being with economic competitiveness.

For workers to share in the prosperity of the 2020s and beyond, they need a seat at the table where decisions are made, responsible representatives to advocate and fight when necessary on their behalf, and the resources to mobilize when employers do not meet their needs. They also need opportunities to develop new skills, benefits that follow them from job to job, and the ability to build coalitions among people dispersed around the globe. Traditional unions can provide some of these things, but not all. It is time for a new type of labor movement.

FEWER UNIONS, MORE PROBLEMS

Organized labor dates back to long before the GM strike. Trade associations existed in some form in many premodern societies—the *collegia opificium* of the Roman Empire, the *shreni* of the Indus Valley, the *za* of classical Japan, and the guilds of medieval Europe. Though these groups operated with different models and rules, they served the same core function: bringing workers together to advance their interests.

Modern labor unions emerged during the Industrial Revolution, beginning in the United Kingdom and eventually spreading to the United States, France, Germany, Australia, and beyond. As workers moved from the farm to the factory, port, mill, and mine, they encountered conditions that bordered on hellish. Laborers were frequently injured and sometimes killed by the machines they operated. Overcrowded sweatshops left workers vulnerable to disease and fires.

For most people, wages were low, days were long, and the work itself was dirty, dangerous, and demanding.

The writer Upton Sinclair summarized the plight of industrial workers in his novel *The Jungle*.

> Such were the cruel terms upon which their life was possible, that they might never have nor expect a single instant's respite from worry, a single instant in which they were not haunted by the thought of money. . . . In addition to all their physical hardships, there was thus a constant strain upon their minds; they were harried all day and nearly all night by worry and fear. This was in truth not living; it was scarcely even existing, and they felt that it was too little for the price they paid.

Unions offered workers a way to confront the grim realities of industrial society. Alone, no one employee can compel a company to change its pay or working conditions, but by banding together, workers increase their collective clout.

This did not always sit well with the people in power. During the 19th and early 20th centuries, union members were frequently viewed as communists and radicals. Corporations used this portrayal to justify aggressive anti-union behavior. The history of the early labor movement is marked by bloody clashes between workers and various law enforcement groups. In 1921, sixty miles from where I grew up in the coal-filled hills of West Virginia, the largest armed conflict inside the United States since the Civil War took place between coal miners and mine owners. An estimated one million rounds of ammunition were fired, and it took 2,100 army troops ordered in by the president to end the conflict. During these years my great-grandmother was sent away from the coal camp where she and my great-grandfather lived so that she could give birth to my grandfather away from the violence that was taking place as strikebreakers beat or shot anybody they thought might be sympathetic to the unions.

Even as violent strikebreaking tactics fell out of favor in the late 1920s, companies went to great lengths to quash union activity. GM spent $1 million (more than $18 million in 2020 dollars) spying on workers' union activities in the three years before the Flint sit-down strike.

In the early 20th century, the American labor movement began distancing itself from revolutionary politics. This rebranding, spearheaded by American Federation of Labor president Samuel Gompers, helped bring unions into the mainstream. As organized labor became more popular, so too did the policies it espoused. Many cornerstones of the industrial age social contract, including minimum wage standards, eight-hour workdays, and child labor laws, were popularized and otherwise driven by labor groups across the West. While these proposals seemed radical at the time, they proved critical to balancing the scales of power between employers and employees.

After the Second World War, organized labor served as the backbone of the booming industrial economy. Through their union, people without a college education found a track to the middle class. Unions provided safe conditions at work, a good paycheck to take home, health coverage when they fell ill, and a pension plan when they retired. With this economic security, workers could purchase a home, raise a family, and afford the innovative products rolling off the country's bustling assembly lines. In the first two decades after the war, Americans saw their purchasing power double.

It is a period that contradicts the assertions made in favor of Milton Friedman's shareholder capitalism. As Dr. Martin Luther King Jr. accurately put it, "the labor movement did not diminish the strength of the nation but enlarged it. By raising the living standards of millions, labor miraculously created a market for industry and lifted the whole nation to undreamed of levels of production. Those who attack labor forget these simple truths, but history remembers them."

The golden age of American unions, which lasted from the Flint strike to the early 1980s, coincided with the lowest levels of economic inequality the United States has ever seen. During the 1970s, the proportion of income that went to the top 1 percent of earners was approximately half of what it is today. Pay within companies was more equitable too. In 1978, corporate CEOs earned approximately

$30 for every $1 earned by workers. Forty years later, they were making $278 for each $1 that went to workers. During that period, compensation for CEOs grew 940 percent, while pay for other workers increased only 12 percent.

For workers, joining a union directly translates to higher paychecks. Across industries, union members earn 15–25 percent more than they would if they did not join a union. Because unions can influence norms across the labor market, even nonunion workers benefit when there is a strong organized labor presence in their industry. When a quarter or more of an industry is unionized, pay for nonunion workers increases an estimated 5 percent. Among economists, this bump in pay is known as the union effect.

But as union membership in the United States has declined, workers across the private sector have seen their wage growth grind to a halt over the past forty years.

If the golden age of the American union began with the GM sit-down strike, the event that marked its end was the PATCO strike. In the summer of 1981, the Professional Air Traffic Controllers Organization (PATCO) was stuck in heated negotiations with the Federal Aviation Administration, demanding raises and shorter hours for its members. With the talks deadlocked, the union ordered some thirteen thousand air traffic controllers to walk off the job on August 3. Thousands of flights were grounded across the country. President Ronald Reagan threatened to fire all controllers who did not return to work within forty-eight hours. On August 5, he did. The FAA soon had planes back in the air, and the government imposed a lifetime ban on all eleven thousand air traffic controllers fired by the president.

Reagan's decision sent a clear message to employers across the country: do not let strikes intimidate you. Following the administration's lead, company management started simply replacing workers who went on strike instead of conceding to workers' demands. In one fell swoop, the labor movement lost its most powerful negotiating tactic. The unions never recovered. There were 234 strikes involving a thousand or more workers per year on average in the United States in the five years before the PATCO strike. In the five years after it, the number fell to 72. Over the course of the 2010s, the average was 15. Joseph McCartin, director of the Kalmanovitz Initiative for Labor and the Working Poor at Georgetown University, said without the ability to strike, unions lost all their leverage.

"More and more, employers wanted strikes because they could use a strike to break the union or severely weaken it," McCartin told me. "As workers lost the ability to engage in strikes, even when they were in unions, they didn't have the power they used to have. They didn't have the ability to bargain effectively because they no longer had that ultimate weapon."

Though the PATCO strike accelerated their decline, labor unions also helped to sow the seeds of their own demise. Beginning in the late 1950s, public perception of unions started to decline. An early blow came in 1957 when Jimmy Hoffa, the outspoken, mob-connected president of the Teamsters, was wrapped up in a federal investigation that uncovered corruption, fraud, tax evasion, extortion, beatings, and murder. He would later go to prison for attempted bribery, conspiracy, and fraud. In the words of Robert De Niro's character, Teamster assassin Frank Sheeran, in the movie *The Irishman*, "Back then, there wasn't nobody in this country who didn't know who Jimmy Hoffa was." Undoubtedly, many of those people started to link organized labor with organized crime.

Unions also clashed with the counterculture of the 1960s. They came to represent the kind of conformist, workaday lifestyles of an older generation. AFL-CIO president George Meany was the person who coined the phrase *silent majority*, referring to the conservative, working-class white voters who propelled Richard Nixon to the White House.

By the mid-1980s, unions were fighting an uphill battle against economic, political, and social change. Companies' embrace of shareholder capitalism gave the executive suite and boardroom all the leverage it needed to minimize workers' wages. Then, as globalization ramped up in the 1990s, workers lost even more power. The labor movement has been largely constrained by geography, and even within the United States workers have been vulnerable to the sudden corporate relocations. While unions long had a firm foothold in the industrialized north, they did not have as much traction in the south, which incentivized companies throughout the last fifty years to shift their operations to friendlier labor markets in the south if workers ever demanded too much. Unionization levels vary widely and wildly in the United States. Only 3 percent of workers in the Carolinas are unionized, compared with an average of 15 percent in Illinois, Pennsylvania, Michigan, and New Jersey. This is why my wife's car was built in Alabama. When the world opened up rapidly at the end of the Cold War, executives discovered vast new options abroad for less expensive labor, which continued to erode the power of workers, both at home and abroad. American unions have only continued to hemorrhage members and fade into the background, with sweeping effects across society and the economy.

SIX CENTS ON THE DOLLAR

When workers got hammered following the financial crisis of 2008–9, they did not turn to their unions for inspiration and action. They turned to populist political leaders championing economic protectionism and anti-immigrant policies.

This trend came as a surprise to many elites in business, government, and academia, who assumed the globalism that emerged in the 1990s had permanently reshaped the world order for the undisputed better. As experts conducted postmortem studies, wrote think pieces, and made pilgrimages to parts of the country where fiery populists drew support, they discovered a large community of people who were disenfranchised and raging at yesterday's institutions, including their unions. The prosperity that globalization brought to cities like London, New York, Milan, Paris, and San Francisco had not spread to the UK's Midlands, the US's Rust Belt, Italy's south, or France's *communes périurbaines*. This was exacerbated by the fact that coinciding with the movement of manufacturing jobs away from their original industrial bases in the heartland were mergers and acquisitions and tax optimization that pushed executive jobs away to fewer points on the map. More than two-thirds of the job creation that took place in the United States since 2007 was concentrated in just twenty-five cities and counties. Similar dynamics could be seen in the UK where just three or four cities owned all the country's job growth, in Italy where Milan and a few regions in the north owned all the growth, and in other regions across the West. The places that had served as the backbone of the industrial economy played a reduced role in the digital economy, and the people who lived there became politically radicalized in one direction or another.

When I was growing up in West Virginia, the state was one of the most reliably Democratic and left-leaning states in the nation, rooted in the pro-union, pro-worker politics of Democratic tradition. At the beginning of the 21st century, the politics shifted, and today it is reactionary and palingenetic, aspiring to return to a time and place of myth and imagining. Though part of the backlash is rooted in old-fashioned xenophobia, much of it is driven by a pervasive sense of economic insecurity. The well-paid union jobs that bolstered the middle class in the mid-20th century had slipped away, and the opportunities that took their place did not always pay the bills. Alongside this is the emasculation that comes with what philosopher Michael Sandel calls "the tyranny of merit": if you are successful economically, you are seen as having "made it," and that validates whatever you do and whoever you are, irrespective of whether what you do makes a moral contribution to society or not; and conversely, if you are not university educated and wealthy, your standing is diminished.

In the supercities where the wealth creation took place, the politics shifted in the other political direction. To be working-class in New York, San Francisco, or London was to no longer be able to afford to live there. The costs of housing shot to the moon. Every day, you got an eyeful of well-being you did not share in. This formed the basis for the growth of an increasingly powerful political movement on the political left.

A 2020 study by former Treasury secretary Larry Summers (a bête noire of the Left) and Harvard economist Anna Stansbury found that both American economic performance and sluggish wage growth for workers were direct results of workers losing their bargaining power. The loss of worker power went beyond the decline of unions, they argued. It also resulted from the private sector's fervent embrace of shareholder capitalism. "The rise of the shareholder value maximization doctrine increased the power of shareholders relative to managers and workers, likely increasing pressure on firms to cut labor costs and . . . to redistribute rents from workers to shareholders," they wrote.

In other words, companies were making more money, but fewer of those gains benefited their employees. At the end of the Cold War, workers received an estimated eleven cents of every dollar they earned for their employer. Thirty years later, they made less than six cents on the dollar. In effect, the personal returns employees received for their labor were cut in half.

"Declining unionization, increasingly demanding and empowered shareholders, decreasing real minimum wages, reduced worker protections, and the increases in outsourcing domestically and abroad have disempowered workers with profound consequences for the labor market and the broader economy," Summers and Stansbury wrote.

Today many people blame globalization and technological change for the growing inequality we see in the United States, but Summers and Stansbury say that argument misses the point. Every developed country saw its economy reshaped by technology and globalization over the past thirty years, they write, but only the United States experienced such a dramatic increase in the wealth gap between labor and capital. Their report offers an explanation: the real reason the US is so unequal today is that the country elevated shareholders and weakened labor unions to a greater extent than any other nation in the industrial world.

Summers and Stansbury's verdict is that "declines in worker power have been major causes of increases in inequality and lack of progress in labor incomes." To address the problem, they added, the business community and country at large need to rethink their approach to economic prosperity.

"[This conclusion] raises questions about capitalist institutions," they write. "In particular it raises issues about the extent to which corporations should be run solely for the benefit of their shareholders. This would suggest that policy should tip the balance more in the direction of supporting union organizing activities and empowering unions."

The effect of this shapes more than just economic systems—it shapes culture and politics. If you work hard at your job but are falling further behind, and you hear the urban elites telling you that the answer is to get a college degree, you begin to feel like you're being told by the winners of the meritocracy that you are unworthy, that your contribution to society is less valuable than theirs, regardless of whether their high-income work is parasitic or humanitarian. The parallel cultural politics of meritocracy that equates economic success with moral worth and social esteem is a dangerous force in politics, because it means that when inequality rises not only do people get poorer, they also get angrier.

THE STATE OF THE UNIONS

The people who led the sit-down strike against General Motors in 1936–37 would look with dismay at their union today. In September 2019, members of the United Auto Workers again went on strike against GM. Nearly forty-eight thousand workers walked off the job for forty days, making it the longest auto workers' strike in fifty years. Workers eventually won small concessions from GM, but they failed to stop the company from shutting its plant in Lordstown, Ohio. That meant thousands of positions would permanently relocate to Mexico, continuing the decades-long decline in American car manufacturing jobs. While the UAW billed the deal as a win for workers, its members felt less enthusiastic—only 57 percent voted to approve the contract.

Less than a month later, UAW president Gary Jones resigned his post amid federal charges for racketeering and embezzlement of more than $1 million in union funds. The striking GM workers lost hundreds of millions of dollars in wages, while Jones was spending their dues on luxury condos, fancy dinners, and custom-made golf clubs. He pleaded guilty in June of 2020. Just two months later, his predecessor as president of the UAW was also arrested and charged with embezzlement and fraud.

Most union leaders are not brazenly using their organizations for illicit personal gain, but this example illustrates a stark contrast now evident within many of the largest unions. While union workers are seeing the slimmest of benefits, their leaders are living a lifestyle that their predecessors during labor's heyday neither enjoyed nor aspired to.

The men who run the UAW, the AFL-CIO, and the Teamsters are far removed from the factory floor these days. Headquarters for organizations such as the Teamsters and the AFL-CIO are located on prime Washington real estate, with majestic views of the Capitol and the White House. In 2019, the head of the Teamsters, James Hoffa Jr. (Jimmy's son), earned a nearly $400,000 salary—that would be unimaginable to the beer truckers I worked with.

The disconnect between union leaders and their members is also the result of organizational structure. Today, the AFL-CIO represents 12.7 million workers across fifty-five different unions, about three-quarters of all union members in the United States. This consolidation gives it more weight to throw around, but also ends up distancing the decision makers from the everyday concerns of workers. Trumka and other AFL-CIO officials are elected not by workers, but by the presidents of the unions they represent. According to Richard Freeman, a labor economist at Harvard, "one expects them to be 'establishment.'"

The end result is bloat among the top-heavy unions and an all-around failure to keep up with the economic reality of the 21st century. Labor movements in the age of Uber require agility and willingness to try new things. But, as Freeman notes, the major unions lack both. "The existing unions are very bureaucratic organizations," he said.

"The typical union is not very innovative. You have a bunch of fifty-sixty-year-old characters leading these unions—they're not start-ups."

Moreover, as Georgetown professor Joseph McCartin observes, unions have taken so many hits over the years that they are stuck in a defensive mindset.

"In this country, to simply have a labor movement has always been a challenge," he said. "Think about the degree to which the public culture celebrates individualism, think about the size and expanse of the labor market in this country . . . think about how that market has been segmented by race, by immigration. To build a union movement in the United States has always been a very, very difficult project. The law has rarely ever supported it—most of the time the law was adamantly arrayed against it. So it has bred in the union movement a sense of defensiveness among people who rise up to positions of leadership. Often they're most concerned with preserving the institution against the things that would destroy it." Risk taking, that is, "has never been their forte."

In the more than one hundred interviews conducted for this book, none left me feeling more conflicted than the one with AFL-CIO president Richard Trumka. The first thing you see as you walk into the lobby of the federation's headquarters in Washington, DC, is *Labor Omnia Vincit,* a seventeen-foot-tall, fifty-one-foot-wide mosaic mural depicting scenes from a futuristic world, captured in marble, glass, and gold. As I gawked at it, a security guard informed me it was the largest freestanding mural in North America.

Trumka comes from a long line of union coal miners, many of whom died from black lung, as my great-grandfather did after decades of work around the mines after emigrating from Italy. Trumka's gruff voice hearkens back to his own time in the Pennsylvania coal mines, where he worked through college. Now in his seventies, with a stocky build and Mike Ditka mustache, Trumka looks like a seasoned football coach.

When I asked Trumka how unions could combat economic inequality in the 2020s and increase jobs for their members, he said the answer was "to change the labor laws in this country. We have labor laws that were written in 1947—nothing has been static in this country since 1947 except the labor laws." When I pressed him for more specifics, he pointed to pending legislation that would strengthen penalties for companies that retaliate against workers who organize, expand collective bargaining rights, and weaken so-called right-to-work laws. "You also have to look at the trade laws, you have to look at the tax laws, you have to look at all the economic rules that have been written," he added.

He's not wrong, but the fact that you have to, in his words, "look at all the economic rules that have been written" and rewrite labor laws that have not changed in seventy-five years highlights not just how much dramatic change is needed, but also how little progress Trumka and his peers have made in the last few decades.

We stood together by his window so he could show me his dramatic, unobstructed view of the White House, and he told me, "When people talk about inequality they only talk about inequality of income. We talk about it in three levels: inequality of income, inequality of opportunity, and inequality of power. And unless you solve the inequality of power, you'll never solve the inequality of income and the inequality of opportunity. So right now we have an economy that is on a trajectory towards implosion. If inequality continues to grow, the system will implode."

Trumka held up his Apple iPhone and remarked, "We don't get the benefit of this telephone. Every component in that telephone was made with taxpayer dollars, every component in that phone. Now you can argue, 'well you get the benefit of a good phone, if you can afford it,' but they're making a whole lot of money. And the taxpayers aren't getting any of it back. So what does society do? Let's decide how we make sure that those benefits of increased productivity from future technology get shared equitably and fairly with the stakeholders. Because if we don't, the day of implosion is closer, not farther away."

His diagnosis about power was exactly right; his desire to bring the stakeholders back in was exactly right. But as I looked at Trumka's view of the White House and Washington and as I walked past the massive mural after our interview, it felt disconnected. There was something wrong, and ineffective, about how Trumka and the big unions have tried to accumulate and exercise power. In the thirty-five years Trumka has been the president of a union, he has played the insider's game. He attends the World Economic Forum in Davos every year, and while in Washington he frequents the Hay-Adams, a power-meal mecca with twenty-five-dollar lobster omelets on the menu. (In fairness, he notes it's a union shop.) He's making a mistake to think that you have to wear the camouflage of the corporate elite to get the C-suite and the halls of Congress to respond to you. It's the opposite. In my experience, with every mouthful of lobster omelet in Washington and canapé in Davos, the union leaders lose their edge. They are dulled. They are members of the Davos crowd, but junior members. And as the world has become more winner-take-all, Trumka's thirteen million workers have seen their power steadily slide.

Compounding the challenge for Trumka's members is that globalization and technological change are both changing their status as *workers*, since it has changed the very nature of work. Jobs are becoming more mobile and short-term. Young people today are more likely to have thirty employers over thirty years than a single employer for their whole career. As technology evolves, workers must constantly update their skill sets. Many of the jobs that will be most in demand in the year 2050 do not even exist yet. Gone are the days when a single set of skills in a single trade could reliably sustain a worker through her entire career.

Instead of fighting to maintain the status quo, unions must position their members to embrace the change. As low-skill industrial jobs went overseas, unions missed the first wave of opportunities to retrain their members for the high-skill, technology-driven jobs that remain firmly planted in the United States. But they can still reorient to provide such services. Many workers would not even need to switch industries—by 2028, researchers estimate, there will be 2.4 million manufacturing jobs in the US that companies cannot fill due to a skills shortage within the workforce. To succeed in the 2020s and beyond, workers are learning to adapt—and unions can adapt in turn to provide resources that will help workers take charge of the future.

"We see people thinking that the solution is to go back to the manufacturing era model, and really trying to re-create that—I don't think you can," said Sara Horowitz, founder of the Freelancers Union, a nonprofit that provides health insurance and other benefits for freelance workers. "We're at a moment where we don't have the future figured out, but we can clearly see that it can't just be the past."

The same problems are just as visible across the pond as they are in the United States. Britain was home to some of the very first modern labor unions, but the Conservative government led by Prime Minister Margaret Thatcher weakened unions during the 1980s, and they never recovered. Today only 14 percent of British private-sector workers belong to a union.

When I spoke with Paddy Lillis, the general secretary of the United Kingdom's 450,000-member Union of Shop, Distributive and Allied Workers (USDAW), his plans for the future were uninspiring. USDAW represents a range of workers, from delivery drivers, butchers, and meatpackers to retail employees and workers in call centers. One of its primary organizing tactics involves leafleting local shopping centers with literature on the demise of brick-and-mortar retail. Though a time-honored strategy, leafleting does not scale like Amazon and Alibaba or persuade like social media.

The relative progress that Lillis cited meant sitting on committees and having conference calls with people in government. He excitedly noted that the prime minister had name-checked his union. It was all process and protocol, not actual results that required more than an acknowledgment of his union's existence. Organized labor needs new strategies for mobilizing workers and new demands to bring to the table.

To that end, grassroots organizations in the United States are starting to experiment with a new approach.

A LITTLE BIT OF PROMISE

The nature of work in the 21st century is not for traditional unions. Historically, organizing tactics relied on physical proximity and derived strength from numbers. It is easier to mobilize a strike or build support for a union in a large workplace with lots of employees, like a coal mine or an auto plant, than among workers scattered across branch offices, franchise restaurants, and chain stores. If people do not stand shoulder to shoulder on the job, they are less willing to do so on the picket line.

The proximity problem is amplified when businesses outsource operations to contingent workers, freelancers, and independent contractors. These "alternative work arrangements" offer workers more flexible hours and commitments, but they also let companies avoid extending them certain benefits and protections available to full-fledged employees. Contract workers can be found everywhere. They include nearly all the baggage handlers and skycaps at airports, about one in three construction workers, and more than half the employees at Google. Others work in the platform economy, earning money through digital platforms like Uber, Lyft, Postmates, TaskRabbit, and Instacart. We will call these various forms of independent employment *gig work*.

Gig work comes in many different forms, which makes it difficult to measure the exact number of gig workers. The US Department of Labor reports that approximately 10 percent of American workers rely on an "alternative work arrangement" as their primary job, while the Federal Reserve estimates 30 percent of US workers participate in some form of gig work.

When people talk about independent employment, they usually jump straight to the on-demand labor force enabled by companies like Uber, Lyft, Postmates, TaskRabbit, and Instacart. While this is the most visible form of gig work, less than 2 percent of the US labor force make their living through this "electronically mediated work," though the number is higher if you count people who use the platforms as a side hustle. Still, this piece of the job market epitomizes the decentralized workforce. Anyone who has worked through one of these platforms knows it is a solitary affair. You have no coworkers. You set your own hours. You interact with the company only when something goes wrong with the app. For the most part, your marching orders—and your pay—are dictated by software.

But just as technology platforms developed this new way to work, their contractors are pioneering new ways to organize.

On August 22, 2017, more than one hundred Uber and Lyft drivers gathered outside Los Angeles International Airport (LAX) to protest for higher wages. In their effort to lower costs for passengers, the companies had reduced the pay rates for drivers. Between 2013 and 2017, rideshare drivers across the country had seen their monthly earnings fall more than 50 percent.

"Most of us as drivers spend anywhere from 10 to 12 to 15 hours a day in our car six and seven days a week," one protestor told reporters. "We have families that we never see. We have homes that we never see . . . Uber pays us 67 cents a mile, sticks us in traffic and expects us to come up to this airport after sitting up there for an hour to pick up a passenger going to Playa Vista for four dollars. I'm going to ask you, what is your time worth?"

Like many other grassroots initiatives, the protest was organized through a Facebook page. In the following months, the organizers of the event came together to form a new group called Rideshare Drivers United (RDU), with the goal of improving pay and work conditions for Uber and Lyft drivers. To advance the cause, the group needed to build its membership, and that required connecting with drivers who could go days without crossing paths with their fellow gig workers. In short, RDU needed to solve the proximity problem.

To do so, the organizers turned to technology. If they were working through an app, why not strike through an app?

With the help of a freelance developer named Ivan Pardo, the group created an app that served as a one-stop shop for recruiting new members. Through the app, organizers scheduled calls with drivers, communicated with them through encrypted channels, rated their interest in the organization, and gauged their feelings toward company policies. But even with the app, the group still needed a way to connect with more drivers. It found the solution in Brian Dolber.

Dolber describes himself as a scholar-activist. With a bushy beard, receding hairline, thick-framed glasses, and the wardrobe of a disheveled academic, he looks the part. Dolber started driving for Uber on and off between 2015 and 2017. Like many gig workers, he had a day job. Dolber worked as an adjunct professor at California State University San Marcos and was in the process of writing a book on Jewish labor organizing in the early 20th century. Most adjunct faculty—the independent contractors of academia—earn less than $35,000 per year. With his class schedule changing each semester, Dolber needed some extra cash. He also saw rideshare driving as a research opportunity—what better way to study the gig economy than to join it? So off he went in his silver Honda Civic, shuttling passengers around the concrete jungle of Los Angeles County.

Dolber first learned of Rideshare Drivers United at an academic conference. He decided to attend one of its meetings in Los Angeles, and while there he crossed paths with Ivan Pardo. By that point, the organization had connected with only about five hundred of the estimated three hundred thousand rideshare drivers in California. Because Uber and Lyft publish only sparse data on their contractors, identifying and contacting new drivers was a laborious process. Up to that point, the group had recruited most of its members by canvassing parking lots at LAX. However, Dolber and Pardo developed a more scalable strategy for picking out rideshare drivers: Facebook.

"Facebook is able to identify drivers better than anybody else," Dolber said. "They know who drivers are because they have the app downloaded on their phone. It's not that people are necessarily identifying themselves [as rideshare drivers]. On Facebook itself, they're figuring out who drivers are . . . and then [targeting] them with ads."

Armed with an academic grant, Dolber and Pardo set out creating a Facebook ad campaign to target rideshare drivers across Los Angeles. The strategy was simple: when users clicked the ad, they were directed to the Rideshare Drivers United website and invited to join the group. Volunteers then used the app to contact interested drivers and discuss how they could get involved.

As a professor, Dolber ran the campaign with academic precision. Between October 2018 and January 2019, the group recruited 1,147 new drivers, more than doubling its membership. By the end of the campaign, the organization was spending about seventy-three cents for each new recruit. At the same time, the group had more than 1,400 members weigh in on different policies they would like to change in the rideshare industry. Leaders tailored their platform, the Drivers Bill of Rights, based on the responses they received from drivers.

"One of the big problems in organizing in the gig economy is that there's no central space . . . no factory floor where workers meet. Social media has provided an outlet for that," Dolber told me. But while technology can enable an organization, he noted it is not a substitute for motivated members.

"We've been able to bat above our weight in relation to what other unions would expect to have in terms of their numbers relative to the workforce. The trick has been to use the technology as a tool . . . to actually build the relationships. We don't work because of the technology, we work because we actually have some really good organizers who are putting in a lot of time and effort, and because the drivers are pissed. I think the technology in some ways has become a necessity because the gig economy disperses workers. It makes sense that a technology that allows for that disbursement then allows for them to reconnect."

By March 25, 2019, Rideshare Drivers United had grown to three thousand members. After Uber reduced per-mile pay for Los Angeles–area drivers by 25 percent, the group mobilized a citywide strike. Thousands of drivers participated, and hundreds formed a picket line outside the company's LA office. Within weeks, RDU had welcomed 1,300 new members to its ranks. On May 8, 2019, days before Uber was set to make its initial public offering, RDU spearheaded a nationwide strike. Tens of thousands of drivers logged off the platform.

Rallies were held in major cities like Atlanta, Boston, Chicago, Los Angeles, New York City, Philadelphia, San Diego, San Francisco, and Washington, DC, and even spread to the United Kingdom.

On May 10, its first day as a publicly traded company, Uber saw its share price drop more than 7 percent. In terms of dollars lost by investors, it was the worst IPO since 1975. Lyft had not fared much better when it had gone public a few months earlier. To be fair, there are other factors that contributed to the company's poor performance—for one, Uber has never turned a profit. But having your workers walk off the job by the thousands does not exactly look good to investors.

In some ways, that was the point of the strike. Unlike the strikes of the 20th century, which centered on bringing work to a halt or damaging a company's bottom line, modern collective action is just as focused on publicity and its impact on a company's brand and perception by the investment community, leading to a higher or lower stock price. Thanks to digital media, a relatively small strike or protest can get lots of attention. In 1936, GM workers needed to bring car production to a halt to make their voices heard. Today, a few viral news stories can fuel a cause. A day of nationwide strikes will also do more to change public opinion than handing out leaflets.

"I think a lot of the drivers want to impact the bottom line . . . but I don't think that's actually how these companies are organized or necessarily how we can best impact them," Dolber said. "We were able to create enough of a buzz that it scared the investors. The investors don't necessarily need everyone to walk out. They need to have the news story be . . . this is a dangerous business model and the workers are upset."

While RDU's tactics are instructive, one of the difficult realities for its movement is that some of its demands—even perfectly understandable ones—are not possible for Uber to meet. There are real changes that can be enacted for drivers, such as policies to mirror the protections already in place for traditional workers, like pay transparency, an appeal process for drivers who get kicked off the platform, and the right to organize without retaliation. But when you look at more impactful changes, like classifying drivers as actual employees, or raising wages substantially—these would very likely send Uber into bankruptcy. For instance, Uber has more than 3.9 million drivers worldwide; if those workers were classified as employees, the company would be the largest employer in the world, ahead of the US Department of Defense, the People's Liberation Army of China, and Walmart. As of this writing, Uber is a money-losing company: without coming close to these changes, it lost more than $8 billion in 2019. Its business model cannot handle many of the real labor protections we see in other fields. If either the much higher wage or the reclassification of workers as employees were enacted, the company would either serve just the wealthier black-car passengers of its origins or go out of business entirely.

But if the gig economy is any indicator of the many jobs emerging in the 2020s and beyond, we as a society must determine what to do about this paradox. We need to determine what rights and protections will extend to the "alternative work arrangement" workforce and what will be provided by the employer and what will be provided by government. If a company with a business model like Uber's cannot provide all its employees with a living wage and decent benefits, there are essentially four choices left.

1. Compel benefits irrespective of the business model. Gig work like ridesharing then reverts to the black-car model of its roots rather than functioning as a service for the masses.
2. Government fills the gap with a higher and stronger safety net.
3. Government deems gig economy or other forms of contract work illegal (such as in Italy where Uber is confined to being a limousine service in just two cities).
4. New models for financing flexible benefits are enacted into law.

In the same way that capital has become more mobile in the globalized, technology-driven economy of the 21st century, labor has also become more mobile. Gig work and other alternative work arrangements provide people with more flexibility and freedom than they could have ever had with a traditional nine-to-five job. But as with mobile capital, mobile labor has its costs. As we will examine at length in the next chapter, global capital flows allow companies to legally minimize their tax bills and force countries into a race to the bottom on tax policy. Similarly, flexible labor markets mean employee benefits are no longer fixed in place. To guarantee workers a share in the economic prosperity to come in the 2020s, we need to explore models of pay and benefits that are as flexible as their jobs. We cannot solve the labor problem on a company-by-company basis.

In a letter to the *New York Times* entitled "I am the CEO of Uber. Gig Workers Deserve Better," Uber CEO Dara Khosrowshahi wrote, "There has to be a 'third way' for gig workers, but we need to get specific, because we need more than new ideas—we need new laws. Our current system is binary, meaning that each time a company provides additional benefits to independent workers, the less independent they become. That creates more uncertainty and risk for the company, which is a main reason why we need new laws and can't act entirely on our own."

Khosrowshahi's proposal is that gig economy companies be mandated to establish funds that workers can draw on to pay for benefits in an amount corresponding to the number of hours they put in. In his example, if a law enabling this were put in place across the United States, Uber would have paid $655 million into the benefits fund. That sounds great until you extrapolate it across Uber's millions of drivers. In his own example and using his own math, a driver in Colorado averaging over thirty-five hours per week would have accrued approximately $1,350 in benefits funds in one year. That's horrendous given the cost of health insurance and anything else that might be termed a benefit. Give Khosrowshahi credit for acknowledging the problem and proposing a solution, but his own example demonstrates that employer-based benefits on Uber's terms leave drivers in a hellish position.

The game theory here just doesn't work. Uber will never be profitable until it engages in enough mergers and acquisitions to stumble into a better business model or until its cars are autonomous and the single biggest cost (the drivers) is eliminated.

The labor movements that lead us into the future will be those that pioneer models for securing benefits for those who work in the gaps not reached by traditional unions. As people change jobs more often over the course of their careers, it is no longer practical to have benefits tied to their employers. As workers move from job to job, they should carry their health care, parental leave, and retirement plans along with them. We are already seeing this "portable benefits" system emerging with the help of innovative techniques from a new crop of union leaders.

Organized labor is in Sara Horowitz's blood. Her grandfather helped establish one of the most prominent garment workers' unions in the United States; her father worked as a labor lawyer for hire; and her mother was an active member in the teachers' union. As a child, Horowitz would make frequent visits to her grandmother's one-bedroom apartment on Manhattan's Lower East Side to snack on ice cream mashed with instant coffee. The apartment complex, named after New York labor leader Sidney Hillman, housed members of the Amalgamated Clothing Workers of America union.

Growing up in Brooklyn Heights, Horowitz assumed everyone shared the same enthusiasm for unions as she and her family. It was not until college that she was exposed to less rosy perceptions of organized labor. President Ronald Reagan had recently broken the PATCO strike, and attitudes toward worker movements in the United States and United Kingdom were shifting.

"The culture just really stopped seeing the benefits of unions," she said. "There are many legitimate issues with unions for sure, but I think we've now seen that we've thrown the baby out with the bathwater."

In 1995, Horowitz founded the Freelancers Union. Though technically a nonprofit, the group offers independent workers many of the same features as a traditional union. It helps members network and organize, and, most consequentially, it provides benefits. Today, the group offers health insurance, retirement plans, and other coverage to contractors who do not qualify for benefits through their employers. But unlike employer-based programs, these benefits follow workers from job to job.

This is especially valuable given that it is not only gig economy employers that fail to provide benefits. Just focusing on retirement benefits, for example, we see that there has been a massive shift from employer-provided retirement. In decades past, "defined benefit" plans such as pensions were the norm; under these plans, employers would make specific payments to past employees during their retirements. Now the norm has shifted to "defined contribution" plans, which are dependent on employees' own savings. This is especially tough for low-wage workers, who have scarce funds to contribute to their retirement after paying for their basic living expenses. Thirty years ago, more than half of American workers had defined benefit plans; today that number is near 20 percent.

This, in turn, is part of a pattern of greater individualization of the social contract. Both employers and the government are doing less across the whole of society to cushion people from hard-edged developments in our economic life. In addition to guaranteed pension levels dropping, an increased share of both health care and education costs is private. This hyper-individualization of benefits and the social contract contributes to the *Mad Max*–like competition to meet basic needs.

The portable benefits pioneered by the Freelancers Union could serve as a model for other labor organizations to pursue and for government to help support and scale.

"I think that we are going to be really riffing off a guild model in many ways—it's going to be much more about self-help and mutual aid, and using technology to link these things together," Horowitz said. "I think that people are going to come together around the things that they have in common and the things that they need, like training, or education, or finding out about jobs, or that kind of thing. I think that the unit of labor representation is going to be still a collective, but the collective may be geographically based or professionally based and less based on the particular employer."

Policy makers in the state of Washington have developed a possible solution built around a new mandated fee for companies that connect workers with clients or customers. The fee would apply to online or app-based rideshare and freelancing platforms, as well as more traditional non-internet-based employment that would fund portable benefits for those workers. Labor leader David Rolf and venture capitalist Nick Hanauer collaborated to design what they call a Shared Security System, which reflects the nature of labor in the 2020s and is based on social security but includes all the employment benefits that used to characterize a full-time job. These benefits would build up through automatic payroll deductions, regardless of employment classification, and would mirror social security in being portable (moving with you from job to job), prorated (paid in proportion to the amount of work done), and universal (employment classification does not matter). These are compelling ideas that are the necessary starting points for change.

Yet, on the whole, there aren't many precedents for such an approach in the United States or the United Kingdom; it's better to look to the models of central and northern Europe for inspiration.

THE CENTRAL AND NORTHERN EUROPEAN MODEL

In the US, unions negotiate on behalf of the workers at individual companies, but in much of Europe they advocate for and represent entire sectors of the economy. This "sectoral" bargaining has enabled labor unions to penetrate new industries and keep wages high across the economy.

In countries including Denmark, Finland, Norway, and Sweden, unions negotiate with employers at three levels: At the national level, union federations and business associations set standards for workers across the entire economy. At the industry level, select unions and employers do the same for individual sectors of the economy, like manufacturing, financial services, and retail. And at the local level, unions hammer out specific agreements with individual companies. Under this system, the vast majority of workers reap the higher pay and benefits that come with union membership, even if they do not belong to the union themselves. Just as the Freelancers Union offers workers portable benefits, sectoral- and national-level bargaining provides them protections and rights that extend beyond a given employer. Variants of this also exist in other countries in specific industries.

For example, when I asked Italian designer Brunello Cucinelli how much he paid the seamstresses and other workers in his factories, he told me that a national contract was negotiated between fashion entrepreneurs and the trade unions under the supervision of government. Wages were set based on the type of job, and Brunello then added 20 percent more to the wages. Instead of a race to the bottom, wage standards were decided by stakeholders from business, labor, and government and set at a satisfactory minimum standard, which Brunello then took 20 percent higher.

In Denmark, Finland, Norway, and Sweden, more than half the workforces belong to labor unions, and more than 70 percent are covered by collective bargaining. In Denmark, Sweden, and Finland, unions are also responsible for administering unemployment insurance, which gives workers an incentive to sign up and pay dues. Today, these countries have some of the world's highest rates of union membership.

And unlike in the United States and United Kingdom, many of the European states seem to try to outdo themselves by making working conditions better. Finland's prime minister has called for reducing the standard workday from eight to six hours. The prime minister in neighboring Sweden, where 70 percent of the workforce is unionized, is a former union welder who got involved in politics through his work as an ombudsman for the country's metalworkers union, a fact that makes me think back to Richard Trumka looking out his window, talking about power and the potential implosion to come. In Sweden, a union welder holds that power.

In addition to the prominence and power of unions, a handful of European states have found an additional, creative way to ensure companies act with their employees' interests in mind: giving workers seats in the boardroom.

These countries—which include Germany, Austria, Denmark, Sweden, Finland, Norway, and the Netherlands—require private companies of a certain size to reserve a portion of the seats on executive boards for worker representatives. This policy, called codetermination, lets company employees weigh in on high-level decisions.

Different countries set different thresholds for board-level representation. In Denmark, workers at companies with at least thirty-five employees elect one-third of the board of directors. The same goes for Dutch firms with more than one hundred employees. In Germany, companies with between five hundred and two thousand employees must reserve one-third of the seats on their supervisory boards for worker-elected representatives. For German firms with more than two thousand people, half the supervisory board is selected by employees.

Douglas Alexander, a former British Labour Party politician and cabinet member, said this high-level representation directly translates to better economic outcomes for workers.

"There is a strong case for ensuring employee representation on boards," Alexander told me. "In the same way we have learned that diversity and inclusion changes the conversation, if you establish a critical level of representation, simply the presence of divergent voices impacts the conversation. Many of the companies in countries with codetermination have managed to retain international levels of competitiveness while sustaining a social contract more generous to their employees than many other countries and companies have managed."

The data support his claim: board-level representation for employees is linked to greater job security and lower income inequality. During the Great Recession, Scandinavian firms with employees on their boards were more likely to favor short-term cost-cutting measures like furloughs and reduced hours over layoffs. The pay gap between CEOs and workers in the United States is twice as large as it is in Germany and more than four times as large as it is in Sweden.

Codetermination is also shown to promote more long-term

decision-making within companies. Businesses in Denmark, Sweden, Germany, and Austria spend a greater share of their income on research and development than those in the United States. Between 1998 and 2014, American companies announced 11,096 stock buybacks, compared to only 533 in total across firms in Germany, Austria, Denmark, Sweden, Finland, Norway, and the Netherlands. Though many argue that codetermination results in slower growth and lower profits, dozens of studies have found no clear evidence to support this claim.

In Germany, Austria, Switzerland, and other European states, employees are also represented by work councils. These organizations often have close ties to labor unions, but their responsibilities are distinct—while unions bargain with employers over wages and benefits, work councils act more like employee advocates at individual companies. Though their exact responsibilities vary by firm, work councils generally have broad say over issues that directly affect employees. They work with managers to determine employees' hours, holidays, and payment methods. Councils must be consulted before layoffs or other major staffing changes, and they play a major role in setting workplace safety standards. In some cases, councils have the right to veto decisions made by management.

I sit on the board of directors of a publicly traded Swiss company, and the dialogue there between executive management and the work council is more positive and productive than anything I have seen in the United States. The work council advocates for its employees but does so recognizing that the overall health of the enterprise makes for better long-term prospects. It is not a coincidence that our employees are an exception to mass employee mobility, with most choosing to stay at the company for decades.

Compared to unions, which represent workers across one or more industries, work councils are much more intimate. Council members are company employees, elected by their coworkers. Larger companies have larger work councils, but even at the biggest firms the councils have only a few dozen members. Each member has personal relationships with the workers they represent and the managers with whom they negotiate. The system fosters camaraderie—you are more likely to trust the guy you eat lunch with to do the right thing than a union leader eating a twenty-five-dollar omelet in Washington.

"Most workers are more committed to their work council than they are to their union," said Harvard economist Richard Freeman.

That is not to say industries with work councils do not need strong unions. Stephen Lerner, an organizer and fellow at Kalmanovitz Initiative for Labor and the Working Poor at Georgetown University, said work councils sometimes favor their own company's employees over the interests of workers across the industry. To strike a balance, you need both internal and external groups advocating for workers.

Germany was the first to develop this system of employee participation in company decision-making. Though many European states have adopted similar corporate governance structures, the system is still known as the German model. While labor relations in the United Kingdom and United States have been "historically adversarial," countries with strong unions and worker representation have found a "far more consensual approach" to conducting business, said Douglas Alexander.

THE MEDITERRANEAN MODEL

Not all of continental Europe benefits from labor unions that reshape entire industries for the better of both business and employee. To the south and west of the countries employing the German model are workforces with comparably high levels of union participation but near-constant friction between employer and employee—often to the detriment of both.

Italy and France lack codetermination, and their unions see workers as perpetually in opposition to management. I've lived in Italy three different times in my life and on any given day somebody is striking. It could be the rail workers, it could be the taxi drivers, it could be any sector, anywhere.

It's important for workers to have that right, but when strikes happen too frequently and without result, it's also a sign that something in the system has broken. In Italy, strikes happen so regularly, grinding business to a halt for the day, that nobody raises an eyebrow. It's almost treated like a little holiday. Ask about it and you'll just get shrugged shoulders and be told, "È un giorno per uno sciopero"—it's a day for a strike. Workers will often plan vacations weeks in advance, knowing that they will have a long weekend with a strike planned for a Friday or Monday. Yet the strikes tend not to be built around a specific grievance or intended outcome, and nobody is organizing online or out protesting in person. It's basically just a day off.

In France, strikes regularly shorten five-day school weeks to four days. In Spain, Portugal, and Greece, work councils occasionally exist in name but rarely in practice, and all suffer from regular striking to no effect.

The result of this is a chasm between employers and employees that ends up hurting both. The lack of commitment between employees and management leads to dysfunction and a lack of dynamism within the company, the sector, and the economy overall. This is one reason that countries using the German model have achieved substantially higher levels of growth and higher wages for employees than has been the case in Mediterranean Europe. Because it's somewhere between difficult and impossible for employers to fire their employees, a significant chunk of the labor force ends up being pushed into the black market. Many businesses simply are unwilling to hire employees, knowing that once they do so they will never be able to fire them. That shifts many jobs off the books, which in turn has the effect of reducing tax payments and, ironically, the rights of those workers. The system is bad for business, bad for employees, and bad for government. The Mediterranean model is worse than the American and British models, which enable entrepreneurial freedom, and a far cry from the German model, where codetermination gives workers a stake in their company's success and forces management to consider workers as stakeholders in the decisions they make. Union members and management in Mediterranean countries feel no such mutual loyalty.

So far, we have focused almost exclusively on relationships between companies and workers in the United States and Europe. The dynamic is very different in the developing world, as we will discuss later in the book. However, it merits mention here.

While globalization contributed to driving away union jobs in Western countries over the last thirty years, it brought substantial economic opportunity to workers in Asia, Latin America, and Africa. Western multinationals and new local companies created jobs and economic growth in parts of the developing world that had missed out on earlier waves of industrialization. Wages rose and billions of people were lifted out of poverty. We tend to see labor movements take root when the prevailing economic system breaks down, but for the last few decades, the system has worked out comparatively well for a majority of workers in the developing world—if you're willing to take a cold-blooded, purely analytic look at the data. It is also the case that the governments in many of these countries would respond to worker mobilization with violent crackdowns.

As long as wages continue to rise and the economy continues to grow, there will be comparatively few worker movements. However, once growth stalls, you start to see unrest. Authoritarian countries may be able to quell these populist movements, but in democratic countries they are harder to suppress.

THE MAKEUP OF A 21ST-CENTURY LABOR MOVEMENT

The private sector is not going to adopt codetermination or most other forms of stakeholder capitalism of its own accord. A handful of firms may reinvent their business models to become more eco-friendly and more generous to their employees, and some others will make tweaks around the edges. But changing the priorities of business at the scale of a national economy will require intervention. Despite their best intentions, shareholders and executives will be reluctant to give up the power, freedom, and remuneration they enjoy under the current system.

Even if you were to concede every point about the value and virtue of giving labor a stake in governance, the data shows that American and British companies are better for shareholders, and central and northern European countries are better for stakeholders, and as long as we are optimizing for shareholders, labor will be locked out of governance.

"I see very little evidence that absent either effective internal negotiation or external pressure, companies are moving towards a fairer and more equitable distribution of profits," said Douglas Alexander.

It is worth both doing the hard-charging internal negotiation and applying external pressure to fight for a more equitable distribution of profits in the form of wages. Another important opportunity that may be even more achievable is to fight for a more equitable distribution of equity. As big as is the gap in wages between executives and workers, the far greater gap and source of rising inequality is in capital, in equity. Rich people don't tend to grow richer because the paycheck they get every two weeks is getting bigger. It is because of the increasing value of their capital—their ownership of things from stocks to homes to any other asset of appreciating value.

The wealthiest people I know, those worth billions and billions of dollars, pay less in taxes, as a percentage of earnings, than I do. That is because in most cases they may draw some salary, but the way they make their real money is through the appreciation of their assets. I, in turn, probably pay a smaller percentage of what I earn over the course of a year than the twenty-something-year-old researchers who worked for me in the writing of this book. I'm no billionaire, but what I earn is a mixture of wages and capital appreciation, and that mix makes my tax rate lower than the young people at the beginning of their careers who earn only what they make in wages.

It is ridiculous that I pay more in taxes as a percentage of my earnings than the billionaires, and it is ridiculous that I pay less than the researchers for this book. As we will read in the next chapter, we need to massively rewire our system of taxation. It is not in need of tweaks or reforms. It is in need of a complete overhaul. Above and beyond that, though, we need to make sure that a much larger percentage of workers themselves benefit from capital accumulation and appreciation. That has historically come in the form of homeownership. Owning your home became foundational to the American dream and to the growth in wealth of middle classes in Europe and Asia in the 20th century. In the United States, we put a thumb on the tax scale to enable this by making the interest on mortgages tax deductible.

This began with retirement savings accounts like 401(k)s and should just be the beginning. Silicon Valley became Silicon Valley in significant part because one thing that drove talent from other places and industries, like finance and consulting, was employee ownership in the form of stock options. Labor unions ought to recognize that wages are not the only thing worth fighting for. Think about how much better off Uber drivers would have been if they were real beneficiaries of its IPO. And there is nothing keeping employees outside of tech and in established companies from being paid in stock. It's not all tech start-ups.

Basing compensation in part on equity in addition to wages is not zero risk, but it is surprisingly low risk. Stocks recovered much faster than home values after the 2008 financial crisis. Stock markets recovered with stunning speed amid the COVID-19 pandemic and rose to record highs while the pandemic was still surging.

Equity-based compensation for workers can also be a partial antidote to stock buybacks, the dumbest and least effective attribute of shareholder capitalism. Better the stock live inside the portfolios of workers than reside inanimately on corporate balance sheets.

Labor movements played an indispensable role in writing the 20th-century social contract. Again, the list runs from the establishment of a minimum wage to unemployment insurance, the forty-hour workweek, sick leave, antidiscrimination laws, child labor laws, pensions, and even weekends off.

They should play an equally important role in rewriting that contract for the 21st century.

In the United States, United Kingdom, and Mediterranean Europe, the vast majority of the labor unions are past their prime. The organizations have grown too big and their membership too small.

To be successful, the labor movements of the 2020s and beyond must be agile. They need the ability to mobilize a dispersed workforce and quickly move resources to the places where they are most needed. Technology can enable both these things, but it is not a magic bullet. Social media and organizing apps may enable grassroots organizations like Rideshare Drivers United to punch above their weight, but building an effective labor movement requires money, manpower, and, above all, motivation. Many grassroots groups that tried organizing through tech in the 2000s have fizzled out, said Richard Freeman. "I would hope we can get more out of the technology, but that so far has not really blossomed."

While the organizational structure of unions must change, their most powerful tool will still be collective action.

"Workers have to act collectively, they have to act together, they have to be in organizations that are expansive enough to give them true leverage," said Georgetown's Joseph McCartin. Though strikes fell out of favor after the 1980s, they are beginning to make a comeback.

Just as the GM sit-down strike kicked off a wave of labor organizing in the 1930s, a single instance of collective action could catch fire today, according to Richard Freeman. Workers are more likely to mobilize when the economy is hurting, he added. "Historically, that's where a lot of the unions in the West developed strength. Workers lose faith in the rest of the system."

As new worker movements emerge, they will need a different set of demands. They must fight for a system of portable benefits, like those pioneered by the Freelancers Union. But on top of that, they will need to fight for workers' place in the 21st-century economy. Instead of opposing technological progress and globalization, they need to position workers to embrace the change.

"It would seem to me the best kind of workers movement would be one that negotiates in a way that moves along with change rather than without it," said political scientist Fareed Zakaria. "If companies have come up with an amazing machine that can do the work of four people, the answer is not to hold on to those four people's jobs forever. The answer is to negotiate the best retraining and severance package for those workers . . . so that you make sure that these people have another twenty or twenty-five years ahead of them at work. The answer is to say, 'what can you have this talented human being who works hard and is disciplined, what can we do with them?' The best workers movement, it seems to me, would try to do the most to enhance that person's employability over the course of his lifetime."

In addition to companies and unions, the federal government could play a role in funding these retraining efforts, Zakaria added. He thinks we should look back to the GI Bill as a model.

"The GI Bill was so successful because it was so universal, it was so simple," he said. "You could come up with something like that, and think of it as a kind of triangle—the local industries identify the needs for the future; local community colleges and educational institutions provide that training; and the federal government pays the bills. I think the biggest problem in doing this is actually just the money. We have a good community college system that could be revived and reinvigorated with more resources. Industry has already tried to do some of this, and they could easily be made to do much more of it. The issue is just that it would be very expensive."

What Zakaria describes is not a hypothetical based on a theoretical based on a maybe. What he describes exists through much of central and northern Europe. It is expensive, but no more expensive than paying for the alternative in the forms of unemployment, public housing, health care for the uninsured, and the costs that come with the increased likelihood of being in the criminal justice system. There are more than two million people incarcerated in the United States. That is not a coincidence given our thin safety net and few pathways to economic well-being for non–college goers. The more than $32,000 spent per person for one year in prison and the more than $80 billion spent a year to keep these two million–plus people in jail would pay for all the skills training the American labor market could absorb.

It is also the case that in addition to advocating for higher wages, compensation in the form of equity, portable benefits, and training opportunities, organized labor needs to more effectively engage on matters of corporate and public governance. Tomorrow's labor leaders must have greater say in how capital is redistributed, not just to workers but also across the entire economy. That means influencing decisions in corporate boardrooms as well as the halls of government.

"You can't separate the issues of labor rights and workers' inequality and democracy—they're totally intertwined," said Stephen Lerner, the organizer and Georgetown fellow. Lerner's statement reminded me of something the AFL-CIO's Richard Trumka said to me. Trumka pointed to a study by political scientists Yascha Mounk and Roberto Stefan Foa and told me,

> They asked millennials how important it is to live in a democracy. Thirty percent of millennials said it's important to live in a democracy in the US. Seventy percent said it's not and 24 percent said it's bad to live in a democracy. I was startled when I heard those results, I wondered, "Where, where, where are they coming from?" And then I looked at it. It's the first generation to live their entire life under the rules of globalization. They've seen their parents' wages drop, they've seen health care taken away, they've seen their pensions taken away, they've seen record corporate profits, and yet their parents' wages are flat for four decades. They've probably even seen their families lose a home. And then they're told, "It's okay. Go to college, get a good job." So they do. They come out with a mountain of debt, and have three or four or five employers in the same week and can't make it. So they're starting to equate capitalism and democracy with insecurity and poverty.

The findings from Mounk and Foa were all but unbelievable to me, but the data don't lie. They also show that attitudes toward democracy among those in my Generation X and older are vastly different from attitudes toward democracy among millennials.

Lerner reinforced this, telling me "a labor movement that primarily sees its mission as raising wages and winning benefits and being focused on what happens only at work is on its face going to be unsuccessful in developing the kind of society that allows for people to live full lives. The labor movement of the future needs to focus on not just the question of what happens at work, but the question of democracy, the question of inequality and economic concentration."

This hearkens back to the earlier ambitions of the labor movement. The labor leaders of the early 20th century wanted workers to have a say in how companies operated. Back then, the idea was known as industrial democracy. While labor movements in northern and central Europe achieved a form of industrial democracy through work councils and codetermination, their American counterparts did not. Again, the turning point came during a strike against General Motors.

In 1945, members of the United Auto Workers went on strike demanding that GM increase their wages and benefits *without* raising the price of its cars. They also wanted the company to open its books so the union could prove the company would still turn a profit if workers' demands were met. In other words, UAW wanted a say in how GM interacted with both workers and customers. The company resisted the union's demands, and after striking on and off for five years, the two sides reached an agreement: workers secured regular increases in wages and benefits, and management was guaranteed the exclusive right to run the company. The agreement, later dubbed the "Treaty of Detroit," set the dynamic for labor relations in the United States for decades to come.

"Both public and private sector unions . . . settled into a relationship with employers that ceded to employers the big questions of how enterprises were run, and that focused unions only on maintaining workers' wages and benefits," said Georgetown professor Joseph McCartin. "The union movement of the early 20th century had a much grander vision. In the early 20th century, the union movement used to speak a lot about industrial democracy as their goal. What they wanted was not just better wages, but a real say in how their businesses were organized. They thought workers should be part of the decision-making and that corporations not respond solely to stockholders but also their stakeholders."

Today, McCartin and Stephen Lerner are trying to bring back that grand vision. They and other activists have launched an organization called Bargaining for the Common Good, an affiliation of unions and community groups that work to coordinate their actions to secure broader social change. In December 2019, the organization published a list of more than 130 specific demands that unions across the country had adopted to address issues like racial justice, climate change, financial reform, educational inequality, and access to public services. The group is also helping labor leaders coordinate contract negotiations and organizing campaigns through online tools. In other words, it is enabling disparate labor groups to come together and build their collective power.

To achieve real change in the 2020s and beyond, new labor movements must think beyond their own members. They must bargain on behalf of all workers across all communities. Otherwise they may achieve a few one-off wins, but in the long run the economic forces that undermined organized labor in the late 20th century will take them down too. If workers fight for short-term gains while ignoring systemic issues that exacerbate inequality, they are effectively engaging in "assisted suicide," Lerner said.

"We need a much more expansive view of our mission, what we're trying to do and how we're trying to influence how the economy and the country function," Lerner told me. "I think if unions only focus on raising wages, then not only will they fail, but they actually become complicit in the very things that are undermining democracy."

It's easy to think about the state of democracy and the widening gyre of inequality and want to curl up in the fetal position, but only optimists change the world. I'm struck by the fact that Richard Trumka has taken a beating for forty years as a union leader but his focus and optimism are undiminished, even as he concedes the beatings. When I asked whether change is even possible, he told me in his gruff coal miner's voice that "for years we've been told that the economy's like the weather, there's nothing you can do about it. The economy isn't like the weather. The economy's nothing but a set of rules. Those rules have been made by the men and women that we elect. Those rules decide the winners and losers. And for four or five decades those rules by both Democrats and Republicans have been made so that the elite wins, and we lose."

Having taken the beatings for going on half a century and noting repeatedly all the opportunities for "implosion" if things don't get better, he then said something that cut across the grain of all our discussions. "I've never been more optimistic in the last four or five decades," he said, than he is now. He's seen new strikes in recent years that outscale anything he's been involved with for decades. He's seen new efforts at organizing and a whole new generation come along and start demanding change. Even if they're organizing in different ways than he ever has, it gives him hope. "And it's pretty exciting."

4

TAXES AND THE WORMHOLE IN THE GLOBAL ECONOMY

Tax policy is complicated, quantitative, and mind-numbing. No less than Albert Einstein said, "The hardest thing to understand in the world is the income tax," speaking to the accountant who prepared his taxes. Very few people understand it, and the ones who do often work as accountants, bankers, and lawyers for multinational corporations and wealthy individuals. However, taxes are a skeleton key for unlocking the problems that emerge out of using a 20th-century set of policies to solve 21st-century problems.

Ninety-nine percent of the people reading this book could pay less in taxes and our governments would have more to spend if we fixed a system where trillions of dollars in tax go missing each year and entire nations have been captured by outside interests. Tax serves as a microcosm for many of the global issues by which governments are divided and conquered.

The story of its complexity and importance can be illustrated by something as simple as buying a new belt.

Marco was out to dinner with Giulia, a writer he met at the supermarket. It was a perfect date: a plate of spaghetti alla carbonara, a fantastic conversation, even a slice of tiramisu to top it all off. But by dessert, Marco had begun to feel a little snug around the waist. When he leaned forward to grab the bill, the buckle of his belt popped off and tumbled to the floor. He managed to keep his cool, put on his coat, take Giulia by the arm, and walk her home without any first-date disaster stories. But now their second date was coming up, and Marco's trusty leather belt was out of commission.

Back in his flat in central Rome, Marco opened up his laptop and typed "men's Italian leather belt" into Google. The people of the Italian peninsula have been working with leather for thousands of years, and their craftsmanship, through brands like Gucci, is among the world's best. On Marco's screen, a series of ads appeared above the organic search results. At the top was an ad for Gucci. But Marco was not a designer-label guy, and the €360 cost was not in his budget. One link down, he saw an ad for Pelletteria Artigianale Firenze della Famiglia Ascani (which roughly translates to "the Florentine artisanal leather maker of the Ascani Family"). Like Gucci, the Ascani family had spent a century crafting fine Italian leather in Florence, but unlike Gucci their belts cost only €40.

Marco loved the belt that appeared on the screen. It was black, glossy, and functional. And for genuine Italian leather, you could not beat the price. Marco clicked on the ad and made the purchase online through Pelletteria Artigianale Firenze della Famiglia Ascani's website. The belt arrived just in time for his second date, and it served him well, through dates two and three and four, until there was no point counting anymore.

Marco bought his belt in the kind of routine online transaction that happens tens of millions of times per day around the world. It would not have been possible before the internet and e-commerce. Years ago, Marco would have needed to walk to a store, select a belt from whatever they had available in stock, and pay the cashier. Years ago, it would also have been an all-Italian purchase. Italian buyer, Italian seller, plus a portion pulled out as tax for the Italian government.

Now, of course, there's a fourth party in the mix. Marco might not even have heard of Ascani if not for Google, after all. Ascani pays for the service, at a rate of approximately €0.11 per click on its ads. On average, it takes about thirty-six clicks to drive a single sale. So, for each belt purchase, Ascani ends up paying Google €3.96, roughly 10 percent of the belt's cost. When you zoom out, Google—and its peers such as Apple and Amazon—have set themselves up as tax collectors on the traffic that runs through their online fiefdoms. It's virtually impossible to operate a business in the 21st century without making regular payments to at least one of the tech giants.

Smaller businesses have been pushing back against this form of rentier capitalism and making noise about the monopoly power that comes with owning an online marketplace like the App Store or Google's "Search" pages. Others argue that this is just the inevitable cost of doing business online.

But whatever your position, fishier than the cut that Google takes out of Marco's purchase and billions of other daily purchases is what Google pays in taxes. Each party in Marco's transaction is paying taxes: Ascani is still paying the 22 percent in value-added tax (VAT) that it would have before the digital age. Marco is still forking over 41 percent of his own income in tax as well to the Italian government. But the biggest player of all—trillion-dollar Google—has managed to slip out of the deal with a shocking 0.7 percent tax rate. The slimmest of slivers.

That is not because Italy has given Google a special exemption. By Italian law, all corporate income in the country is taxed at 24 percent. But the catch is that Google has assembled a complex set of levers and transfers to shift its profit off its Italian books. That €3.96 is collected by a subsidiary in Ireland, where Google faces a much lower tax rate—and that's just the first trick.

This kind of loophole might look irrelevant or eye-glazingly boring to the average citizen—especially one who's in a hurry to dress himself up for his second date. But when you zoom out and understand the scale of these maneuvers, when you start to see how central they are to the workings of the world's wealth, you begin to understand that Google's trick is less like a loophole and more like a wormhole in the global economy—one that has steadily eaten into the power of social contracts around the world for decades, and shows no sign of stopping.

When Marco buys his belt online, 10 percent of an otherwise all-Italian transaction just vanishes. And once that money slips away into Ireland, it does another disappearing act, followed by another. The full chain of transactions, through which Google has transferred billions of dollars, reveals one of the greatest engines of corporate power and inequality in the globalized world.

Extrapolate that €3.96 over the billions of ads Google serves every single day and you are dealing with big money, both in gains for Google and in losses for the countries where it does business. The tax laws we have today were written for commerce that occurred in the physical world, with tangible goods and national borders. But these rules begin to fall apart when businesses go digital and spread their operations across a global chessboard. Economists estimate that governments around the world lose more than $500 billion each year due to corporate tax avoidance. Even more is lost through the further tax evasion by wealthy individuals, often through many of the same tricks that multinational corporations have mastered.

Of course, tax might seem like a dirty word to you. *Who cares? Maybe if Marco had a choice, he'd be doing the same thing, and then he'd be able to afford Gucci*. But taxes are at the very core of government and what we rely on it for. Without revenue, governments cannot defend the nation, educate their citizens, build public infrastructure, support the economy, or fund social programs. People can debate the scale and scope of the government's responsibilities—but no matter its mandate, a government needs money to carry it out. A fair and just tax system is one that requires everyone to pay their fair share. People of different political stripes can debate what constitutes a "fair share," but when any party pays less than that amount, it undermines the greater good and puts a tear into the social contract. Either the government receives less than it's owed, or somebody else pays more than they should.

Today, we live in a society in which FedEx pays less money in federal taxes than one of its delivery drivers and Starbucks pays less than one of its baristas. Over the last fifty years, a massive proportion of global corporate income has begun to route through tax havens rather than to the countries where major corporations do the bulk of their business. Yet how far would FedEx have gotten without public roads to deliver its packages? How valuable would Google be without a steady stream of technologists graduating from universities with federally funded research? Would the company even exist were it not for the federal grant that enabled its founders to develop their famous search algorithm? And where would any of these companies be without strong courts to defend their intellectual property and effective militaries to protect their physical assets? As US Supreme Court Justice Oliver Wendell Holmes Jr. put it, "Taxes are what we pay for civilized society."

I do not like paying taxes any more than anybody else, and the 41 percent of his €55,000 annual income that Marco pays to the Italian government must sting. If Google, FedEx, Starbucks, and their peers paid anywhere close to the level of taxes that you, Marco, I, and everyone else reading this book paid, we could pay much less.

Each transaction has real-world consequences, even the €3.96 Google gets from a belt. Every dollar that multinationals or wealthy individuals keep from tax authorities is a dollar that is not being spent on infrastructure, health care, education, public safety, and other government programs that benefit not only society but the companies themselves.

Yet the bulk of the tax avoidance we see is not obviously illegal. As major corporations have become larger and larger, they've become ever more capable of gaming the tax policies of any individual nation and finding the best deals by shuttling money around the world. As they've done so, they've been able to accelerate their own growth and then put pressure on nations to loosen their tax mandates even further. This cycle has been going on for at least a half century, in a long-running race to the bottom.

We are nearly at rock bottom. And the only fitting response will need to be global: a worldwide effort to remove incentives for companies and wealthy individuals to dodge billions of dollars in taxes, leaving everyday citizens to come up with the balance.

TAX HAVENS 101

Tax avoidance is not a new phenomenon. People have found ways to avoid paying taxes for as long as their sovereigns have been collecting them.

The merchants of ancient Sumer avoided their kings' extensive tax regimes by working through an equally extensive black market, smuggling cows, sheep, and grain. In medieval Japan, landowners lobbied the emperor's government to extend a tax exemption created for Buddhist temples to their own private estates. Later, these tax-free estates, called *shōen*, became so large that the imperial court ran out of land to tax and went bankrupt.

Tax avoidance is a game historically mastered by society's elites. With money and political connections, they can push for laws that work in their favor and circumvent the laws that do not. Just as the aristocrats of Japan leveraged this power to acquire massive, tax-free estates, today's elites use it to operate through an opaque, lightly regulated financial system that lets capital dart around the globe out of the reach of authorities.

The jurisdictions that cater to the offshore world are known as tax havens.

Tax havens as we know them emerged in the early 20th century. They proliferated after World War I as stashes for Europe's wealth, then started to become a staple of the global economy in the 1960s and '70s. They come in all shapes and sizes: tax havens can be countries (Ireland and Luxembourg), individual states (Delaware and South Dakota), or semi-sovereign territories (Bermuda and Hong Kong). They might specialize in certain areas: hedge funds like the Cayman Islands, insurance companies prefer Bermuda, Wall Street financiers gravitate to Delaware, and their European counterparts flock to Jersey, Ireland, and Luxembourg. They often target certain geographies: elites in the US and Latin America funnel their money through Panama and the Caribbean; the Chinese send theirs to Hong Kong, Singapore, and Macau. Wealthy Europeans and Gulf royals are serviced by the famously secretive banks of Switzerland, though reforms in the Swiss system bringing more transparency have pushed those really seeking to hide their wealth into Singapore and the Cayman Islands. And as we will read, the United States is as big a culprit as the Caymans.

But no matter their status or specialty, all tax havens offer their clients one thing: an escape from the laws of someplace else.

For instance, when Google received €3.96 from the Ascani family, it likely would have avoided paying a dime to the Italian government. As soon as the transaction was completed, that money departed the country. The payment did not go directly to Google LLC, the corporation headquartered in Silicon Valley, nor to Alphabet Inc., the company that owns Google and its various side projects for self-driving cars, drone delivery, biotechnology, and the like. Instead, the Ascanis' €3.96 worked its way through a chain of corporate entities scattered across three different countries, none of which played any role in getting Marco his belt.

The reason Google and other multinational firms shuffle their money around the map in this way is to minimize their taxes, allowing them to generate billions of dollars from customers around the globe without giving a cut to the countries where they do business. Tax havens like the Cayman Islands, the Netherlands, Bermuda, Luxembourg, and Ireland offer drastically reduced tax rates and regulations to lure in foreign businesses or wealthy individuals. Following a model set by Switzerland in the wake of World War I, most tax havens also promise secrecy, outlawing even officials from prying into the details of offshore accounts.

HOW IT WORKS

There are countless financial hoops that companies can jump through to ensure the money they make in one country appears in a tax haven. Corporations generally pay taxes only on profits. Thus, they can save a lot of money by reducing profits in countries with high tax rates and increasing profits in jurisdictions where they pay little or no tax.

The strategies for moving earnings from one country to another fall under the broad umbrella of "base erosion and profit shifting." And as convoluted as these maneuvers may sound, most of them do not blatantly violate the law.

One of the most common techniques companies use to shift their profits around the globe is called transfer pricing. In short, this allows one branch of a company to pay another branch of that same company for goods and services that it provides, at a price basically set by the company itself. For multinational corporations, that often entails a subsidiary in one country making a payment to a subsidiary in a different country. Today, these sorts of intra-company payments are extremely common—about one-third of all international trade happens within the same company.

Transfer pricing has many legitimate applications. If you are a multinational citrus producer and your Brazilian subsidiary sends ten tons of oranges to the US, it is reasonable for the American subsidiary to pay its Brazilian counterpart for product and shipping costs. That said, transfer pricing can easily be abused.

In 2019, American corporations reported earning $577 billion in profits outside the United States. Nearly 60 percent of that money—some $330 billion—was "earned" in just seven low-tax jurisdictions: Ireland, Luxembourg, Switzerland, the Netherlands, Singapore, Bermuda, and the British Caribbean (the Cayman Islands, British Virgin Islands, Turks and Caicos, and Montserrat). Only 7 percent of that profit was reported in Germany, France, Italy, India, Japan, and China.

In other words, on paper, US multinationals "earned" nine times more profit in seven small jurisdictions than in six of the world's largest economies. That is not because the customer base in Bermuda is nine times bigger than the one in China. It is because transfer pricing allowed them to move profits to tax havens and lower their profits in high-tax jurisdictions.

To explain how this works, let's imagine what this kind of profit shifting might look like in a conventional business using analogous tricks of creative but legal accounting.

Imagine you were hired as a delivery driver for a local pizza shop. Each delivery comes with a tip, but you have to share 20 percent of your tips with the owner of the restaurant. Before the owner takes her cut, you are allowed to deduct any job-related costs. At a basic level, this is how corporate taxes work. Your company earns a profit (revenue minus costs), and a portion of the proceeds goes to the government.

We will say on your first night, you made $25 in tips and spent $5 on gas. You would immediately get back the gas money, and then the remaining $20 would be divided between you and the owner. She would get $4—20 percent of the total—and you would pocket the remaining $16. In this situation, you are the multinational corporation and the pizza shop owner is the government.

Now imagine you wanted to game the system through transfer pricing. The car that you use to deliver pizzas belongs to your parents. Normally they let you drive it whenever you want, but you could instead ask them to charge you $1,000 to "lease" the car for pizza deliveries. Your mother drafts an invoice and you bring it into the shop. The owner allows you to count that $1,000 as an operating cost, which you can deduct from your profits.

Now the next night that you make $25 in tips and spend $5 on gas, you get to keep the whole thing. You would get $5 back for the gas just as before, but you also count the remaining $20 toward the car lease. Your "profit" is zero on the night; you're still $980 in the red on that car lease. So there is nothing for the pizza shop owner to tax.

In this case, your mother is acting as an offshore subsidiary of your multinational company. You would "pay" your parents the $20, and because you live in their house (a jurisdiction with no taxes), nobody else takes a cut. In reality, your parents would never even need to touch the money.

After that first shift, the balance on the car lease is knocked down to $980. The same thing happens the next night, and now the balance is $960. After the next night, it drops to $940. At that rate, it would take fifty shifts to pay off the lease. That is fifty shifts in which the pizza shop owner is not getting 20 percent of your tips.

By the time the lease is paid off, you will have successfully transferred $1,000 in profit from a high-tax jurisdiction (the pizza shop) to a tax haven (your home). The pizza shop owner did not take a single penny.

The lease was a purely paper transaction—neither you nor your parents spent any extra money—but it nonetheless eliminated the "taxes" you would otherwise have owed. Without the lease, you would have taken home only $800 in profits. With the lease, you made an extra $200.

This is essentially how multinational firms abuse transfer pricing. They make payments from one subsidiary to another to shift their profits toward countries with low tax rates and raise their costs in countries with high tax rates. The difference is that multinationals have the accountants, lawyers, and international footprints to build paper trails that span oceans, and you can only draft invoices across town. If you are a pizza delivery driver, the offshore world is out of your reach.

With that in mind, we will go back to Google.

THE DOUBLE IRISH WITH A DUTCH SANDWICH

Between 2004 and 2019, Google used a pair of profit-shifting maneuvers—the "Double Irish" and "Dutch Sandwich"—to move the vast majority of its global earnings into Bermuda. Different versions of the Double Irish were also used by Facebook, Pfizer, Coca-Cola, Cisco, and other American multinationals. The maneuver follows the same basic logic as your pizza delivery scheme: raise costs in high-tax jurisdictions and move profits to low-tax jurisdictions. However, instead of a car lease, Google used licenses for its own intellectual property. Its Bermuda-based division was given ownership of Google's search algorithms and essential technology, and other divisions of the company had to lease out the intellectual property.

Google was forced to abandon this specific practice in 2020, after Ireland closed one of the necessary tax loopholes, but for fifteen years it used the Double Irish with a Dutch Sandwich to reduce its tax bill by tens of billions of dollars. In 2016 alone, the arrangement helped Google keep an estimated $3.7 billion away from European tax authorities.

We will say Marco bought his belt in the summer of 2018, while Google was still using the setup. This is how it would have worked.

When Marco (and the thirty-five people who did not make a purchase) clicked on the ad for the Italian leather belt, the Ascani family was charged €3.96 by a Google subsidiary called Google Ireland Limited. Created in 2003, this Irish company acts as the hub of Google's ad business across Europe, Africa, and the Middle East.

Google maintains corporate offices in dozens of countries including Italy, but the company argues these outposts are not full-fledged businesses but rather satellites of its European headquarters in Dublin. This semantic maneuver helps the company justify funneling revenue to its Irish subsidiary, where Google can take advantage of Ireland's comparatively lax tax structure.

Ireland's low tax rates and permissive corporate laws have made it something of a mecca for American technology companies looking to expand their presence across the Atlantic. Google's glassy European headquarters (where Google Ireland Limited is based) ranks among the tallest buildings in Dublin, towering over the city's Grand Canal. The surrounding neighborhood, a former industrial yard turned tech-bro hot spot, is also home to the European headquarters of Twitter, Facebook, LinkedIn, and Airbnb. Apple set up shop in Cork, where it is the city's largest private employer. According to the most recent data, American companies booked more revenue in Ireland than in the sixteen largest European countries, combined.

Had the transaction between Google and the Ascani family taken place in Italy, the profit it generated would have been subject to the country's 24 percent corporate tax rate. Instead, Google immediately shifted the revenue to Ireland, where the corporate tax rate is only 12.5 percent.

That does not mean Google pays no tax in Italy—the company's total tax bill is just much lower than it would be otherwise. In 2018, Google's Italian subsidiary—Google Italy s.r.l.—brought in €107 million in revenue, recorded €15.4 million in pretax profit, and paid €4.7 million in taxes to the Italian government. The catch is that almost all of that revenue came from "sales and services" in Ireland, not Italy. In other words, Google's Italian subsidiary makes almost all its money by helping Google's Irish subsidiary sell ads in Italy, not by selling the ads itself. Again, this is an instance of transfer pricing.

By shifting the €3.96 in ad revenue from Italy to Ireland, Google effectively cut its tax rate in half. If the buck stopped there, Google Ireland Limited would have deducted its expenses, paid the Irish government its 12.5 percent corporate tax, and called it a day. But the journey is far from over—Google does not pay anything close to the Irish rate either.

Technically, Google Ireland Limited makes its money by using the technologies and services developed by Alphabet Inc., the parent company of Google and its dozens of subsidiaries. Alphabet owns the intellectual property for software that powers Google Ads, Google Search, Google Maps, and other technologies. In order to use that software, subsidiaries must obtain the right to use that intellectual property.

But Google Ireland Limited does not lease the right to use this intellectual property directly from Alphabet. Instead, it obtains the license through another subsidiary, called Google Netherlands Holdings B.V.

In 2018, Google Ireland Limited generated about €38.1 billion in total revenue. The company logged €1.4 billion as profit and paid €272 million in taxes to the Irish government.

The company claimed that the other €36.4 billion got eaten up by operating costs, which are not subject to taxes in most jurisdictions. That included the usual expenses like employee salaries and office rent, but it also included a €16.1 billion royalty payment to Google Netherlands Holdings B.V. You read that correctly: Google used more than 40 percent of its earnings in Europe, Africa, and the Middle East to buy the rights to use its own software.

This Dutch subsidiary does not actually own this software either, but rather leases it from another Google subsidiary. It is a shell company in the purest sense, a conduit for distributing intellectual property licenses and transporting the profits they generate around the globe. In 2018, Google Netherlands Holdings B.V. did not employ a single person, yet it received a multibillion-dollar royalty fee from the Irish subsidiary in exchange for a software license.

But Google Netherlands Holdings B.V. then needed to pay for its own software license. Where did it receive that license? Another Alphabet subsidiary called Google Ireland Holdings. This company is officially incorporated in Dublin, at an address just a short walk along the canal from Google Ireland Limited. But thanks to a loophole in Irish tax law, the company is not required to be managed in Ireland. In this case, it legally operates out of Bermuda.

Here we have another game of semantics: the company is "incorporated" in Ireland, where it benefits from the European Union's trade policies, but it is "domiciled" in Bermuda, where the corporate tax rate is 0 percent.

In 2018, Google Netherlands Holdings B.V. paid this Irish-incorporated, Bermuda-based holding company a €21.8 billion royalty fee for the right to use its software. This entire sum came from the Dutch company's own royalty fees—the €16.1 billion from Google Ireland Limited and another €5.7 billion from Google Asia Pacific Pte. Ltd., a Singapore-based entity with which it has a similar arrangement.

The Netherlands did not tax royalty payments at the time, so those billions were routed from Ireland and Singapore to the Netherlands and then back to Ireland (but actually Bermuda) without losing a penny to taxes. From Ireland to the Netherlands to Ireland—a Double Irish with a Dutch Sandwich.

Like its Dutch counterpart, Google Ireland Holdings (which is domiciled in Bermuda) does not employ a single person. The company shares its registered address—70 Sir John Rogerson's Quay, Dublin 2—with nearly a thousand other businesses. Yet in 2018, Google Ireland Holdings took in more than $25.7 billion (€22.4 billion) in revenue and recorded profits of more than $15.5 billion (€13.5 billion).

Of the remaining $10.2 billion, nearly 95 percent was spent on Google's own R&D and the rest went to cover other costs.

Because the company is technically based in Bermuda, it paid no taxes to either the Irish government or the Bermudan government.

Google Ireland Holdings is where the buck finally stopped. Through an agreement with Alphabet, the company held the rights to license all of Google's intellectual property outside the United States. And while on paper it "generated" billions of dollars in annual revenue, the company's only physical presence on the island of Bermuda was a post office box in a nondescript four-story office building in the capital city of Hamilton. The number of the PO Box is 666.

To summarize:

Marco clicked on the Google ad for Pelletteria Artigianale Firenze della Famiglia Ascani, and he bought one of the company's belts. Thirty-five other people clicked the same ad but did not buy the belt. Each of those thirty-six clicks cost the Ascani family about €0.11, for a total bill of €3.96. For the sale of Marco's belt, the Italian government also received €8.80 in sales tax paid by the Ascani family. Italy would have collected that tax regardless of whether the sale took place online or in person.

Google Ireland Limited received €3.96 from the Ascani family. From there, the company spent €3.78 on what was classified as operating expenses, kept €0.15 in profits, and paid roughly €0.03 in Irish taxes. The Italian government received no taxes from this transaction, which involved an Italian citizen and an Italian business and took place entirely within the borders of Italy.

Of the €3.78 that Google Ireland Limited spent on operating expenses, €1.67 was wrapped up in a royalty payment to Google Netherlands Holdings B.V. and €2.11 went to other costs.

Google Netherlands Holdings B.V. took that €1.67 and funneled virtually all of it to Google Ireland Holdings, withholding only a tenth of a penny to cover its own costs. The Dutch subsidiary paid about €0.0003 in taxes.

Finally, Google Ireland Holdings, an ostensibly Irish company with a PO Box in Bermuda, received the €1.67. From there, about €1.01

was recorded as profit and the rest was mostly used to fund Google's own research. Google Ireland Holdings paid no taxes.

In total, of the €3.96 that Google received from the Ascani family, only €0.0284 was paid in taxes. That is an effective tax rate of roughly 0.7 percent. Instead of going to Italy, where the transaction occurred, that paltry sum was split between Ireland and the Netherlands. Keep in mind that Italy's corporate tax rate is 24 percent, Ireland's is 12.5 percent, and the Netherlands' is 25 percent. Yet—like magic, and with the help of Bermuda—Google found its way to 0.7 percent.

THE COST OF TAX AVOIDANCE

When companies get to pick and choose among the laws of hundreds of jurisdictions, their money will flow to wherever it is offered the most tax breaks. This is a choice that the pizza delivery driver does not get to make. As convoluted as it sounds, the financial wizardry employed by Google and other multinational companies is not overtly against the law. Such *tax avoidance* contrasts with *tax evasion*, where wealthy individuals hide money that is due by law as tax—though both make use of the same tax havens and follow the same labyrinthine process of disguising money flows, relying on bank secrecy to avoid detection and turn profits.

The technical legality of tax avoidance is used by many business leaders to justify their strategies. Eric Schmidt, CEO of Google at the time it adopted the Double Irish, pointed out that it was commonplace among major companies to use such techniques. "We were following the global tax regime in the same sense that European companies follow the things that benefit them when they operate in the U.S."

In a later interview, he noted that of course "businesses will respond to the tax stimulus made available to them." He has a clear point. He's not wrong. If countries are putting money on the table, why should a company just leave it there? "Europe did this to itself," Schmidt stated, noting that the Europeans themselves created the "race to the bottom" tax treatment for a then-struggling Ireland to stimulate investment there. "The global tax system is incredibly complicated, and we are required to follow the tax rules," he continued. "When the tax rules change, of course we would adopt them. But there was a presumption that somehow we were doing something wrong here."

Schmidt is correct. For whatever finger wagging may be directed against him and Google, the culpability rests principally with the countries that enable these activities by making them legal in the first place in the race to the bottom.

Still, just because something is legal does not make it right. "Where there is an income tax, the just man will pay more and the unjust less on the same amount of income," Plato wrote more than two thousand years ago. An argument rooted in moral philosophy is difficult to make successfully in a world of shareholder capitalism, though. Harm has to be demonstrated to win the moral argument, which Columbia University Law School professor Tim Wu makes by pointing out that "if everyone just does what's legal in their marriages or families or even their conduct as a consumer, you pretty quickly turn into Hobbesian chaos. I think ethics have long been the oil that lubricates the social contract. When you have a dedication to doing that which is legal and nothing else, that I do not think makes for a very cohesive society."

Many times, corporate tax avoidance schemes are considered legitimate only because they have not been challenged, said John Christensen, director of the Tax Justice Network. "So much of what [multinational corporations] do in terms of tax planning falls into an untested grey zone, with many avoidance schemes, claimed to be perfectly legal, falling apart under investigation."

In other words, when it comes to tax avoidance, companies are innocent until proven guilty. They are more than happy to take advantage of these shades of gray. Unpacking the intricate, global tax structures of multinational corporations requires a significant amount of time and expertise. Some governments have the resources to devote to these investigations, but many others do not.

"In countries where the fiscal authorities are powerful, multinational companies and their tax planners are likely to be more conscious of risk and therefore more likely to steer towards safer tax planning," Christensen told me. "In countries where the tax authorities have weaker transfer pricing investigation capability, multinationals are much, much more aggressive."

Nations offering major tax breaks are in a tough spot themselves. To attract capital in a globalized world, countries have been sucked into a race to the bottom, neutering their laws to compete for investment. The result is that both individuals and companies have figured out how to operate beyond the reach of any government. "Companies and capital migrate not to where they are most productive but to where they can get the best tax break," Nicholas Shaxson, a journalist and tax justice advocate, wrote in his book *Treasure Islands*. This process undermines the ability of governments to make sovereign economic policy decisions, as well as the efficiency of free markets. "There is nothing 'efficient' about any of this," said Shaxson.

Indeed, every dollar that they keep from tax authorities is a dollar that is not being spent on infrastructure, health care, education, public safety, and other government programs that benefit not only society but the companies themselves.

Given the complexity of these tax structures, it is difficult to know exactly how much tax revenue governments are losing. Companies are not exactly lining up to share those figures either. But looking at the data, researchers estimate that governments around the globe lose between $500 billion and $600 billion each year due to *tax avoidance* by corporations, and another $200 billion to *tax evasion* by individuals.

The United States and European Union each lose about $190 billion in taxes every year thanks to the offshore system, but countries in the developing world are hit even harder. Developing countries in Latin America, South Asia, and Africa have much more to gain from corporate tax—it typically comprises 15 percent of their total tax intake, versus 10 percent in developed countries, and is more reliable when it can be collected. But tax evasion and avoidance costs these countries drastically more, since they have fewer resources to plug leaks. When wealthy individuals and multinational corporations make money in developing countries and then send it to a tax haven, it cuts economic growth off at the knees. It quashes real investment in infrastructure and health care, undermines democracy, magnifies inequality, and destroys public trust. And while the cost to developed countries might seem like a steady leak, in much of the world the loss is an outright flood. One think tank estimated that developing countries in 2008 lost as much as $1.2 trillion in illicit financial flows—a figure that dwarfs the $100 billion in total annual foreign aid to these same countries.

Fixing the global tax system would have a greater impact on the developing world than any acts of philanthropy or foreign aid.

The reason we know about Google and its Double Irish with a Dutch Sandwich is largely because the company continued to use the setup for years after it had been exposed. It sparked outrage, but it was still technically legal.

In 2014, under heavy pressure from the EU, Ireland stopped letting multinationals domicile Irish subsidiaries in a different country. No longer could an Irish company be managed out of Bermuda. However, businesses that already used the setup—like Google Ireland Holdings—were allowed to continue doing so until 2020. It was only on December 31, 2019, that Google's parent company confirmed it would abandon the structure. And by then, similar maneuvers had already started cropping up to replace the banned scheme.

A further reason the Double Irish, Dutch Sandwich got so much attention in the first place was that Google and the other multinationals that used it were among the highest-profile and most closely scrutinized companies in the world. This one avenue for tax avoidance was filled with streetlights and neon signs, but the vast majority are not as well lit. Even so, it took years for journalists, the public, and policy makers to pressure the Irish government to close the loophole.

The coverage of Google's tax strategies prompted a crackdown from other European governments as well. Italy and France both implemented a digital services tax, which gives the government a small cut of the profits generated by digital advertising and other online transactions. The two countries also launched tax fraud investigations against Google, which led to the company paying more than a billion euros in back taxes for tax strategies that apparently did not pass the legal test in addition to the laugh test. The Netherlands also introduced a 21.7 percent tax on royalties and other payments that flow to low-tax jurisdictions like Bermuda, effectively taking the Dutch Sandwich off the menu.

These measures addressed the specific techniques used for a particular type of tax avoidance but did not solve the underlying problem. For every Double Irish with a Dutch Sandwich, there are dozens of equally tricky maneuvers that are known only to the lawyers and accountants who dream them up, as well as the companies that put them to use. The offshore world is like an iceberg, with the vast majority out of sight. Even right in Ireland, just as the Double Irish was phasing out, a replacement quietly entered stage left. When one Irish lawmaker, Matt Carthy, pointed out to the finance minister that revised legislation still left major loopholes wide open, he was told to "wear the green jersey." That is, he should quiet down and do what's best for Ireland. Ironically, that meant catering to the tax bills of US multinationals.

Without building a cohesive framework for taxing companies that operate across the globe, money will continue to flow to the jurisdictions with the lowest tax rates. Paul Monaghan, CEO of Fair Tax Mark, compares the existing system to a leaky dam. "The water's spilling through the holes and . . . as [you] plug some holes, other holes appear," he said. "As we close loopholes and create new legislation, other loopholes will open up."

To see this leak in action, look no further than the iPhone.

For years, Apple saved billions on its tax bill through its own Irish arrangement. By the early 2010s, Apple had achieved what economist Brad Setser calls "the nirvana of global tax planning." Its main Irish subsidiary was considered Irish for US tax purposes and American for Irish tax purposes—thus, it lived nowhere. Other offshore affiliates were so well disguised they did not need to file tax returns in any country. In 2014, the company paid a tax rate of roughly 0.005 percent on its global profits. This was not a Double Irish arrangement, but a close cousin that was later ruled to be an inappropriate sweetheart deal that Irish authorities had granted. Apple and Ireland won an appeal of that decision, but remain entangled in further litigation.

When a US Senate investigation shined a light on the company's practices and European tax authorities prepared to crack down, Apple started looking for a way to reshuffle its tax structure. After reaching out to lawyers in six different low-tax jurisdictions, Apple decided to take its business to Jersey, a speck of land in the English Channel with a hundred thousand residents and zero taxes on corporate profits.

From the outside, Jersey does not seem like a place a major tech company would set up shop. The island is forty-six square miles of lush, hilly pasture bordered by some of the best beaches north of the Mediterranean. You can drive to the ocean from any point on the island in ten minutes or less. The fishing villages and resort towns that line its coast are home to more shopkeepers than coders. Prior to the 1980s, Jersey had the sleepy, self-reliant economy typical of a small island. But today, Jersey is among the world's most popular tax havens.

In late 2014, Apple had two of its three "stateless" Irish subsidiaries claim tax residence in Jersey, and then a third Irish subsidiary claimed residence in Ireland. Around the time of this restructuring, nearly $270 billion of intangible assets suddenly appeared in Ireland. This influx of wealth—more than the value of all the residential property on the island—was so significant that it boosted Ireland's GDP by 26 percent that year.

At the time, nobody was sure what had caused this economic spike. Eventually, tax experts recognized it as a sign that one of the world's biggest companies had landed on the shores of the Emerald Isle.

Upon organizing its corporate structure, Apple had its Irish subsidiary borrow more than $200 billion from one of its Jersey affiliates, and then use the loan to buy the intellectual property owned by the other Jersey company. The Irish subsidiary was then able to deduct both the interest on the loan and the depreciation of the intellectual property from its taxes.

In effect, Apple lent itself money to buy its own intellectual property, and then generated billions of dollars in tax credits as the loan accumulated interest and the intellectual property became less valuable. Economist Brad Setser, who covered these issues at the White House and Treasury Department, told me it was a "classic paper transaction," and it left Apple with an effective tax rate in Ireland that likely sits between 1 and 3 percent.

This new tax avoidance maneuver was one of the very loopholes that Irish lawmakers had quietly left open when reforming the Double Irish. Fittingly, the scheme has been dubbed the "Green Jersey," and it is gaining popularity among companies that trade in intellectual property. It lets companies knock billions of dollars off their tax bills, just like the Double Irish, but now their profits and intellectual property never have to leave Europe. The Green Jersey does not rely on an Irish company based in a tax haven, the now-outlawed arrangement that underpinned the Double Irish. Instead, the Irish company is borrowing money and buying intellectual property from separate tax haven subsidiaries. The 2014 reform does not apply.

Like other tax avoidance strategies, the Green Jersey was not publicized by the companies that used it. It came to light only after journalists received a trove of leaked documents from a law firm that advised Apple on the restructuring.

Technology platforms like Apple and Google are not the only companies that engage in tax avoidance, but they do present especially difficult targets for tax collectors. There are a few reasons for this. For one, their products are ubiquitous. Unless the government blocks the site, you can become a customer of Google or Facebook or any other consumer internet company from anywhere in the world with an internet connection. When a company can operate in virtually every jurisdiction without a physical footprint, figuring out where to tax it is difficult.

At the same time, technology companies derive most of their revenue from intellectual property. Unlike corn, oil, and other commodities, intellectual property is often intangible. It is a creation of the mind—the patent, trademark, copyright, or other special sauce that differentiates your product from all the others. For Coca-Cola, it is the recipe for its signature soft drink. For Walt Disney, it is the copyrights for Mickey Mouse and Donald Duck. For tech companies, it is the code that makes their software tick. Intellectual property is incorporeal, easy to move from one country to another, and hard to pin down in terms of value. This makes it an ideal product for transfer pricing abuse.

By hiking up the licensing fees—in Google's case, €16.1 billion for a single year—tech companies can shift huge amounts of profit to the offshore havens where their intellectual property legally resides.

Just how much does this intellectual property offshoring cost the world's governments? Fair Tax Mark estimated that between 2010 and 2019, the big American technology platforms used transfer pricing and other strategies to collectively shave between $100 billion and $155 billion off their international tax bills.

Though the big tech companies get a lot of attention for their low tax bills, they are far from the only perpetrators of international tax avoidance. In large part, they are simply putting their own spin on the strategies that other multinationals have used for decades.

In 2017, the Institute on Taxation and Economic Policy found that nearly three-quarters of Fortune 500 companies operated at least one subsidiary in an offshore tax haven. At the time, 293 Fortune 500 firms used those subsidiaries to store more than $2.6 trillion in profits offshore. On average, those profits were taxed at only 6.1 percent. At the time, the US corporate tax rate was 35 percent.

Had the 293 companies brought those earnings back to the US before Congress changed the tax code in 2017, they would have owed the government a combined $752 billion. Even after the new tax law reduced the repatriation rate (the taxes companies pay when they move assets back to the US), the government would have received more than $200 billion in corporate tax revenue if that $2.6 trillion had come back to the States. And that is just from the Fortune 500.

This does not even begin to address the tax optimization strategies of companies headquartered throughout much of Africa, East Asia, and the Middle East. The reason we know about the Fortune 500's tax maneuvers is that the US government requires a certain amount of transparency and disclosure from its publicly traded companies. The same thing happens in every other part of the world. We just do not have the view into their financial activity.

While American companies get much of the attention, some European multinationals have recently come under fire for their own aggressive tax practices. The European Commission launched an investigation into IKEA over allegations that the company had avoided €1 billion in Dutch taxes. Similarly, German journalists found that Volkswagen stashed billions of euros in Luxembourg-based subsidiaries to avoid paying taxes back home.

As of this writing, among the Fortune 500 firms, Apple had the most profit stored in tax havens, with about $246 billion scattered across its three offshore subsidiaries. However, US financial institutions were by far the tax havens' most prolific customers.

America's largest banks and investment banks operated more than two thousand offshore entities and held about $149 billion offshore. That is nearly as much as they received in government bailouts after the global financial crisis.

Like technology platforms, pharmaceutical companies derive most of their value from intellectual property, and their patents have a similar tendency to wind up in tax havens. The four largest pharmaceutical companies in the US—Abbott Laboratories, Johnson & Johnson, Merck, and Pfizer—held a combined $352 billion across their 443 tax haven subsidiaries. According to Oxfam International, the companies use their offshore structures to avoid more than $3.8 billion in global taxes every year, including $112 million in taxes to developing countries.

While bashing tech platforms, banks, and pharmaceuticals is very much in vogue, it is important to realize that the offshore world plays host to firms in virtually every sector. Even companies that are inextricably linked to the US and its national identity—brands like Coca-Cola, Nike, and General Motors—used offshore subsidiaries to avoid paying billions of dollars in taxes to the US government. But as with

Google and its tax practices, none of these companies is breaking the law. The behavior may be objectionable, but it is still legal, so the only solution is to change the law. Period.

When they avoid paying taxes, multinationals not only avoid paying their fair share into government programs, but they also gain an unfair edge on small businesses. Hiring accountants, lawyers, and bankers to optimize your offshore tax structure is not cheap. Only the biggest companies can afford to do so, and those that cannot are left at a significant disadvantage.

If a local coffee roaster is forced to hand over 21 percent of its profit to the US government, while a globally tax-optimized competitor like Starbucks receives a $75 million tax *rebate*, the playing field is tilted at a 45-degree angle.

"It's the big players that get rewarded on a fact that has nothing to do with productivity or entrepreneurship or real, genuine stuff," said journalist and tax expert Nicholas Shaxson. "It's just about transferring wealth offshore," where even the most powerful nations can't touch it.

THE RACE TO THE BOTTOM

But if nations are roundly hurt by tax abuse, then why does the web of tax havens still have so much influence? It siphons billions per year away from developed and developing countries alike, weakening their ability to serve their citizens and granting free passes to the world's largest companies and wealthiest individuals. Yet even as the enormous costs have come to light, and even as regional powerhouses like the European Union have made serious efforts to plug major loopholes, the offshore system has suffered hardly a scratch. If anything, it continues to grow bigger and stronger.

To understand why, and to begin to approach solutions to the problem, we need to look at how the modern offshore system came to exist. Over the course of the last half century, tax havens have gone from peripheral actors to central hubs in the global economy. Many nations have tried to take a stand against them in one decade or another, but no efforts have made a lasting impact. And the constant slipperiness of the offshore world is best understood by two themes that keep recurring: a country becomes captured—or even simply influenced *just enough*—by outside interests. And it is then pulled into the global race to the bottom, where it competes against other nations to see who can offer the most enticing tax policies.

It has become increasingly difficult to find countries that are saintly actors. If you're looking for a villain, it's difficult to finger just the tax havens themselves or the corporate lobbyists or accountants. Two of the most prominent players in establishing the offshore world as we know it are major countries that are now losing billions to it every year: the United Kingdom and the United States. These would seem to be two of the few countries that would be powerful enough to start fixing the leak, and perhaps they still can do just that.

The starting gun for the global race to the bottom, if we are seeking its beginnings, was fired in London during the aftermath of World War II. Tax havens certainly existed before then; Switzerland, for instance, was a mecca for tax evasion from the late 19th century on. But, prior to the 1950s, tax havens largely catered to wealthy individuals and organized crime. They held plenty of money, but it was illicit money—which limited these countries' global economic power. That is, until the City of London helped tax havens go mainstream.

A common theme among tax havens is that they rarely choose to become havens. They tend to make the shift at the behest of a powerful outsider. And while the City of London might not sound in the slightest like an outside interest, it's worth making a clear distinction. The City of London should not be confused with London, the city.

London is the capital of the United Kingdom, and the City of London is a square-mile district inside the capital that houses much of the country's financial industry. And it is something else entirely.

The City of London has a peculiar history, tracing its roots to the Roman Empire. It has been a powerful force in British politics since the Normans invaded the island in the 11th century. And as the United Kingdom grew up around it, the City of London used its financial clout to maintain a degree of autonomy from the rest of the country.

It elects its own government (the City of London Corporation), maintains its own police force, and remains exempt from certain laws of the UK Parliament.

In addition to the geographic area, "the City" is also used as a shorthand for the UK financial industry, similar to "Wall Street" in the United States. Not all British banks fall within the City of London's geographic limits, but the City and its officials act as the banks' chief representatives in the UK and abroad.

The official responsibility of the City's top executive—the Right Honorable Lord Mayor—is to serve as "an international ambassador for the UK's financial and professional services sector." The Lord Mayor is also the president of the leadership council of TheCityUK, an industry group established in 2010 to "champion and support the success" of the British financial sector. The organization, which represents dozens of global financial services firms, acts as a "fusion of the City of London Corporation and the private financial sector," according to Nicholas Shaxson.

Reuters called TheCityUK "Britain's most powerful financial lobby group." The organization proudly displays the assertion on its website.

The City of London Corporation also appoints an official called the Remembrancer to serve as a lobbyist in the House of Commons—he has a special seat across from the Speaker. Members who raise questions about financial services and other matters related to the City can expect a call from the Remembrancer within hours. It's also important to note that the businesses residing in the City have a hand in electing its local government, the City of London Corporation. In municipal elections, the City's eight thousand human residents each get a single vote, but the *businesses* that reside there get thirty-two thousand votes. That means international banks like Barclays, JP Morgan Chase, Central Bank of China, Bank Sepah International, and Moscow Narodny Bank can directly participate in one of the UK's most important local elections.

Though the City has assimilated into the greater UK in many respects, its loyalties reside with the financial industry. Given its constituents, the City is perhaps the most powerful special interest organization in the UK, if not the world. Shaxson calls it a lobbying organization "so deeply embedded in the fabric of the British nation-state that it has made it very hard for Britain . . . to confront or even seriously check the power of finance."

This is partly a result of the City's aggressive lobbying efforts. John Christensen, director of the Tax Justice Network, said that when compared to TheCityUK, the US National Rifle Association "seems quite shy and timid." The City's sway over British politics also stems from its importance to the national economy.

"Most [members of Parliament] . . . think that the City of London is the goose that lays the golden egg," Christensen said. "It's a sector that generates . . . the most wealth in the UK economy, and if we were to take action against it, our economy would tank because it's that weak. It's the sense that there is no option other than to continue to kowtow to financial services. It's almost complete state capture."

This influence extends beyond domestic politics as well.

"On the list of things most important to the United Kingdom in its relationship with the European Union—number one on the government's list, I suspect—was to protect the City of London," said Jonathan Luff, a former top aide to UK prime minister David Cameron. "At the top of the list of any British prime minister, any chancellor of the exchequer, any diplomat representing the United Kingdom in Brussels, would have been 'how is this going to affect the British financial services industry?'"

Both sentiments were confirmed by one of the exchequer's former top officials.

"We very much saw it as a golden goose that you don't want to kill, but you want to pluck—that basically has been the UK attitude for a long time," the former official said. "The UK pursued a . . . policy of trying to promote and protect the City of London, particularly from EU regulation, while at the same time seeking to try and tax and extract rents in a way that didn't undermine the international competitiveness of the City."

One of the major contributors to the City's lasting influence was its role in creating the world's offshore system after the Second World

War. At the time, the United Kingdom's empire was coming apart at the seams. It was ravaged by war, deeply in debt, and rapidly shrinking as its colonies declared independence. It needed a way to maintain its position as a world power, and the City, which had served as the economic hub of the once-sprawling empire, offered a solution: finance.

The British banking sector began courting international clients, and appealed to them by offering a way around the rules and regulations back home. By doing business in London, American bankers could circumvent Depression-era regulations, the Soviet Union could confidently invest in Western markets, and criminal organizations could launder their money until it was squeaky clean.

But as the City revved up its financial services, it needed access to way stations where clients could deposit, store, and withdraw money. Preferably, these would be at arm's length, to allow banks, clients, and the UK a few layers of plausible deniability if other governments came calling.

The banks did not need to look far. Despite losing the vast majority of its empire after World War II, the UK managed to cling to a few scattered islands, concentrated in the Caribbean and the English Channel. Through lobbying by the City of London, these islands found a new purpose.

Consider the Cayman Islands, one of the world's top tax havens today. The Caymans have been controlled by the United Kingdom since the 17th century, but for most of its history the territory was nothing more than a sun-kissed, tropical backwater. Fewer than 6,500 people lived on the islands when they got their first airport, bank, and hospital in 1953. In 1966, cows still wandered through the town center of its capital, George Town. That same year, foreign bankers petitioned the British-led government to enact banking secrecy, and the City of London paved the way. By the 1970s, the Caymans were on their way to becoming a global financial hub. Note that this evolution was not driven by the Caymanian people—but by outside bankers and the City of London.

Some officials back in London objected to the Caymans' overt appeal to offshore capital, but their concerns had less to do with ethics than maintaining control over the British currency and financial industry. "We need to be quite sure that the possible proliferation of trust companies, banks, etc., which in most cases would be no more than brass plates manipulating assets outside the Islands does not get out of hand," Bank of England officials wrote in a 1969 letter. "There is of course no objection to their providing bolt-holes for non-residents, but we need to be sure that in so doing opportunities are not created for the transfer of UK capital to the non-Sterling Area outside UK rules."

Eventually, the Cayman Islands adopted their own currency, alleviating the Bank of England's concerns. Since then, the islands have continued to act as a honeypot for foreign cash. And many of Britain's other remaining territories followed the same route. Bankers and accountants from abroad would offer a raft of new business if these jurisdictions rewrote their finance laws, exploiting loopholes in other nations' tax laws along the way. The City would pave the way for these reforms to pass, and its banks would soak up much of the new business. So, with the tacit approval of the British government, the City refashioned the empire's islands into some of the world's top tax havens.

Notably, these havens were increasingly appealing to foreign banks and the skyrocketing number of multinational companies, and they were working within the lines of international law to exploit loopholes that would allow their clients to maintain legality. Over time, this would turn tax havens from peripheral to larger players in the global economy.

CITY IN ACTION TODAY

There are now thirteen jurisdictions across the globe that do not have a general corporate income tax. Eight of them—Anguilla, Bermuda, the British Virgin Islands, the Cayman Islands, Guernsey, the Isle of Man, Jersey, and Turks and Caicos—are British territories or Crown dependencies. "They're all little outposts of the British Empire that have managed to sort of find a way to give wealthy people advantages and wealthy companies advantages in their battle to reduce their tax burden," said Jonathan Luff, the former top aide to UK prime minister David Cameron. These jurisdictions have their own legislatures, but their chief executive is appointed by the British monarch, and their top court is the Privy Council, a group of British politicians primarily responsible for advising the Crown. In other words, though these jurisdictions present themselves as independent states, they are very much linked to the United Kingdom. And, given its weight in UK politics, according to Luff, the City of London can wield "extremely significant" influence over regulations (or the lack thereof) in the territories.

There are a number of channels the City can use to exert its influence over the British domains. The most overt is its presence in Parliament, but most of its methods are more subtle. By exploiting the peculiarities of island politics, the financial industry can make these territories impervious to reform and hostile to those who question their behavior.

Few people know this better than John Christensen, who saw firsthand how the City drove the policies of Jersey, the site of Apple's latest tax havenry, in the 1990s and 2000s. A tall, gray-haired Brit in his midsixties, Christensen is a Jersey native and the sort of guy you would hope to run into at a pub. He is quick to laugh and brimming with stories, each one drawing you further in than the last. Some are adventurous, like the accounts of riding motorcycles along the Jersey coast and racing sailboats on the choppy English Channel. Others are more solemn, like returning to an island whose main newspaper declared him an "enemy of the people" and hearing his estranged brother call him a traitor. Christensen bears the stern features of someone who has spent decades battling forces more powerful than himself. But even after fighting the odds for so long, he remains optimistic they will soon turn in his favor.

Christensen now leads the Tax Justice Network, a nongovernmental organization that investigates the offshore industry. But before he joined the group in 2003, Christensen worked inside the offshore system itself. He started out as a private account manager at Touche Ross (now a part of Deloitte) and became an economic adviser to the island of Jersey in the early 1990s. There, he was astounded by the level of corruption he witnessed.

Christensen describes islands like Jersey as "a perfect environment for complete political capture" by outside organizations like the City of London.

Island governments are organized in a way that makes them easy to influence, he said. Jurisdictions like Jersey, Bermuda, and the Cayman Islands lack a free press, strong political parties, bicameral parliaments, independent judiciaries, and other "foundations that you would regard as essential to democracy," he said. Their elected officials are also easy to "bamboozle."

"Most of the politicians in these very small islands are reasonably decent people, but they don't have a particularly sophisticated professional background," Christensen said. "Few of them could look at revised company law and critically examine it. Lawmakers are more likely to spend hours and hours debating relatively trivial things, like the location of a new school, and pass very high-level financial legislation through on the nod because they do not feel in a position to challenge it. They don't see the big international picture. What they're told is 'this will bring business to the island in terms of newer clients or big companies booking tax in the island, and the island will benefit from that additional tax revenue.' As far as they're concerned that's all that's of interest."

When Christensen served in the Jersey government, many members of Parliament who did understand the financial industry were themselves closely tied to the banks, at times in insidious ways. In 1996, Christensen helped the *Wall Street Journal* uncover a slew of regulatory missteps that allowed a currency trader at a Jersey-based subsidiary of UBS to commit numerous financial crimes. The multimillion-pound scandal implicated two of the island's senior senators and its top civil servant, who also happened to be Christensen's boss. Both the senators implicated in Christensen's whistleblowing—Reg Jeune and Pierre Horsfall—had separately presided over the island's financial regulatory committee while simultaneously working for the bank at the heart of scandal, Horsfall as a director and Jeune as a senior partner with the bank's law firm. So close were the ties between the banks and the government that many elected officials "were acting almost as the lobbyists within the Parliament," Christensen said.

Once Christensen had blown the whistle, he knew his days on the island were numbered. "Within twenty-four hours, I went from being the head of the government economic service to knowing I was going to have to leave the job, sell my house, leave the island. There was no way I could continue. Once you start challenging really powerful people, and if you are in a position where your evidence is plausible and credible and is backed up, then you become an enemy and they will bore you to the knife." It took Christensen about eighteen months to finally leave Jersey. By the time he departed, many friends and relatives had severed ties with him, and he had dropped thirty pounds in weight. The government attempted to discredit him by circulating stories in the media that he was just a disgruntled employee operating on his own personal agenda.

Instead, he was trying to reveal how Jersey's agenda was not its own. Combine pliable island politics with London's direct control over executive appointments and judicial decisions, and you are left with jurisdictions that will bend to the will of the UK government and to the City of London's outsize power over British financial matters.

"The idea these are independent places frankly doesn't hold water," Christensen said. "Territories will say 'we are independent,' and the UK will say, 'Yeah, they're independent, we can't interfere with their affairs.' That's a lie. It's all part of creating a theater where the UK can plausibly deny responsibility for what happens in Cayman or in Jersey. There's no way that anything could happen in Jersey without London's nod."

Oftentimes, he added, that means a literal nod. During his time in the Jersey government, Christensen said British officials took care not to keep paper records of their efforts to influence matters in the territories. Instead, "Brits have this language, this coded language. They wouldn't necessarily say, 'you cannot do that,' but they would over a cup of tea say something along the lines of, 'well, we don't think it's in Her Majesty's interests,'" Christensen said. "Very tongue-in-cheek language, very ironic. Our ears are tuned to that kind of language, so we know, 'don't do it.' They don't want to be seen to be putting things down in writing, because you then have a paper trail which can expose that actually this is being controlled from London."

These ties to "elsewhere" are a defining feature of most global tax havens, Nicholas Shaxson said. They make it especially difficult for the international community to force offshore jurisdictions to reform their ways. It would be one thing to pressure a small chain of Caribbean islands to adopt transparency measures and close tax loopholes, but when those islands are controlled by a global power like the United Kingdom it becomes more challenging. It's even more challenging when the UK itself has one of the most powerful financial lobbying organizations, the City of London, built into its Parliament.

By transforming its territories into flytraps for foreign cash, the United Kingdom played a critical role in creating an offshore world that lets individuals and corporations escape their domestic government's taxes and laws. And once any jurisdiction is sufficiently captured, the history of the offshore industry shows that it is a slippery slope.

When one jurisdiction lowers its tax standards, others must compete to keep companies from testing new waters. Over time, virtually every country in the world has been drawn into the race to the bottom, trying to outmaneuver one another to lure money from companies and individuals with as few questions asked as possible. Even the most powerful countries in the world, which might have enough weight to turn the tide, have instead been roped in—either because corporate interests have lobbied to prevent action or because they are afraid of losing business. The United States serves as the perfect example.

UNITED STATES

The United States loses at least $225 billion every year due to tax avoidance and evasion. You would think that this would provide enough of an incentive for the nation to use its muscle to crack down on tax haven abuse. While there are plenty of voices in the States who would like to do just that, a haphazard policy has emerged instead. The ultimate result is that the US has taken half measures against other tax havens while quietly sprinting ahead in the race to the bottom. In many ways, it is now one of the world's leading tax havens.

In its 2020 financial secrecy index, the Tax Justice Network named the United States the world's second-most secretive jurisdiction, outdone only by the Cayman Islands. At the federal level, the country is unwilling to share information on foreign companies and individuals who transfer money into the US. And because states like Delaware, Nevada, and Wyoming grant corporations and their owners extensive anonymity, foreigners find the US to be an extremely attractive destination for ill-gotten funds.

After the Second World War, as the UK was laying the foundation for the offshore system, the US government remained staunchly opposed to tax havens. In 1961, President John F. Kennedy called for legislation that would "[eliminate] the 'tax haven' device anywhere in the world." But as the expanding offshore markets and escalating war in Vietnam drew more US money abroad, the government chickened out. It needed a way to bring more capital into the country and keep the dollar strong, so it joined right in. The US started adopting the lax regulations that banks enjoyed in London in an effort to corner a piece of the global financial market. It made an even bigger shift in the arena of financial secrecy. In the 1960s, non-Americans could already invest in the US without fear that banks would share information with their home governments. In the decades that followed, federal and state lawmakers enacted policies to give foreign investors greater secrecy and more tax exemptions. Money began to pour into the country, much of it from corrupt officials and criminal organizations in Latin America.

"Anonymous companies . . . can be formed in any state in the United States. That allows wealthy individuals, corrupt officials, money launderers, etc., to set up companies to stash wealth . . . completely anonymously and without any accountability whatsoever," said Clark Gascoigne of the FACT Coalition, a nonpartisan alliance of more than a hundred state, national, and international organizations working toward a fair tax system that addresses the challenges of a global economy. "That's a very real policy choice that we have made in the United States, to allow these entities to exist."

As it expanded secrecy for foreign investors, the US government pushed for laws and tax treaties that forced foreign jurisdictions to share more information about American investors abroad. In 2010, the US passed the Foreign Account Tax Compliance Act (FATCA), a law that required foreign financial institutions to automatically share information on American clients with the IRS. Foreign banks that did not comply with the act were slapped with a 30 percent tax on all interest and dividends paid by the United States.

Interestingly, this was a major step toward shining a light into every shady tax haven or hiding hole in the global economy. Except for one problem. The law did not require American banks to share information on their own foreign clients. In fact, since FATCA was enacted, the US has pushed back against measures that would force its banks to open their books to international tax authorities.

In effect, the United States is trying to have its cake and eat it too. It wants to fight non-American tax havens while acting as a tax haven for non-Americans.

This approach to global tax is particularly harmful. The US participates in the race to the bottom while punishing other countries for competing. And as long as it serves as a sieve, the problem of tax avoidance will inevitably continue and every country will continue to feel pressure to keep cutting taxes on corporations and foreign investment to compete. If we look at just the last half century in the United States, we can already see the cost of the race clearly.

In 1952, corporate taxes accounted for approximately 32 percent of the US government's total tax revenue. In 2019, less than 7 percent of federal tax revenue came from corporations. During that same period, the proportion of federal revenue that came from individual income and payroll taxes rose from 52 percent to 86 percent. If you adjust for inflation, American companies paid less tax in 2018 than they did in 1989. During that time, their total profits more than doubled.

Most of those reductions were not made because policy makers wanted to give companies tax breaks and put a higher burden on individuals. But that is exactly what happened. Since these trends began after World War II, they have not stopped. In the first two decades after the war, taxes and regulations were at their stiffest in developed nations, and growth was at an all-time high. But the UK's offshore organizing let banks and companies start to dodge those rules, setting up a competition between countries. If nations resist lowering taxes and reducing regulations, they will hemorrhage capital. As a result, between 1980 and 2019, the average corporate tax rate across the globe fell from 40.4 percent to 24.2 percent. Since 2000, only 6 of the world's 196 countries have increased their corporate tax rate—Chile, the Dominican Republic, El Salvador, Hong Kong, Lebanon, and Papua New Guinea.

The companies and individuals who can afford to take advantage of the global financial system might benefit, but most of us do not. Many small countries have "mostly given up" trying to bring in taxes from multinationals, according to University of Chicago economist Austan Goolsbee.

Today, governments around the world rely more on sales and individual income taxes than corporate taxes to fund their programs. The result, Goolsbee said, is that the burden of funding the government has shifted from big companies to everyday people. Government policy enables concentrated power in markets to avoid contributing to society, and as a result that burden is borne by citizens even as their public benefits are constrained by a drop in tax revenue. When countries are forced to compete on tax, their citizens lose the ability to determine the size of their government programs, the strength of their safety net, and the distribution of their wealth. The power and potential of good governance evaporate.

Nowhere is this cost greater than in the developing world.

ANGOLA

As we turn to the developing world, it's worth remembering the distinction between corporate *tax avoidance*, which does not blatantly violate the law (albeit contortedly), and *tax evasion*, which does. Both tax evasion and tax avoidance rely on the same basic strategy: use the laws of an offshore jurisdiction to get around the rules of your home country. While companies use the offshore system to lower profits in high-tax countries and raise profits in low-tax countries, many of the ultra-wealthy use it to make their wealth disappear from view altogether.

When it comes to tax evasion, the name of the game is secrecy. The more cash, stocks, bonds, and other assets you can hide from the government, the less income you declare on that wealth, and the less you pay in taxes. By obscuring the paper trails that can tie them to their assets, some of the wealthiest individuals in the world can make it seem like they make a lot less money than they do.

Certain jurisdictions specialize in these disappearing acts. The funds that reinvest this hidden wealth are located mostly in Luxembourg, Ireland, and the Cayman Islands. The anonymous shell companies, trusts, and foundations where elites deposit their money are concentrated in the Caymans, Panama, Singapore, Hong Kong, and the British Virgin Islands. The United States is also becoming a top destination for non-Americans looking to set up anonymous companies. This secretive banking industry traces its roots to the early 20th century, when wealthy families flocked to Switzerland to avoid the new taxes European governments imposed after the First World War. Because Swiss banks did not communicate with other countries' tax authorities, foreigners could earn interest and dividends on their assets without tipping off anyone back home.

The secrecy of Swiss banks also attracted less savory clients from across the pond. After federal authorities locked up Chicago gangster Al Capone on tax evasion charges, mobsters found themselves in desperate need of a place to stash their ill-gotten money. They found refuge in Switzerland. Beginning in the 1930s, mobsters started moving their assets through anonymous companies into Swiss banks, often in suitcases stuffed with cash, diamonds, and cashier's checks. They then took out loans from the same banks and wrote the interest payments off their taxable business income.

The effort was orchestrated by Meyer Lansky, a Russian-born mob financier who inspired the character Hyman Roth in the *Godfather* movies. Lansky would later spearhead the mob's expansion into Cuba and, after Fidel Castro came to power, the Bahamas. His gambling and banking operations brought so much money to the Bahamas that the territory's British officials were willing to turn a blind eye to his criminal ties. In the 1960s, Finance Minister Stafford Sands, who had previously taken a $1.8 million bribe from Lansky, pushed for legislation that made it a criminal offense to disclose the owners of bank accounts and other financial information. The measure passed with the tacit approval of London, making the Bahamas one of the first Caribbean tax havens.

The secretive banking system created for mobsters in the Bahamas would later expand to the Cayman Islands, the British Virgin Islands, and beyond. It also started attracting new clients. By the 1980s, Latin American drug traffickers, African dictators, and American entrepreneurs were using the offshore system to invest their fortunes in the global market, invisible to tax authorities and law enforcement. The banks that provided these services were (and still are) mostly regional offshoots of larger institutions in London, Zurich, and New York City. While it still caters to organized crime, the offshore system now serves the whole array of global elites, and the scale of the tax evasion is massive.

Gabriel Zucman, an economist at the University of California, Berkeley, estimated in 2015 that about $7.6 trillion in private assets is hidden in global tax havens. That means about 8 percent of the planet's personal financial wealth is invisible to tax authorities. If it were taxed, this hidden wealth would generate an extra $200 billion in revenue for governments worldwide, every single year. And this is a conservative estimate. Researchers at the Organisation for Economic Co-operation and Development uncovered more than €10 trillion ($11.4 trillion) in personal wealth stashed offshore. Economist James Henry places the figure in the range of $24 trillion to $32 trillion. One estimate holds that if the wealthiest 1 percent paid just 0.5 percent in extra tax each year over the next ten years, it would equal the investment necessary to create 117 million new jobs.

But not every country feels the impact of tax evasion in the same way. According to Zucman's estimates, Europeans have the most money stashed offshore—$2.6 trillion—but that represents only about 10 percent of the total financial wealth on the continent. In the United States and Asia, only 4 percent of financial wealth is located offshore. Make no mistake: personal tax evasion still costs these governments tens of billions in revenue. But wealthy nations can weather the loss of revenue more easily.

As previously stated, it is the developing world that suffers the most from tax evasion. In Latin America, about 22 percent of personal financial wealth is kept in tax havens, and in Africa the figure is 30 percent. In both Russia and the Gulf states, more than half of all financial wealth is stashed abroad. Developing nations often lack the necessary resources to ensure that the tax they're owed makes it into their coffers—especially when tax havens and even the US and UK make it so easy to move money to their shores without a trace. And in developing nations, individual tax evasion and corporate tax evasion often go hand in hand. There is a long history of companies engaging in downright abusive schemes to drain profits out of the developing world without giving a cent back. In Africa alone, a High Level Panel on illicit financial flows estimated that companies drained $50 billion from the continent annually. And while the US or EU might have the tools to investigate a Double Irish scheme or more brazen money laundering, this is much rarer in poorer nations, especially as the globe continues to race to the bottom.

Financial secrecy exacerbates poverty, government corruption, and organized crime. Over the years, journalists have uncovered countless stories of oligarchs in developing countries using the offshore system to enrich themselves at the expense of citizens. Nowhere is this more evident than in Angola, a prime example of the tax abuse woes that plague the developing world.

Angola's geography bears some resemblance to California: it boasts rain forests in the north and desert in the south, connected by nearly a thousand miles of beautiful coastline. Like many countries in sub-Saharan Africa, the vast majority of Angola's wealth comes from beneath the ground. Oil accounts for more than 90 percent of the country's exports, diamonds make up another 5 percent, and the rest is coffee and other agricultural products. Despite the riches that lie beneath Angola's soil, half of its citizens live on less than a dollar per day, and the country has one of the highest rates of infant mortality in the world. The suffering of the Angolan people is attributable to the country's ruling class, which has spent decades funneling Angola's wealth offshore.

Immediately after gaining independence from Portugal in 1975, Angola descended into a twenty-seven-year civil war. By 1993, the forces loyal to President José Eduardo dos Santos were in desperate need of weapons. With his government under an international arms embargo, dos Santos and his associates set up an under-the-table deal with French officials to exchange arms for oil. In the following years, nearly $800 million in Angolan oil money was transferred out of the country through anonymous accounts in Switzerland. Subsequent investigations found that much of the money ended up in the hands of French and Angolan officials, after routing through tax havens. At the same time, the forces opposing dos Santos were smuggling diamonds into the Congo and Belgium to finance their own war effort. Though the exact figure is impossible to know, researchers estimate some $4.7 billion was smuggled out of Angola during the last decade of its civil war.

Dos Santos emerged victorious from the civil war and held on to the presidency until 2017. All the while, he and his family used Angola as their personal piggy bank.

José Filomeno dos Santos, the president's son, served as the head of Angola's sovereign wealth fund from 2013 to 2017. He was later accused of siphoning more than $500 million out of the fund during his tenure.

In 2020, Isabel dos Santos, the president's daughter, was charged with embezzling some $57 million from the state-run oil company she once directed. She is also wrapped up in a scandal involving Angola's state-sponsored diamond producer, Sodiam.

In 2012, Sodiam and dos Santos's husband, Sindika Dokolo, agreed to buy a stake in the Swiss jeweler De Grisogono. It was intended to be a fifty-fifty partnership, but it later came out that Sodiam poured nearly $150 million into the deal while Dokolo put up virtually no money. To pay for the investment, Sodiam took out a loan from a private bank in which dos Santos herself was the largest shareholder.

As of April 2020, dos Santos was still considered the richest woman in Africa, with an estimated $2 billion in assets scattered across some four hundred companies in forty-one different countries. I spent time with Isabel dos Santos on two occasions, once in Gabon and once in Nigeria. In both cases she moved through the country like a head of state, with an absurd sense of entitlement and dripping in jewelry.

The problem of families like the dos Santoses is not unique to Angola. The offshore system has allowed corrupt officials and business leaders to plunder the continent for decades.

"Corruption continues to be a major problem in Africa," said Johnnie Carson, a career diplomat who served as US assistant secretary of state for African affairs. "If you steal all of the major income of a country . . . then you're going to have a weak and fractured society. You're going to have endemic corruption that goes up and down, not just at the top, but through the system, and the social contract will break down."

The Western firms that assist elites in siphoning money out of the developing world appear happy to ignore the consequences of this theft.

Before his time in the Jersey government, John Christensen worked for Touche Ross, a professional services firm that is now part of Deloitte. While there, he administered the offshore accounts of about 120 clients, none of whom resided in Jersey. Given his access, Christensen said, he quickly realized most clients were engaged in some kind of illicit activity. He voiced his misgivings on more than one occasion, but each time they were met with a shrug. Once, he remembers alerting his boss to potential fraud involving an oil company in Nigeria and a string of trust companies in Jersey and the Caribbean. He was told to drop it. "That client is a very good client—and frankly I don't give a shit about Africa anyway," his boss said.

Each year, tax evasion costs African governments $14 billion in revenue. When you factor in the money African leaders directly siphon out of their governments, the total losses are much greater. Among economists, this outflow of national wealth through tax avoidance, tax evasion, and other means is known as capital flight.

A dollar invested abroad is a dollar that does not support local businesses and entrepreneurs. Researchers at the University of Massachusetts Amherst found that between 1970 and 2015, Africa lost more money to capital flight than it received in foreign aid. That makes the continent a "net creditor" to the rest of the world.

"A major constraint to economic development in Africa is the lack of adequate financial resources in the face of immense needs in public and public investment in infrastructure and social services," researchers wrote. "Capital flight undermines efforts to alleviate that constraint."

You cannot stop wealthy Africans from investing abroad. But by reforming tax havens and the secretive banks that they empower, you can ensure that a piece of their returns gets injected back into the local economy. Increased tax revenue would also enable governments in developing countries to more effectively investigate tax evasion and avoidance, creating a virtuous cycle. We have already seen that a small increase in resources can go a long way. In 2015, the Organisation for Economic Co-operation and Development (OECD), an organization comprising thirty-seven of the largest economies, and the United Nations launched Tax Inspectors Without Borders, an initiative that supports developing countries' tax authorities with outside expertise. By 2019, the program had helped participating nations collect almost $500 million in additional tax revenue. Every dollar invested in the program returned $100 in extra taxes, which is then reinvested in citizens and the economy. These results show that strengthening tax authorities may be among the most cost-effective ways to improve governance and expand social services in developing countries. According to John Christensen, countries participating in the program see multinational companies adopting "far less aggressive" tax structures than they had previously.

Much of the money flowing out of developing countries is flowing illegally. It is not companies cleverly navigating the rules of different jurisdictions to lower their tax bills; it is often individuals using financial secrecy laws to hide their wealth entirely, or shady companies keeping illicit deals off the books and absconding with the money.

In these cases, "we're not talking about tax competition, but of theft pure and simple," said Gabriel Zucman, the economist and author of *The Hidden Wealth of Nations*. "Luxembourg or the Cayman Islands offer some taxpayers who wish to do so the possibility of stealing from their governments. It is their choice, but there is no reason that the United States, Europe, or developing countries should pay the price for it."

That's the reality right now. That's what happens when nations like the US talk about cracking down on tax havens while welcoming anonymous foreign money.

HOW DO WE START TO FIX THIS MESS?

So how do we start to fix this mess?

The world we know today is not the world our tax system was built for. When financial activity and wealth traverses national borders, the tax system must do the same. Right now, it does not.

When it comes to tax, a multinational corporation is treated not as a single entity but rather as a loosely affiliated group of subsidiaries distributed around the globe. As such, countries can tax only the subsidiaries that fall under their jurisdiction. The government of Italy can levy taxes on Google Italy s.r.l. (the search giant's Italian arm), but Google Ireland Limited, Google Netherlands Holdings B.V., and the dozens of other subsidiaries under the Google umbrella are out of its reach. So too is Alphabet Inc., Google's parent company.

If you think of multinational companies as a forest that spans the globe, national governments today can levy taxes only on the tree trunks within their borders. But the companies can ensure the fruit falls well beyond those borders. When the bulk of the harvest is funneled to low-tax jurisdictions, it is easy to see how other regions will starve.

Given this complexity of international tax law, some people think countries would be better off shifting away from corporate taxation altogether.

"I think some legitimate mutual gain that can be had by continuing to creep towards clamping down on some of the more egregious corporate tax structures, but it's not going to solve the issue around corporate tax because it's just unsolvable," said a former top official with the UK chancellor of the exchequer. "The coordination problem is too hard—there's too many jurisdictions willing to be the low tax jurisdiction. If you're actually really serious about using the tax system more effectively to be redistributive . . . corporate taxation is not where it's at."

However, some economists think they have already figured out a system that prevents countries from falling victim to multinationals' profit shifting. It is an elegant solution with an unwieldy name: unitary taxation with formulary apportionment.

The system is actually a combination of two separate but related policies: *unitary taxation* and *formulary apportionment*.

Under unitary taxation, governments treat a multinational corporation not as a collection of affiliates but as a single organization.

Instead of looking at the profits of each individual subsidiary, a unitary tax system focuses on the profits of the company as a whole. In Google's case, that means it does not matter if profits come from Google Ireland Limited, Google Ireland Holdings, or Google Netherlands Holdings B.V. Tax collectors consider only the profits for Alphabet Inc. In other words, you acknowledge the trees but tax the forest.

That said, countries would be able to tax only their fair share of the forest. This is where formulary apportionment comes in. The process can get quite complex, but at its core, formulary apportionment is a way to determine where a multinational's revenues and costs were generated geographically. The calculation can be based on different metrics—the simplest formula considers only sales, but others factor in payroll and property. After crunching these numbers, governments can figure out what percentage of the company's total profit was generated within their borders, and thus what they have the right to tax.

Armed with those two numbers—total profit and proportional allocation—countries can determine how big their slice of the pie should be. Theoretically, if 15 percent of Google's overall business were conducted within the borders of Germany, then the German government would apply its taxes to 15 percent of the company's total profit.

Under this system, countries still get to decide how to tax corporate income, but the race to the bottom would end. The Cayman Islands could still offer companies a 0 percent corporate tax rate, but no matter how hard they try, multinationals can conduct only so much of their business in a territory with seventy thousand people. Similarly, a company can decide not to pay the 30 percent corporate tax rate in Germany, but that would mean forgoing one of the world's largest markets.

Unitary taxation with formulary apportionment is not without kinks. In the words of economist Austan Goolsbee, "There's no system of tax policy that's un-gameable." Depending on the definitions of profit and formulas for apportionment, companies could find ways to reduce their tax bill, and countries could undercut each other's tax laws to compete for business. We have already seen this competition play out in the United States, where the fifty states use formulary apportionment to tax interstate companies. The system uses three metrics for apportionment—sales, payroll, and property—but states can give different weights to each factor. Companies take advantage of differences to lower their tax bills. As a result, you see firms concentrating employees in states that underweight payroll and buying buildings in those that underweight property.

Under a global formulary apportionment system, companies might also drive up sales in low-tax countries by expanding their offerings, but that can go only so far.

"Grocery stores in Bermuda suddenly become very valuable, because you'll increase your sales in Bermuda and thereby dilute the amount of tax you pay," said economist Brad Setser. "But there's sort of a limit to how many supermarkets you can buy in Bermuda."

While companies will always optimize their tax bills, unitary taxation with formulary apportionment would eliminate most of the profit shifting we see today, said Setser. That means global governments would get hundreds of billions of dollars in additional revenue every year.

Beyond tax revenue, the system also forces companies to be more open about their operations.

When companies report their profits on a country-by-country basis, and that information is made public, every government official, journalist, academic, and everyday citizen knows exactly where their business is being done. This transparency would lead to more effective business strategies, more informed government policies, and more responsible corporate behavior. To paraphrase US Supreme Court Justice Louis Brandeis, sunlight is the best disinfectant.

John Christensen, the Jersey whistleblower, thinks investors also have a lot to gain from this transparency. Aggressive corporate tax structures carry a lot of risk, leaving companies vulnerable to changing laws and international investigations. "Not many people . . . understand that there is a risk attached to tax policies. Yes, investigations can damage your reputation, but also if you have a full-blown investigation leading to a court trial, it might very seriously materially affect your balance sheet."

The thirty-seven-nation Organisation for Economic Co-operation and Development (OECD) has already paved the way for these reporting standards.

In 2015, the OECD released an action plan for reducing profit shifting, which included a framework for country-by-country reporting standards. The problem is that the rules apply only to the companies that earn more than €750 million per year. These companies are also required to file reports only with their home government, and those governments can share the information only with countries that meet minimum standards for information security. Most developing countries do not.

In other words, the measure lets wealthy countries observe the behavior of wealthy companies, but neither developing countries nor the public gets to see anything.

"Even if [countries] are able to get ahold of this, they're only getting information on the largest companies—there may or may not be any of those operating in your country," said Clark Gascoigne of the FACT Coalition. "Those thresholds have been set at a level that doesn't work for developing countries."

This underscores a key point. In international tax, as with every other area of policy, it matters who writes the rules.

Though every country loses revenue to tax avoidance, developing nations suffer a disproportionate amount of the loss.

"The folks that are oftentimes making the rules about the international system, it's generally the G20 or the OECD . . . the largest economies in the world. So you end up with a bunch of rules that are very skewed towards thinking about the world as if the world were all wealthy developed countries," Gascoigne said. "Oftentimes, developing countries don't have a seat at the table. If you're going to enact something that takes into consideration the concerns of developing countries, then developing countries should be at the table on equal footing."

He and Christensen both believe the proper forum for reforming international tax is the United Nations, not an exclusive group like the OECD or G20. In a more representative body like the UN, it will be harder for the United States and United Kingdom to stonewall or water down tax reforms. The G77, a coalition of 135 developing countries, regularly speaks out against tax havens and voices its support for reform. However, it has yet to take any actions that have produced a real result.

Some members of the OECD are pushing the organization to take stronger action against tax avoidance. Today, the group is updating its original framework to curb aggressive profit shifting by technology platforms like Google, Apple, and Facebook. The Base Erosion and Profit Shifting Project or "BEPS 2.0" initiative was still in development at the time of this writing, but it is expected to focus on two policies.

The first policy, called the Unified Approach, would create a formula for dividing the profits of multinational technology companies among the different jurisdictions where they operate. The calculation would take into account different types of profit. This should sound familiar to you: it is formulary apportionment.

Gascoigne thinks the final scope of the Unified Approach will be narrow, applying to only a small fraction of the profits from a small fraction of companies. Nevertheless, it is the first time countries have entertained the idea of formulary apportionment, Gascoigne said, and it has "enormous potential" to push the international community toward a more holistic system of unitary taxation with formulary apportionment.

The second policy is even more radical: a global minimum tax. This measure guarantees that all companies pay a minimum tax rate no matter where they do business—if a company's offshore profits are undertaxed, its home country can step in to make up the difference.

The OECD has yet to finalize the rate, but Gascoigne said it will likely be between 10 percent and 15 percent. For the purposes of this book, we will say it is 10 percent. This is how it would work.

Let's say you own a German company that recorded $1 million of profit in Bermuda. You do not pay any taxes in Bermuda, because the corporate rate is zero. But under a global minimum tax, the German government could step in and take $100,000 in tax (10 percent of your profits). If the profits were made in Hungary, where the corporate tax rate is 9 percent, you would owe $90,000 to the Hungarian government and $10,000 to the German government—a combined tax rate of 10 percent. If they were made in Canada, where the 26.5 percent corporate tax rate exceeds the global minimum, you would pay $265,000 to the Canadian government and owe the German government nothing, because you already hit the global minimum. In effect, a global minimum tax sets a floor on what companies must pay and helps direct those taxes to the real centers of economic activity.

"Currently, the global minimum tax is 0 percent—countries can set tax rates as high or as low as they want to. What that has led to is a global race to the bottom on taxes. It's just bringing everybody down, and . . . we get to the point where we bankrupt ourselves," Gascoigne said. "Now, I'd say 10 to 15 percent is a pretty pathetic corporate tax rate. That said, the current floor is 0 percent. If we can raise the floor to 10 to 15 percent, well I mean, that's an enormous shift."

The idea for the global minimum tax came from an unlikely source: the United States.

In 2017, the US Congress passed the Tax Cuts and Jobs Act, which cut the country's corporate tax rate from 35 percent to 21 percent and lowered taxes on offshore assets that companies bring back to the US. In many ways, the Tax Cuts and Jobs Act was one more descent in the race to the bottom, another tax cut in a long line of cuts to try to stay "competitive." But the act also contained a brand-new provision.

It placed a 10.5 percent tax on so-called global intangible low-taxed income, or GILTI. Supporters hoped that the provision would serve as a minimum tax, capable of incentivizing multinationals to bring their foreign cash back home, while landing a blow against tax havens. The GILTI essentially guarantees that all companies pay a minimum tax rate (in this case 10.5 percent) no matter where they do business. If a company's offshore profits are taxed below that rate, the US would step in to make up the difference. And while it was a first step toward a global minimum tax, it ended up being just a half measure that allowed multinationals to lower their tax bill.

Before the 2017 law, the United States taxed offshore profits and onshore profits at the same rate—the only difference was that companies did not owe taxes on foreign profits until they were returned to the US. This is why companies like Apple, Pfizer, and Google stored trillions of dollars in tax havens: as long as the money was offshore, they did not need to pay the US corporate tax rate.

But while the GILTI was great in theory, it served as a major tax cut in practice, reducing the tax rate on foreign profits by half. Profits made in the United States are taxed at 21 percent, while profits made abroad are taxed at only 10.5 percent. If you make $1 million from a patent in the United States, you pay the US government $210,000. But if the patent is in Bermuda, you owe only $105,000. After the GILTI is paid, you can move the money back to the United States without owing another penny. So a dollar made overseas becomes more valuable than a dollar made back home.

Through this mechanism and a handful of other loopholes, GILTI ended up rewarding companies for basing their operations abroad, rather than convincing them to come home. Even so, it represented a step toward a new approach to tax abuse. When Congress enacted the GILTI in 2017, it made the United States the first country in the world with a global minimum tax. Yes, "it's like a Swiss cheese of a global minimum tax," said Clark Gascoigne, but "if you plugged those holes . . . it could mean you'd pay the same rate whether you book your profits abroad or domestically."

Like the Unified Approach, any global minimum tax the OECD agrees to will likely be modest at the beginning, Gascoigne said, "but I would say it's an enormous step that over the long term is going to be hugely impactful. And it's a completely unintended consequence of the tax law in 2017. Even two years ago, I would have told you that we are thirty years off from discussions about a global minimum tax, and yet here we are."

Even if the OECD's programs go through, the measures will only address the behavior of corporations. Wealthy individuals, who are responsible for the majority of global tax avoidance and evasion, will remain largely untouched.

The way to help governments spot individual tax evaders is through transparency, specifically international information-sharing programs. Under such programs, countries agree to share foreigners' financial information with their home country. If a Brazilian citizen opened a bank account in Germany, the German government would share their financial activity with Brazilian tax authorities.

Both the OECD and the United Nations endorse information-sharing agreements as a key tool for dealing with tax avoidance and evasion. The OECD created standards for reporting financial information to international tax authorities. The group also created a portal for countries to share this information with one another. Some 160 countries have either adopted or committed to adopting the framework, called the "common reporting standard."

It is important to note that not all information-sharing agreements are alike. Countries can choose to share foreigners' financial information with tax authorities automatically or on demand. Automatic exchanges promote more transparency—authorities do not request information unless they already suspect bad behavior.

As of November 2019, nearly one hundred jurisdictions have adopted automatic information-sharing programs. The list includes Bermuda, the Bahamas, the Cayman Islands, Jersey, the British Virgin Islands, Ireland, and other top tax havens, as well as the vast majority of the world's largest economies. However, the United States is conspicuously absent.

The United States has agreed to share information with certain countries that comply with FATCA, but only on request. Clark Gascoigne said that the position of the US is that it wants to share sensitive information only with countries that "have the technology and rule of law to protect that information as sacrosanct." But the result is that its agreements exclude most of the developing world. "The countries that are losing the most from tax evasion from their own countries . . . they're not getting information back from the US. [The United States is] getting information from everybody else in the world, but we're not sharing it with the vast majority of the rest of the world."

Again, the United States is fighting foreign tax havens while serving as a tax haven for non-Americans. The US opposition to automatic reporting reinforces its role as one of the world's top secrecy jurisdictions. The door is open for foreigners to set up anonymous shell companies or bank accounts knowing that information will likely never make it back home. Until the United States gets on board, meaningful solutions to tax abuse are going to sputter out. And all the while, the US loses billions per year in taxes.

To significantly reduce tax evasion, the international community needs to chip away at banking secrecy. Economist Gabriel Zucman thinks he knows the place to start.

In his book *The Hidden Wealth of Nations*, Zucman proposes creating a "global financial register," a consolidated log for "recording who owns all the financial securities in circulation, stocks, bonds, and shares of mutual funds throughout the world." Using the registry, international tax authorities can verify that banks are reporting all the information they have at their disposal. Similar registries already exist, but they are privately controlled and only cover individual countries. By combining these disparate logs into a single repository, Zucman said, countries can build a system that does not "exclusively rely on the goodwill of offshore bankers."

The policies needed to build a coherent international tax system are straightforward: treat each multinational as a single unit, let countries tax their share of profits, and automatically share information about individuals who bank across borders. But bringing the entire international community on board is a much heavier lift.

"In terms of what needs to be done, none of it's rocket science," said John Christensen. "The problem lies entirely with political will."

Making real progress on international tax reform requires buy-in from many different stakeholders, both developing countries that lose the most to tax avoidance and wealthy nations where the global economy is concentrated. Among the latter is a handful of countries that are either tax havens themselves or direct supporters of the offshore system: Ireland, Luxembourg, Switzerland, the United Kingdom, and the United States.

Countries that oppose global tax reform are finding themselves at odds with the rest of the world. Amid growing economic inequality, recent backlash against globalization, and modest yet noteworthy steps by the OECD, change seems inevitable. What remains unclear is how it will come. Small countries might bend under enough international pressure, but forcing the United Kingdom and United States to reverse course could get messy.

Considering the United States remains the biggest roadblock to global information sharing and the United Kingdom controls the world's top tax havens, they could bring about change almost unilaterally. "You can't have a global norm without the United States being on board, and likewise if the United States acts, they can pretty quickly make something a global norm," Gascoigne said.

But if the US and the UK refuse to lead, it will likely take a global effort. The Group of 77, led by emerging global powers including China, India, Brazil, and South Africa, would have an enormous amount to gain if it could force global tax reform through the United Nations. Creating this unified bloc would be a logistical challenge, Gascoigne said, but "with enough political will, they could absolutely do it."

This highlights another key point. There are both moral and economic arguments for building a cohesive and fair tax framework: more tax revenue benefits democratic societies, and international competition on tax leads to economic inefficiency.

Creating elaborate, globally optimized tax structures is costly, and more and more companies are having a difficult time defending them in court. For example, Google's Double Irish with a Dutch Sandwich did not escape the attention, and anger, of European tax authorities. The company has been sued in several jurisdictions, and in 2017, Google settled a $335 million tax bill with the Italian government following an investigation into its Irish arrangement. In 2019, it reached a similar settlement to pay the French government more than $1 billion in back taxes after a four-year fraud investigation.

Though the existing global tax system benefits multinationals in the short term, it creates a significant amount of uncertainty in the long term. Every country that a company routes its money through is an additional variable the company must consider in its long-term planning. When laws change or government investigations launch, companies are left scrambling.

After the French court's decision, Google released a statement saying, "We remain convinced that a coordinated reform of the international tax system is the best way to provide a clear framework for companies operating worldwide."

When governments lose tax revenue, societies suffer the consequences. Every dollar that companies or wealthy elites stash offshore is a dollar that is not contributing to the economic growth of their home country or the well-being of their fellow citizens. When money can flow freely across borders, it pools in places that are best for capital, not people.

If we want to build a more equitable, inclusive, and just society in the 2020s and beyond, we need to start with tax reform, so that wealthy companies can no longer transcend national tax authorities, wealthy individuals can no longer bank with anonymity, and wealthy countries can no longer siphon off resources from the developing world. A fair and just tax system would ensure that each group pays its fair share and each country receives its rightful slice of the pie. It is also the best way to avoid raising tax rates for existing taxpayers and to make sure the gods of rentier capitalism actually pay taxes on the rents they collect.

It is said death and taxes are the only certainties in life. For more and more of the world's largest corporations and richest people, the latter no longer applies. Without more cohesive tax laws and the resources to enforce them, the cost of building a better society will fall not on the people and institutions with the greatest means to effect change, but on those who need change the most.

5

FOREIGN POLICY: DOES EVERY COMPANY NEED ITS OWN STATE DEPARTMENT, PENTAGON, AND CIA?

In the months prior to the outbreak of civil war in Syria, I led a State Department delegation on a controversial trip to Syria that included a sit-down with Bashar al-Assad. Our intention was to muscle the Syrian dictator on a serious of security issues in the field of technology. The weaponization of widely available consumer technology was making it easier to surveil, spread disinformation, and both develop and destroy political movements. Our delegation was there to apply political and economic pressure to try to get Assad moving in the right direction.

The thing that made this delegation walking into Assad's office different from any other was that it was not composed of diplomats or government officials from the Pentagon or CIA. It was comprised of senior executives from American companies including Cisco Systems, Verisign, Microsoft, and others. Our view was that the companies held the power to be more persuasive under the circumstances and given the topic.

Not all the world's problems can be solved by governments and citizens alone. Tax avoidance offers a fairly unique issue, where the world's governments all lose out and stand to gain together by ending the race to the bottom. But other issues we face as the 21st century unfolds are far knottier. Some—like the weaponization of AI and data and cyber war—break along geopolitical fault lines, pitting major powers against each other with citizens hanging in the balance. Still larger dangers, like climate change, loom so totally and immediately that all hands are needed on deck—governments, citizens, and corporations of every nation.

In the case of Assad and Syria, digital technology did end up having deadly effects. The Assad regime followed digital organizing on open social media platforms, including Facebook, and then targeted attacks at the locations of protests organized online. When they detained people, they would take their mobile phones, force them to log on to Facebook, and then make a kill-or-let-live decision based on the person's posts and Facebook friends. The Syrian government developed Android apps that outwardly appeared to be apps tied to the COVID pandemic, in one case masquerading as an app to take users' temperatures, but which also served as powerful spyware, accessing users' data, texts, and contact lists and providing real-time geolocation data to the Syrian government.

America and our technology companies did not persuade Assad. Instead, he stood with Russia, and in the same way that Russian aircraft bombed Assad's Syrian opponents, Russia and hackers who worked inside and outside government conducted the cyber war for Assad. Companies and countries were combatants. The entire cyber war in Syria blurs the distinction between what is being done by business and what is being done by government.

Companies have carved out a unique place for themselves on the global stage in recent decades. This new role can be harnessed to exploit gaps in geopolitics, as we saw with the subject of tax avoidance. Or it can be used to plug those holes, by using companies' expertise and scale to help create a more stable social contract. In this chapter we will largely use the subject of AI and cyber war as a case study in the stabilizing effect that companies can have on international issues. But we will also examine the risks and difficult trade-offs that emerge when companies enter the global arena, and explore how to navigate them. First, however, it is worth stepping back and looking at how the role of the world's companies has shifted over the past thirty years, giving them unprecedented independence.

HISTORICALLY, COMPANIES HAVE been subservient to the state. This has been the case for 99 percent of the era in which government and commerce have coexisted. Loyalty to the state was simply a cost of doing business, and every company was expected to serve its country at home and abroad as part of its responsibilities under the social contract. In the case of our State Department delegation to Syria, the companies were acting as loyal American institutions—flying to Syria and going face-to-face with a genocidal dictator because that was what would advance US national security interests. It was corporate patriotism.

For centuries, countries relied on that loyalty to project and exercise power beyond their borders. During the age of exploration, European nations used companies as tools of empire. Monarchs from Portugal to Russia granted different "chartered companies" monopolies over trade with certain parts of the world. Indeed, the very first companies were embodiments of the state—that's the literal sense of the word *corporation*. They were created by rulers with the explicit purpose of serving the Crown.

There has always been a link between the grand strategy of countries and their economic philosophies, binding state and company together.

But in the rise to modernity, the nature of companies changed. They gathered distinct legal rights and protections, inhabiting a niche between the state and individuals. In the United States, for instance, corporations gained many of the rights of individuals—such as freedom of speech and protection against unwarranted search and seizure. Still, the general rule held that businesses owed loyalty to their home countries and served them in times of need. During World War II, Allied and Axis nations alike tapped into their private sectors to be able to wage war, and the fate of the war hinged on how robust and flexible their industrial powers would prove.

In the United States, General Motors, Ford, and Chrysler stopped assembling cars and started building tanks, airplanes, guns, and ammunition. The Lionel toy train company built compasses for warships. The Mattatuck Manufacturing Company went from producing tacks to making rifle clips. General Motors president William Knudsen, who became the government's wartime production chief, summed up the expectations of the business community in a 1941 speech to industry executives: "Gentleman, we must out-build Hitler."

Meanwhile, the German private sector worked to help Hitler outbuild the Allies. Daimler-Benz, BMW, and Volkswagen supplied the Nazis with cars, motorcycles, and airplanes. IG Farben, then the world's largest chemical company, manufactured synthetic rubber, fuel, plastics, and the poison gas Zyklon B. On the Pacific front, massive corporate conglomerates known as *zaibatsu* provided the war materiel for imperial Japan.

With the advent of the Cold War, the bond between state and commerce only strengthened. The high stakes of the Cold War forced multinational businesses and democratic governments to work in lockstep on foreign policy issues. They represented two faces of the same political and economic model—democratic capitalism—and they both stood to lose if communism spread across Europe, Asia, Africa, and Latin America. It was at the dawn of this era that General Motors president Charles E. Wilson famously said, "What was good for our country was good for General Motors, and vice versa. The difference did not exist."

Throughout the Cold War, there was an expectation that Western multinational companies working around the world would assist the government, or at least not get in the way. The Cold War created a mostly binary world for both government and business: either you supported American-sponsored democratic capitalism (or at least American-aligned capitalism) or you supported Soviet-sponsored communism. Each side of the Iron Curtain developed its own unique sets of economies, and for decades there was little crossover between the two. American consumers drove Chevys, drank Budweiser, and smoked Marlboros. Their Soviet counterparts drove Ladas, drank Zhigulevskoye, and smoked Belomorkanals.

When the Cold War ended, however, the rules that had held for centuries started to change rapidly. With the dissolution of the Soviet Union, capitalism became the triumphant economic model. In the "end of history" euphoria, the United States, United Kingdom, and other Western democracies rolled back many of the financial and legal guardrails that tethered businesses to the government. They simultaneously set out to build the infrastructure for a global economy based on free-market capitalism. The European Union was created in 1993, the North American Free Trade Agreement (NAFTA) went into effect in 1994, and the World Trade Organization kicked off its operations in 1995. China, the world's largest nominally communist country, joined the WTO in 2001.

The West's companies, now free from constraint and with the whole world accessible to them, increasingly set up global operations. The number of multinational companies around the world increased from approximately seven thousand in the late 1960s to thirty-seven thousand in the early 1990s. By the United Nations' last count in 2008, there were eighty-two thousand multinational corporations operating around the globe, and there are probably twice that again today. The growth of multinationals is exponential.

As these companies grew and invested across global markets and built relationships with foreign governments, their ties to the community back home grew weaker. Once bound by the patriotic obligations of the Cold War, companies' loyalties now shifted to the countries that most benefited their balance sheets. With enough resources, a multinational company can effectively customize its social contract. It can choose to adhere to the tax laws of the Cayman Islands, the labor and environmental regulations of China, and the trade policies and capital markets of the United States. It can tap into the educational institutions of virtually any country and leverage whatever human capital and research funds it provides. Its customer base is global, and its political alliances are flexible.

If businesses have been subordinate to the government for 99 percent of history, we are now in the other 1 percent. Large corporations can now act as sovereign players on a 196-country chessboard.

"The mid-20th century stands out as a period where there's the sort of near identity between the interests of big companies and the big governments where they reside," said historian and Stanford University professor Niall Ferguson. "It only really starts to change in a meaningful way, I think, in the '80s and '90s as exchange controls and capital controls were gotten rid of. It just becomes easier to invest in other countries—the Europeans were actually in some ways pushing as hard as the Americans in this respect.

"There's this tremendous shift away from national bases, and I think that gives rise to a very different corporate culture. Facebook . . . Google and Apple think of themselves as global companies and not American companies. They don't say 'what's good for the United States is good for us.' They say 'we're building a global community.'"

But what exactly does this mean? There are obvious ways in which this shift can cause problems, as we saw in the case of international tax avoidance. But there are also ways in which an air gap between companies and the state—so long as it is not abused—can be beneficial and even make for a more stable social contract. When companies are not operating in lockstep with government, they can serve as a check on the abuse of power or a push toward addressing global problems where government might be lagging. For all the ways in which shareholder capitalism has twisted businesses' ability and incentives to help address the world's problems rather than exacerbate them, it is still possible to turn the corner and harness corporate power. Doing so requires companies to accept the responsibility that comes with their power, and it also requires governments and citizens to monitor that power.

To wrap our arms around what this can look like, we can turn to one of the most complicated problems to emerge out of the last two decades of foreign policy—the explosive potential of artificial intelligence, ubiquitous data, and the new theater of cyber war. The dangers of weaponized code have been approached very differently in the world's two protagonist nations—the United States and China. And the difference offers a glimpse of both the perils ahead and the role that the corporate sector needs to grow into.

THE PENTAGON IS not the most inviting place for first-time visitors, and it was no different for Chris Lynch. When he rode the escalator out of the Pentagon metro station, Lynch was greeted by guard dogs and security personnel wearing body armor and toting machine guns. He lost cell service upon entering the building and was forced to run through more than a half mile of hallways to make his meeting in the office of the secretary of defense. He showed up late and out of breath, his hoodie and gym shoes soaked with sweat.

It was a surreal experience, Lynch said, and it marked the beginning of "the most delightful detour of my entire life."

Lynch had just completed a forty-five-day posting in the United States Digital Service (USDS), an organization formed in 2014 to fill what many officials viewed as a critical gap in the government's technology expertise. That year, the White House had launched Healthcare.gov to help enroll Americans in government health insurance, but it had been a technological debacle that almost derailed the Affordable Care Act. The website was so buggy that on its first day only six people were able to sign up through the site. In response, and to prevent similar flops from occurring in the future, the White House created the USDS. The group is meant to act as a SWAT team of technologists who can come in whenever a government system needs fixing.

Chris Lynch's first project at the USDS involved building software to let the Pentagon and Veterans Affairs Department (VA) more reliably share veterans' medical records. The problem his team sought to solve was a simple one with severe consequences—the VA could accept the records only in PDF format, but sometimes the Pentagon would send them as JPEGs. As a result, doctors sometimes mistreated patients and overlooked underlying conditions simply because they had incomplete records. Lynch said, "If you have cancer, it could be literally the difference between life or death."

Lynch and his team set about building file conversion software that would reformat such misfiled records, and the effort was a success—so much of a success that when Defense Secretary Ash Carter wanted to spin up his own military-focused branch of USDS, the Defense Digital Service, he tapped Lynch to lead it.

The Defense Digital Service was the reason Lynch found himself at the Pentagon that day in the summer of 2015. Before moving to DC, Lynch knew nothing about the military. The closest he had come to the national security world was watching *Saving Private Ryan* and *Full Metal Jacket*. He does not fit the stereotype of the military man, either. Lynch is five-foot-nine, slim built, and in his own words, "very, very average for a human being." He smiles often and boasts a pair of geometric tattoos, a Fibonacci spiral on his left biceps and a spirograph down the length of his right arm. His days begin with a trip to a coffee shop in DC's hip Shaw neighborhood. His dog—a miniature pinscher named after the film producer Dino De Laurentiis—is afraid of motorcycles. When I went on a walk with Lynch and Dino in March 2020, Chris wore a black fitted T-shirt, white Ray-Bans, and gym shoes with tie-dye laces. The look spoke more to his background in the Seattle start-up scene than his current role as one of the top technologists in US national security.

Lynch also came in with the same skepticism of the government that many in the tech industry share. There is a perception that "you can't do anything in government . . . bureaucrats don't care about technologists . . . it's a waste of your talents," Lynch told me. When his friend first announced he was joining the US Digital Service, Lynch told him flat out "that is the dumbest fucking idea I've ever heard."

It was not until Todd Park, the White House's chief technology officer, personally flew to Seattle to recruit Lynch that he decided to join the organization himself. After spending a month and a half building file conversion software for military doctors, Lynch had a change of heart.

The experience was "the turning point in my entire life," he said. "I realized that having a mission is meaningful work. Just because a bunch of nerds did the most seemingly simple project, somebody would not potentially die."

But it also showed just how far the American military had fallen behind the rest of the world in its technology expertise. The same year Facebook released software that could describe images to the blind, the Pentagon needed help converting JPEG files to PDFs. If a small team of programmers could make this much of a difference in forty-five days, Lynch thought, something was very wrong.

Lynch was right. Traditionally, a military's power has been defined by its strength in air, land, and sea. For decades, the United States had raised a military that could outmatch any other global fighting force in each of these domains. However, over the last twenty years, we have seen a paradigm shift in the domain of national security. No longer is a country's military strength defined solely by the size of its fleets, the speed of its vehicles, or the destructive power of its munitions, as it was in the 20th century and every era before. In the 21st century, militaries must also project their strength in a new domain: cyberspace.

In every era before our own, physical damage could be dealt only by physical force. But in the 21st century, militaries can deal a physical blow with a digital signal. With the right lines of code, you can cripple a nuclear reactor, destroy a munitions factory, or knock out power to an entire country. You can infiltrate the computer networks of your enemy, surveil their every move, and stop them from launching attacks your way. The digital warrior never needs to look up from their keyboard.

Cyber weapons are not the only digital technology that is transforming national security. Artificial intelligence is also revolutionizing how militaries do battle and spy agencies conduct espionage. Using AI systems, governments can spot individuals in a crowd, locate facilities to attack, detect intrusions on a computer network, predict civil uprisings, and identify potentially violent extremists.

While the United States can best any other country in the four physical domains—land, sea, air, and space—it faces a much more level playing field in cyberspace. The Pentagon has been slower to adopt national security technologies like artificial intelligence than certain other countries including China. One major reason is that the leading developers of these new digital tools are not members of the traditional military-industrial complex—companies like Lockheed Martin, Raytheon, and Northrop Grumman. Instead, they are in the technology industry.

This is a major difference. Traditional military contractors have worked for decades in lockstep with the Pentagon. But the leaders in the tech industry were people like Chris Lynch, skeptical of government bloat and bureaucracy, whose hackles were raised by the ways in which the same technology they were making could be turned toward destructive ends.

Lynch's experience at the Pentagon began to change his mind. As we've seen in recent years, democracy is a fragile thing, especially in the face of cyberattacks we are not prepared for. Someone needed to do the work to help prepare for the worst—and Chris Lynch realized that he was made of the right stuff.

In 2015, Lynch became director of the Defense Digital Service, and in 2019 he left the government to found his own company, Rebellion Defense. His company is one of several to emerge in recent years to provide countries with the technologies needed to protect national security in the 21st century. This industry includes a handful of big-name players like Microsoft and Palantir, as well as countless smaller companies that few people outside the national security world would know, like Rebellion Defense. This new breed of government contractor is changing the way the US and its allies conduct foreign policy around the globe, and they are upending the traditional relationship between sovereign nations and their defense businesses.

Lynch's overall aim with Rebellion Defense is to provide the US military with much-needed digital tools while also helping young technologists reach the same epiphany about public service that he did.

His strategy is encapsulated in the name of the company.

While leading the Defense Digital Service, Lynch fashioned the organization into something of a haven for *Star Wars* geeks. Team members gave projects names like "BOBA," "AT-AT," and "JEDI." The group had an office in Augusta, Georgia, called Tatooine. Lynch's going-away party was attended by a group of Pentagon staff dressed up as *Star Wars* characters. During our walk, he showed me a photo from the party that included him, his dad, General Paul Selva (who was at the time the nation's second-highest-ranking uniformed officer), Chewbacca, and a fully robotic R2-D2.

But what really set the tone for the group was the sign outside Lynch's office, which read "Defense Digital Service, Rebel Alliance." According to Lynch, the plaque was intended to signify to the team that they were the "rebels" bringing change to the bureaucracy that surrounded them. To continue the *Star Wars* analogy, the Defense Digital Service was Luke, Leia, and Han, and the department's culture was Darth Vader and Emperor Palpatine.

Lynch saw the idea of rebellion as the central theme of his tenure at the Pentagon, and he looks to bring the same mentality to his new defense business.

The name Rebellion Defense "is a recognition that there's something new that has to be created. Now more than ever, this will be the team that does it, and this will be the time that we do it," he said. "It's something where we're the outsiders, but we're part of the system as well, because defense is owned by all of us."

There is a certain irony in naming a defense technology company after the destroyers of the Death Star, and Lynch himself is quick to acknowledge it. Still, it has helped bridge the gap between Washington and Silicon Valley, he said. "Who doesn't want to be part of the Rebel Alliance?"

Lynch also acknowledged that in today's world, the line between good and evil is much less cut-and-dry than it was a long, long time ago in a galaxy far, far away. Even compared to the Cold War era, the landscape that Rebellion and its counterparts navigate today contains many shades of gray. Arms controls are not nearly as clear-cut for digital technology as they are for old-fashioned ballistics, so modern defense companies have much more that they need to figure out on their own.

Throughout the Cold War, the United States created a broad regulatory regime to limit the export of weapons and national security technologies to foreign countries. For example, the International Traffic in Arms Regulations (ITAR) prohibits non–US citizens from accessing technical data or physical materials for certain defense-related technologies. (As of August 2020, the US Munitions List was more than one hundred pages long.) Other measures—like the Arms Export Control Act and Export Administration Regulations—restricted the export and use of national technologies to foreign countries. The goal behind such standards is clear: to prevent national security technologies developed by the United States from winding up in enemy hands. The government could customize its arms control agreements to fit its relationships with different countries. The regulations for the United Kingdom differed from those with Turkey, which differed from those with Iran. During the Cold War, these laws cemented the lines between militaries of liberal democracies and communist states, and in the post–Cold War period, they have (mostly) prevented traditional weapons from falling into the hands of terrorists and adversarial nations.

But the arms control regime of the 20th century largely does not apply to the national security technologies of the 21st century. One of the main reasons is that digital tools like AI are more difficult to categorize than traditional defense technologies.

Fighter jets and warships are used for one thing: the projection and exercise of military power. But artificial intelligence is a general-purpose technology with both national security applications and completely benign commercial uses. A computer vision algorithm can be trained to spot enemy combatants on a battlefield, but it can also be used to tag friends in social media posts and power self-driving cars. AI takes on the values and intentions of its human masters. The same AI-enabled facial recognition technology that can identify known terrorism suspects can just as easily profile and track members of an ethnic minority. The technology is also imperfect. The accuracy of artificial intelligence depends on the quality of the data used to train it, and it is not always clear how the software reaches a particular conclusion. While you can tolerate a certain number of errors in a system that provides online shopping recommendations, the consequences of an error on the battlefield can be lethal.

These are core concerns of Rebellion Defense's work. It makes traditional IT and cybersecurity tools, but its bread and butter is AI. This includes software that can read text, classify images, analyze video, and process the enormous amount of information flooding into the Pentagon from every corner of the globe.

However, when it comes to arms control, the "dual use" nature of artificial intelligence software creates a conundrum for US policy makers. Subject all AI systems to the same regulations that apply to nuclear warheads, and you stifle innovation and cripple the American tech industry. But leave them completely unregulated, and you could enable terrorists and enemy militaries to get their hands on powerful weapons of war, made in the USA.

To effectively regulate the sale of AI and other emerging technologies, policy makers must first agree on which narrow applications pose a national security threat if they wind up in enemy hands. But today, the definition of "security sensitive" technology varies widely based on whom you ask, said MIT's R. David Edelman, a former White House senior official who led policy making at the intersection of technology and national security.

"That question about what's really sensitive is a fundamental debate that is taking place . . . at the government level, which is not always informed by technology; at the industry level, which is certainly not always informed by government; and at the researcher level, which is sometimes not informed by either of them," Edelman told me. "You've seen little blips where these communities get out of sync."

He continued, "If you were to go ask researchers what constitutes an AI technology, they would give you exactly as many answers as the number of researchers you asked, possibly plus five or six. The reality is that something like AI means everything and nothing."

The confusion is compounded by the lack of technical expertise in the halls of government. Today, the thirty students in my son's high school class could compete in technology know-how with the 535 members of the US Congress. Informed policy decisions require informed policy makers, and most of the government is still interpreting the national security challenges of the 21st century through the lens of 20th-century technology.

In January 2020, the US Commerce Department issued its first export control on an artificial intelligence system. The rule limits the sale of AI software that can automatically analyze geospatial imagery, ostensibly collected by military drones and satellites. While this is a significant step, it is important to recognize that the government did not exactly break new ground. Geospatial technology was already highly regulated. Companies could not sell imagery above a certain resolution, and both drones and satellites are themselves subject to ITAR and other export controls. Policy makers simply amended an old framework to accommodate a new technology.

However, there are many applications of AI for which there is no precedent in the existing arms control regime. AI systems can help authoritarian regimes consolidate power within their own borders. While facial recognition and surveillance technology may not fit the traditional description of national security technologies, they are no less threatening to free and open societies. Yet Western companies have freely exported these technologies for years, Edelman said, and "I think most members of the American public and certainly a lot of public policymakers wish they hadn't." Beyond this gray area, there are algorithms that can be even more consequential. Today, companies are developing systems that can identify enemy combatants on the battlefield, power semiautonomous weapons, and coordinate drone swarms.

Edelman explained that certain types of AI can be more easily weaponized than others and that "those are the sorts of implementations that it is entirely appropriate to regulate, and frankly, government's a little bit behind the ball in identifying them."

US military leaders have begun to stress the importance of AI ethics, and in 2020 the Pentagon signed on to a set of five broad principles for the ethical application of the technology. However, these principles are vague, stating platitudes such as "personnel will exercise appropriate levels of judgment and care" when developing and using AI.

As we have discussed, today's geopolitical landscape is not as binary as it was during the Cold War, and countries cannot be classified as either "allies of democracy" or "allies of communism." Political and economic models fall on a spectrum from open to closed, and national alliances are not as fixed as they once were.

The members of the new cyber-military-industrial complex are navigating this new world largely on their own. This puts them in a unique position where they need to formulate clear principles for the types of technology they are willing to develop, and what goes too far. This is a lot to ask of a company, and they cannot handle it wholly on their own. The challenge is exacerbated when the technology executive is very young and may be a great engineer but does not have much experience in the world of geopolitics. There is a difference between intelligence and wisdom, and I have seen too many mistakes made by technology executives who are very intelligent but not yet wise.

At the same time, when the technology sector has so much more expertise than the traditional defense sector, it is worth harnessing that expertise and ensuring that technology companies shoulder the responsibility for what they are making. As we will see, a system that allows companies to weigh in and even lead allows more informed innovation and implementation—and provides more checks and balances than a system where government decides and drives everything.

For Rebellion Defense founder Chris Lynch, that sense of responsibility is a motivating force. "If you have strong opinions about national defense and security and the utilization of all these technologies that are ultimately going to change the world over the next fifty years, you have an obligation to show up at the table," Lynch said. "You are providing the things that people need, and you're helping craft the strategy, the policy, the implementation, and the execution of how those technologies will be used."

Like most other technologies, artificial intelligence is neither inherently good nor inherently bad. It takes on the values and intentions of its creators and users. Given the Pentagon's lack of technological expertise, the companies that develop its AI tools have a responsibility to steer it in the right direction.

"Every technology company has a responsibility to think through the implications of the things that they're building," Lynch told me. "We need to be thoughtful . . . with what we build and why we build it. We need to care because we are dictating defense. We are dictating how technology gets used."

At Rebellion Defense, employees meet once a month to discuss the types of projects and customers the company would refuse to take on. For example, Lynch said, the company has already determined it will not build domestic surveillance technology, nor will it aid US officials in rounding up undocumented immigrants. Lynch was reluctant to disclose Rebellion's other lines in the sand, though he said the company has turned down multiple offers based on feedback from employees.

Of course, when this decision-making lands with companies, there can be major differences in how it is applied.

In September 2017, Google began working with the Pentagon on a broad artificial intelligence initiative called "Project Maven." Google's particular project sought to build AI software that could sift through the troves of footage collected each day by military drones. The system would save intelligence officers from the tedious task of analyzing the footage frame by frame. This is the sort of geospatial analysis software that would fall under the government's January 2020 export controls.

Within months, Google employees began protesting the project, which they argued would help the Pentagon better target its drone strikes. In April 2018, some 3,100 employees signed a letter demanding that Google stop participating "in the business of war." Soon after, Google declined to renew its contract with the Pentagon.

Chris Lynch disagreed with that decision. Google may have seen it as its own line in the sand. But as Lynch saw it, Google gave up an opportunity to directly influence how the Pentagon uses artificial intelligence. Instead, the contract went to Anduril Industries, a defense technology company founded by Palmer Luckey, a controversial libertarian in his twenties who helped invent the Oculus Rift virtual reality headset.

Anduril was contracted to build an AI-powered sensor network that would provide troops with a virtual view of the front lines. The sensors would be mounted on drones, fixed towers, and troops themselves, and used to identify potential targets and direct autonomous military vehicles into combat. The software helps troops in the field make real-time operational decisions. It might not directly decide who lives and who dies, but it will significantly influence how troops arrive at that answer.

Anduril applied different principles to its work than Google or Rebellion Defense would have. The company went on to build a similar AI-sensor network to help US Customs and Border Protection to coordinate operations along the US-Mexico border. When asked in 2018 whether there were any Pentagon projects Anduril would turn down, Luckey said, "that's not really totally up to us. We are working with the U.S. government."

That said, Anduril CEO Brian Schimpf told me there is one thing the company would not do: they would not build systems that execute "lethal force" without a human in the loop. In other words, Anduril will not create robots that can kill on their own accord.

"This is a military decision-making responsibility—it can't be outsourced to a machine," he said. "Everything else is one of these questions where I think it's mostly a matter of the controls on how the technology is employed. There are very few other technology areas that I think have those sort of bright lines."

Schimpf thinks it is the responsibility of military leaders to set those controls, and he trusts them to make the right call in the end. "Any of these [applications] that are too out there, they eventually get shut down, they eventually get stopped. The US system may take a while, but it is quite robust to keeping a lot of these overreaches in check."

That all three companies end up resolving on different principles in the development of AI might seem worrying—but that is also part of the debate that needs to happen with such new technologies. There are not clear-cut ethical answers at the outset. But realistically, the Pentagon does not have much of a choice as to whether to develop its artificial intelligence capabilities. China and Russia are investing heavily in military AI, and the national security of the US and its allies will suffer if they do not do the same. Russian president Vladimir Putin remarked to a group of students, "Artificial Intelligence is the future not only of Russia but of all mankind," and added that "whoever becomes the leader in this sphere will become the ruler of the world."

For companies that build facial recognition and other technologies that can empower authoritarian regimes, that also means being responsible about their customer base. Claiming ignorance is no longer a valid excuse, said R. David Edelman, the former White House senior official. "It is no longer an acceptable excuse for a tech CEO to say, 'well, I didn't know what use they were going to put it to.' The sort of near-criminal negligence that we heard from tech CEOs of even three years ago is simply no longer plausible in today's era."

Technology companies have the expertise in which technology applications are possible and reliable. But it is also important for technology companies to have the autonomy to decide how their relationships with the national security community will proceed, and to develop clear principles for how what they build can be used. If they have an objection to specific applications of AI, it is worth voicing those broadly, in a way that other companies and policy makers alike can weigh.

"Now more than ever, we need to bring technologists into a place where they can help shape and craft the policies and the direction of not only how these technologies will be built, but how they will be used," said Rebellion Defense CEO Chris Lynch. "If the conversation is only happening in the Department of Defense . . . that is not a long-term strategy. If the conversation is only being had in a coffee shop in San Francisco with a bunch of people who have never spent a moment thinking about the mission of defense, those people are failing just as much. If you don't bring those two sides together, there is one thing I am one hundred percent certain of, and that is that nobody will be happy with the outcome. If you don't have that discussion, and if you don't participate in that discussion, we end up in complete and total failure."

TO GRAPPLE WITH exactly why, we need to look across the Pacific to a wholly different model—that of China. Even the ability to debate the ethics of technology is a luxury of Western democracies.

While Western democracies work to define the expectations and responsibilities of their technology companies, this debate is nowhere to be found in China. That is because in China, the government and private sector act as one and the same.

To draw a line between state and capital in China is to make a distinction without meaning. Politicians and business leaders operate in tandem, with each doing their part to execute national strategies dictated by Beijing. Over the last forty years, the Chinese Communist Party used its command-and-control system to transform China from a poor agrarian backwater into an industrial powerhouse. And today, it is using it to advance a model of techno-authoritarianism that threatens the very foundation of liberal democratic society.

Modern China was built on the wave of globalization that began near the end of the Cold War. Beginning in the late 1970s, the Communist government implemented a series of market-based reforms to modernize China's economy. Local entrepreneurs began launching their own businesses, and foreign multinationals flocked to the country's coastal cities to take advantage of their cheap, lightly regulated labor markets. Within a few decades, China became the world's factory, producing everything from German cars to American flags.

In 1990, when the Fortune Global 500 list was first published, it included zero Chinese companies. In 2020, the number of companies on the list from China and Hong Kong surpassed those from the United States, 124 to 121.

Over the last fifteen years, China has also emerged as a global leader in the industries of the future. The Chinese technology industry began as something of a counterfeit Silicon Valley, populated by copycat companies producing cheaper, less functional knockoffs of American technology, often with stolen intellectual property. But with close supervision and substantial assistance from Beijing, the industry came into its own. Today, companies like Alibaba, Baidu, Tencent, and Huawei are competing with Western technology giants for global market share. The US and China are near peers in technology, and in some areas the Chinese technology industry is outpacing Silicon Valley.

Like the manufacturing boom of prior decades, the ascendance of the Chinese technology industry was engineered by government policy makers. Unlike the United States government, the Chinese Communist Party does not need to bother with the messiness of the democratic process. Party leaders sit at the helm of a massive state apparatus, steering the country's economic and political system free from the constraints of political parties and public consent. When party leaders want something done, the government and private sector immediately fall in line. There is no kludgeocracy or vetocracy in China.

This centralized control of the private sector gives China certain advantages. The Chinese government can mobilize investment in strategic areas in a way that Western democracies cannot. Hundreds of billions of dollars flow as a result of the national strategies set out by Beijing. Between 2007 and 2017, the government marshaled the construction of more than twenty-five thousand kilometers of high-speed railway, double the combined length of high-speed track laid by every other country up to that point.

In recent years, the Chinese government has devoted similar attention to building the country's domestic artificial intelligence industry.

In 2017, President Xi Jinping unveiled a national strategy to transform China into the global leader in artificial intelligence by the year 2030, with a domestic industry worth more than $150 billion. The plan included a detailed roadmap of the policies that would lead the country to AI dominance, as well as billions of dollars in government funds to inject into promising start-ups and moonshot AI projects.

As soon as the plan was released, the government and private sector kicked into gear. Local governments started pouring funds into AI start-ups, and industry partnerships began to form. The following month, the government drafted a "national AI team," selecting four domestic companies to take the lead in strategic AI fields including autonomous vehicles (Baidu), medical imaging (Tencent), natural language processing (iFLYTEK), and smart city technology (Alibaba). By August 2019, the team had expanded to fifteen members, each with its own area of expertise. These national champions are granted special access to government funds and databases. They collaborate with one another in a manner that does not exist in a serious way in Silicon Valley, sharing research insights and setting standards for the Chinese AI ecosystem.

China's foray into artificial intelligence and other emerging technologies has also been bolstered by the aggressive acquisition of technology and intellectual property from foreign competitors, particularly in the United States. In some cases, Chinese firms can gain access to an American tech company's crown jewels of intellectual property by offering capital investments, entering joint ventures, poaching employees, or acquiring companies outright. Foreign companies that want to do business in China are often required to share technical data and intellectual property directly with government agencies, which can then offer it up to domestic companies. But Chinese companies also steal competitors' trade secrets, internal communications, and other sensitive data through cyberattacks. This economic espionage is often committed at the request—and with the direct assistance—of the Chinese government.

Through overt and covert technology transfer, China can effectively co-opt other countries' research and development efforts for its own gain. The theft of foreign assets has enabled the Chinese economy—as well as its military—to keep pace with the rest of the world at a fraction of the cost.

As it bolsters its own economy through direct investment and state-sponsored tech transfer, the Chinese state and capital apparatus also works behind the scenes to wall off the country from foreign competition. With its 1.4 billion citizens, China is one of the most attractive global markets for multinational companies. Over the years, numerous technology companies have tried to gain a foothold in China to little avail. By way of illustration, when Uber launched in China in 2014, its CEO Travis Kalanick hoped his ride-sharing app would become one of the first American consumer technology firms to succeed in China. Having watched US tech giants like Google, Amazon, and Facebook fail to expand into China, Kalanick sought to avoid making the same mistakes.

He set up a Chinese subsidiary—Uber China—which he hoped would avoid government restrictions that had kneecapped other Western tech companies. He made frequent visits to the country to court investors and study the local landscape—in 2015, Kalanick reportedly spent one in five days on the ground in China. The company catered its service to local consumers, allowing riders to pay for trips through Alipay, a popular third-party payment system. It entered into a joint venture partnership with the Chinese tech giant Baidu. It based its servers in China in an attempt to prevent any interference from the country's Great Firewall.

"Travis structured something that worked within the construct of China . . . he was willing to make those compromises," said Shervin Pishevar, an early Uber investor who introduced Kalanick to Baidu CEO Robin Li on a trip to China in 2013.

However, Uber faced a powerful local competitor—Didi Chuxing—and even with the support of local partners like Baidu, it could not overcome the realities of the Chinese market.

"Didi tried to destroy them," Pishevar told me. The two companies entered "a massive war," with each pouring billions of dollars into discounts and incentives to attract new drivers.

By 2016, Uber China had expanded to sixty cities, but Didi had set up operations in some four hundred. Both companies were burning through capital, but Didi had deeper pockets. The company received billions of dollars from China's sovereign wealth fund and state-controlled banks. At one point, the Chinese tech giant Tencent blocked Uber on its massively popular app WeChat, but Didi remained embedded in the platform. In July 2016, the Chinese government issued regulations that prohibited driver subsidies that both Didi and Uber were using to expand their business, effectively freezing their existing market share. The regulations also applied more stringent government oversight to foreign companies. It was death by a thousand cuts.

Uber China was sold to Didi in August 2016. Kalanick and his partners retreated from the country with an equity stake in their victorious competitor and a $1 billion investment in its US business.

"Uber saw the writing on the wall," Pishevar said. "They were like, 'this is a war of attrition . . . we've got to make some kind of peace.' The peace was only 'twenty percent of Didi and get the fuck out.' That's what they did, and it was smart."

By all accounts, Uber fought a good fight. It played by the rules and avoided the mistakes that hobbled other US tech companies in their pursuit of Chinese customers. But it occupied a strategic industry, and its success would have encroached on the technological ambitions of the Chinese government. China's public-private capital apparatus kicked into gear, and the foreign rival was run out of town. After beating out Uber, Didi Chuxing opened AI research labs in Beijing and Silicon Valley. In July 2020, the company announced it would partner with the Chinese central bank to test a new digital currency.

It was a familiar story that has played out with countless Western technology companies: Western company enters China; company cuts promising deals with local partners; company slowly loses market share to a homegrown rival; company retreats from China; homegrown rival entrenches its dominant position.

China is proving to be as impenetrable to great Western technology companies as Afghanistan has been to great geopolitical powers like the Soviet Union and United States.

By keeping Western technology companies from gaining a foothold inside its borders, and by bolstering domestic companies through direct investment, economic espionage, and the state-sponsored acquisition of foreign technology assets, China is constructing a technological universe entirely removed from the Western sphere of influence. It is a world with its own companies, its own trends, and its own norms. And its values are dictated by the nationalistic ambitions of the Chinese government.

Over the last two decades, the Chinese government has used technology to construct an apparatus of surveillance and social control that would surpass the wildest dreams of despots from any prior century.

As of 2019, China has deployed approximately one surveillance camera for every four people, with that number expected to double by 2022. Most of the footage they collect is fed into AI systems trained to identify "antisocial" behaviors, ranging from murder to jaywalking to reading the Koran. Through facial recognition, the government can track every citizen throughout their daily lives, taking note of every place they go, every person they interact with, and every protest or meeting they attend.

Though controlled by the state, the Chinese surveillance apparatus is constructed and operated by the country's myriad AI companies. It embodies the symbiosis between government officials and Chinese business leaders.

Building effective artificial intelligence requires lots and lots of training data, and you would be hard-pressed to find a government with fewer qualms about general public data collection than China's. Companies share data with the government, which then shares data back with other companies, which then refine their algorithms and continue collecting more data. The CEO of the Chinese computer vision company SenseTime, which helped construct the Xinjiang surveillance apparatus, referred to the government as the company's "largest data source."

More data beget better algorithms, which beget better data. The surveillance state feeds itself and becomes more effective as it goes. As fifth-generation broadband networks enable China to embed more sensors on its streets, in its vehicles, and around its offices, homes, and public spaces, the panopticon will become more total.

In a real sense, China reveals the hazard that comes with perfect alignment of the business sector with the state. In the digital age, this arrangement puts all of our data in one set of hands, which can lead to frightening levels of control.

In most countries around the world, as we have seen the internet rise and spread, citizens have come to rely on companies as a buffer between ourselves and the state when it comes to our data. The private sector certainly is not a perfect buffer, and technology companies undoubtedly collect more data than most of us would like. But even so, the data habits of a Google or an Apple are a far cry from what can happen when there is no daylight between the government and the private sector. China's example shows how that can hurtle a society into a real-world *1984*.

China is also packaging its surveillance state for export. Thanks to state subsidies, Chinese technology companies can sell their products at artificially low prices, which has attracted foreign governments that want to construct their own apparatuses of social control. One of their customers is Zimbabwe.

Zimbabwe is no stranger to repressive regimes. The landlocked southern African nation was controlled by the British South Africa Company before becoming a British colony. It gained independence in 1980 after a fifteen-year civil war, only to fall under the thirty-seven-year rule of strongman Robert Mugabe. When Mugabe resigned in 2017 under pressure from the military, Zimbabweans rejoiced in the streets, hoping his ouster would set the country on a new trajectory toward democracy and political freedom. But less than six months later, the government of Zimbabwe signed a contract with the Chinese AI start-up CloudWalk Technology to install facial recognition systems in the country's airports, bus stations, financial institutions, and other facilities. The government also planned to use the technology to build a national database of citizens' faces. As the state integrates biometrics into its election system, the technology could become a tool for voter intimidation and control.

The biometric data from Zimbabwe can also be sent back to

China, where it can help the Chinese private sector better train its algorithms to recognize African faces. China has engaged in similar partnerships with political leaders in the Philippines, Malaysia, Sri Lanka, Singapore, Mongolia, Serbia, Kenya, and other countries, and it is beginning to make inroads in Latin America. Once they hone their algorithms to identify people of additional races and ethnicities, Chinese companies will have an easier time selling their surveillance technology to authoritarians anywhere in the world and their own intelligence agencies will grow stronger.

It is not difficult to see the harm that persistent surveillance can inflict on democratic societies. A dynamic social contract hinges on citizens being able to express dissent through collective action. They mobilize against the government through opposition political movements and protest. They check the power of corporations through organized labor. But when the state and the private sector have such intimate insights into every person's life, this sort of collective action becomes impossible. The group that controls the surveillance state can nip dissent in the bud before it ever blossoms. With enough data and processing power, they can even anticipate dissent and respond, like something out of a Philip K. Dick novel.

As China exports its techno-authoritarian model abroad and continues to refine it back home, it presents a fundamental threat to the future of democracy, particularly in the developing world. Fledgling democratic governments in Asia, Africa, Latin America, and even Europe are more likely to give in to authoritarian tendencies if they are equipped with the technologies of control.

In addition to software, China is the world's top manufacturer of computer chips, telecommunications equipment, and other high-tech hardware. Using its position in the global technology supply chain, China can project its own power and kneecap its competitors. The US dependence on Chinese hardware for military equipment, medical supplies, and digital infrastructure remains a significant national security threat. American companies would have few places to turn if the Chinese government decided to cut them off from its factories.

The United States is beginning to recognize the threat and has tried to stop its allies from installing Chinese telecommunications equipment, fearing that it could be used as a data collection channel for Chinese state intelligence services. In 2020, the White House announced it would rescind visas for Chinese students and researchers with ties to China's military universities. The government is also applying greater scrutiny to Chinese business ventures involving American companies.

In 2016, a Chinese gaming company called Beijing Kunlun Tech paid $93 million to acquire a 60 percent stake in Grindr, a popular dating app for gay men. But three years later, the Committee on Foreign Investment in the United States ordered the company to sell its stake in the app. The reason: its data could be used to blackmail American national security officials.

If you were to open Grindr in Washington, DC, odds are you would stumble upon profiles of intelligence analysts, members of the military, and government officials and contractors who hold security clearances. Those profiles include your standard online dating details—age, height, personal interests, and location—but also more sensitive information, like sexual orientation, HIV status, unusually precise location data (down to the foot), and whether or not the user is in the closet. Combine that information with a few personal photos (sometimes with minimal clothing), and you can build a potentially compromising dossier.

Given the close ties between the Chinese government and private sector, US national security officials feared that Grindr data would ultimately pass from Beijing Kunlun Tech to the hands of the Chinese government, which would use it to blackmail US officials. The risk was especially great for people who are not open about their sexuality.

"We know there's plenty of people who aren't honest and open about who they love," one thirty-year-old intelligence analyst who uses Grindr told me. "The risk of personal trauma or losing your career, losing your job, losing your family—people will do a lot to protect that, which is something adversaries know full and well."

Grindr is not a physical US security asset. It does not explode or fly or sail, like the technologies developed by defense contractors during the Cold War. It does not power nuclear reactors or control sophisticated fighter jets or support critical infrastructure. What Grindr does is generate valuable data.

In a sense, the injunction also suggests that we need a serviceable buffer in the social contract, between citizens and states, to handle the data that underlies the internet and the rapidly advancing AI industry. It is not safe for such data to be turned over to state-affiliated entities, the United States is arguing. Of course, on that matter, the US intelligence networks would be pleased to have comparable data. But that makes the Grindr scuffle all the more interesting. It underscores the special role that we have already come to expect from companies in our lives.

There are things many of us are comfortable having companies know about us, provided they do not misuse that data. Yet we would not be comfortable sharing the same information with governments, whether foreign or our own. Fostering the kind of autonomy we see in the work of Rebellion Defense, and pushing technology companies to be transparent about their policies and principles surrounding data, has great value. It can offer a check against the frightening power that centralized data can have, and this is especially the case if policy makers keep reasonable checks on these companies in turn. That gap between corporation and state, where each can constrain the other, ends up serving citizens in the long run. Because, as we have seen in China, when there is no meaningful separation between government and business, the door springs open for full-on authoritarianism.

WHERE DO WE GO?

If the geopolitical landscape during the second half of the 20th century was defined by the Cold War between the United States and the Soviet Union, the first half of the 21st century is being defined by the Code War between the United States and China. This rivalry is unlikely to grow as tense or as binary as the Cold War, but it will still draw nations and companies to one side or the other. Chinese and American technology companies will compete against each other for talent, market share, and first-mover advantages in new branches of artificial intelligence and other emerging technologies. The Chinese and American governments will each strive to outdo the other in setting global standards for digital technology and adopting the latest innovations into their defense and intelligence agencies. Each country will form its own sphere of influence through international alliances, business partnerships, intelligence sharing, and academic collaboration.

The vision put forth by China is clear. The Chinese government sees artificial intelligence and other emerging technologies as instruments of political and social control. It seeks to build a surveillance state so total that it becomes impossible for citizens to organize meaningful opposition. The Chinese model strengthens its control over the social contract.

Moving through the 2020s, Western democracies must figure out how to maximize the democratizing potential of digital technology and minimize its abuses through legal and regulatory guardrails. Europe has taken the lead through measures like the General Data Privacy Regulation.

Eric Schmidt, the former chairman and CEO of Google, who has led two government panels on national security and technology, warned in a February 2020 article that "ultimately, the Chinese are competing to become the world's leading innovators, and the United States is not playing to win." Without "unprecedented partnerships between [the United States] government and industry" on artificial intelligence, biotechnology, and 5G, China will likely come out on top.

Others have argued that to prevail over China's techno-authoritarian model, and to keep the flame of a democratic social contract alive, it will be necessary to turn to the type of strong international alliances that bound together liberal democracies during the Cold War.

My former State Department colleague Jared Cohen has proposed the idea of building an alliance of "techno-democracies" that he dubs the T-12. "There's not a single democratic country that's big enough to compete with China on a one-to-one ratio—China has too much flexibility in terms of rules, and too much capacity," Cohen told me. "The only way to compete with China is through collective action, and the best way to compete with collective action is to organize like-minded states."

This organization, composed of democratic nations that lead in strategic technology fields—including the United States and key European nations, as well as India, Japan, and South Korea—could shape international norms, pool resources, and coordinate policy around export controls, supply chain security, and AI ethics. Together, these countries could build a unified front against China's techno-authoritarianism.

I see the appeal of this type of approach, but the loss of standing of the American government on technology policy issues in the eyes of its likely partners—especially the Europeans—would make this exceedingly difficult, though it is still worth pursuing. The US government just is not trusted to guide international alliances in the days of the Code War the way it was during the Cold War. Advancing democracy during the Code War will be a whole-of-society effort, and the global corporations that have emerged out of and thrived in democratic societies cannot shy away from the fight, particularly those in the technology industry.

This is true across the broad sweep of global concerns that we are facing in the coming decades—from climate change to human rights to inequality, as well as tax avoidance and the stewardship of AI and data. These issues require governments to act and citizens to speak up, but they cannot realistically be solved within a reasonable time frame without leadership from the world's most influential companies as well. A good deal of corporate responsibility actions under shareholder capitalism are window dressing. But when companies like Unilever, Apple, and Microsoft commit to becoming carbon neutral—and hit that goal—it proves that a paradigm shift is possible. Such changes in the standards by which business is done can push authorities to standardize them across other industries (like technology), codifying them into law. And when global companies set clear standards and explain the rationale behind them, they can help jump-start changes across a number of countries.

It is one thing to say that companies need to step up and grow into their new role in the social contract. But how do we ensure that it can actually happen?

First off, we will get nowhere unless corporate leadership embraces stakeholder capitalism. If companies are going to meaningfully weigh in on the biggest problems the world is facing, then they need to do so without a short-term, profit-only motive. Otherwise they can justify building anything and selling to anybody. And such a shift needs to come with transparency and metrics, such as the generally accepted accounting principles discussed in earlier chapters. We can develop analytics that measure companies' environmental and human rights records; we can do the same for foreign policy records. There also needs to be oversight from several angles. Company boards will be the very first line of defense, ensuring that companies have stronger standards for the goals and implications of the products they create. Board oversight will be even stronger if it includes workers' input, as we discussed in the labor chapter.

Lawmakers will also need to continue to establish guardrails and guidelines, which will require dialing up their expertise on these subjects, above what you will find in my son's high school classroom. Even as companies can use their expertise and scale to help address sweeping societal questions, this cannot come without government playing a role. Antitrust measures should not fall by the wayside, and it's worth even extending anticompetitive standards to cover the danger around regulatory capture as well.

While many companies see themselves as global actors, unconstrained by the domestic and foreign policy concerns of their home countries, it does not take much collective action from the world's leading governments to correct that notion. According to political scientist Fareed Zakaria, it would be fairly easy for a government to disabuse them of that idea.

"People need to understand that at the end of the day, whatever power that these companies have is power that has been ceded by the state," Zakaria told me. "The state can very easily recapture that power at any moment. None of these companies have the ability to flaunt state authority in the way that the British East India Company might have been able to do. The reality is all these companies live in fear of regulation. They're constantly adjusting themselves to abide by state authority."

People tend to become chiefs of global companies because of their expertise in fields such as management, sales, finance, or product—not in navigating the geopolitical landscape. But that is exactly what success in the 21st century demands. The world's most successful CEOs are those who adopt and adapt the toolkit of a world leader.

Expanding into new global markets and helping to establish industry standards requires the skills of diplomacy. Different cultures require different business strategies, different customer experiences, and different government relations. If companies do not learn how to do business in different cultural contexts, they will fail.

Multinational companies must also develop something of an intelligence apparatus to help them see around the corner. In today's global supply chains, civil unrest in southeast Asia could impact sales in North America and civil unrest in North America could impact sales in Europe. Effective geopolitical forecasting could make a significant difference to a company's bottom line.

At the same time, companies on the global stage now need to know how to defend themselves when it comes to cybersecurity. Any company that handles valuable information is a potential target of digital attacks, whether it is a defense contractor or a dating app. They need to work proactively to protect that information from falling into the wrong hands.

"Every company needs its own State Department, Pentagon, and CIA," said Jared Cohen, my former State Department colleague turned tech executive, who proposed the idea of the T-12.

Lastly, companies need to be able to articulate their principles, policies, and lines in the sand. And they need to do so transparently with customers, regulators, and employees alike. Accounting principles and standard regulations will help keep companies honest, and the days when a large company does not need to articulate its own ethical groundings are over.

All these shifts are ways in which companies stand to learn from policy makers—and that is fitting. Because for us to account for the dangers of AI and mass surveillance, or of climate change, we need buy-in and action from the world's largest companies. They are not in the periphery of geopolitical power; they have used their gains over the last thirty years to become protagonists, and now it is time to live up to the responsibilities that come with their great power.

6

THE GEOGRAPHY OF CHANGE: THE CONTEST FOR POWER BETWEEN CLOSED AND OPEN SYSTEMS

For more than six thousand years, people have worked to balance the rights and responsibilities of the state, the people, and businesses. The social contracts that have emerged out of that balancing act have taken different forms in different places at different times, but their existence remains a constant throughout world history. Strong social contracts tend to reinforce themselves while weak ones give way to new models. The contracts established a basic equilibrium: governments provided the security and stability needed to maintain a free market that let citizens and companies flourish, while citizens held the power to choose their leaders.

As we have seen throughout this book, however, that equilibrium has been lost in much of the world. In the United States and many European countries, companies took on responsibilities we have traditionally reserved for the state, and government institutions became less effective and less responsive to citizens. Inequality grew out of control, and economic mobility declined. As a result, we have seen disaffected citizens respond with xenophobia and populism. All the while, the world has grown massively interconnected. News can spread from a village in Brazil to the rest of the world in an instant; a market crash in London can affect lives and livelihoods in every other continent on the planet; the fuel burned in one corner of the globe affects the entire atmosphere. As the world grew more interconnected, global poverty fell massively and new opportunities opened up for billions around the world, but we are still just coming to terms with how the rapid networking of the world affects us all. The basic equilibrium of decades ago has lost hold, and in the developed and developing world alike social contracts are increasingly frayed.

Countries around the world have responded to the tumult by shifting their social contracts in one of two directions. Either nations have closed off and adopted a more controlled, authoritarian model of government, or they have opened up—welcoming innovation, investment, immigration, free speech—while simultaneously enacting reforms that can shelter their citizens from the greatest risks that openness can bring.

While the United States seemed to emerge as the only model worth emulating in the wake of the Cold War, it has failed to adapt its model to reflect the raging forces of the 21st century. It has instead seen its own brush with authoritarianism and populism in recent years, and from the perspective of the other 195 countries in the world, it has lost its status as the go-to model for stability and prosperity.

In this chapter, we will look at the fork in the road that countries around the world are facing. For much of the book, we have focused on nations that are caught in the tumult, needing to find a way to fix their problems. Here, we turn to the nations that have already chosen their approach. Some, like China, have embraced a controlled model, while adding key adaptations that allow them to thrive in the global economy. Others, like the Nordics, have built a new template for the open model, one that balances capitalism and stability. Moving through the 2020s and beyond, every country will have to make difficult choices about how to adapt their social contracts to our new age. Countries like the United States and most of those in Europe will need to find ways to right the balance. Meanwhile, many of the fledgling democracies that emerged across Latin America, Africa, and South

Asia in the late 20th century are beginning to give in to their more authoritarian tendencies.

We will come to understand the nations around the world that offer crucial examples—both positive and negative—of how to rebuild a global social contract for the 21st century. We'll examine the tough trade-offs that need to be made, the high stakes for the planet, and the work that every country needs to undertake to be able to thrive in the raging 2020s.

CHINA

We will start by looking at the siren-song appeal of the controlled model, and at its most powerful proponent: China.

The controlled model seems to many in the West like a regression to a bygone era. It is a social contract that is drafted, signed, and executed entirely by the state. The people have very little say in laying out rules and responsibilities for their governments and businesses. Those who do not comply face the consequences.

Throughout history, you can find examples of kings, queens, emperors, sultans, religious leaders, and political party strongmen imposing their will on entire societies, unchecked by public opinion or democratic consent. Authoritarianism is the world's oldest form of government, and it has taken on many guises over the years. But no country has more effectively adapted the model for the 21st century than China.

In part, this follows from the country's history. A strong central government has ruled the Chinese people for more than 3,500 years. The country was led by a succession of 557 emperors from antiquity through the early 20th century, descended into infighting, civil war, and foreign occupation for several decades, and then reemerged in 1949 under the control of the Chinese Communist Party. There is no history of democracy in mainland China. Its 1.4 billion people remain subject to whatever social contract the state forces upon them. And for the last four decades, it has been defined by the marriage of economic liberalization and political control.

China's transition to authoritarian capitalism began in 1978 as the country emerged from the brutal reign of Chairman Mao Zedong. Ravaged by famine and political purges, China lagged far behind the developed world on nearly every quality-of-life statistic. At the time, the country had an economy slightly smaller than that of the Netherlands, but it was home to 950 million more people, almost 90 percent of whom lived in extreme poverty. Hoping to pull the country out of its backwards existence, Mao's successor Deng Xiaoping gradually started opening China for business. The state loosened its grip on the agriculture sector, allowing rural farmers to rent land and equipment, and sell their surplus on the free market. Private companies, previously outlawed by the Communist Party, began popping up around the country. In coastal cities, the government established "special economic zones," which provided tax breaks and exemptions from the restrictive business policies of the rest of the country. As foreign investors flocked to these free-market hubs, China's exports skyrocketed and its economy began to grow. China turned its back on economic communism some ten years ahead of the Soviet bloc, and the word *communist* ceased to have any meaning tied to its actual ideological origins. But while Moscow's economic reforms were soon followed by the dissolution of the Soviet Union, Beijing managed to open the Chinese economy without weakening the Communist Party's grip on political power.

The story of China's ascent over the last forty years is by now common knowledge, but that does not make it any less remarkable. The country sustained an average annual growth rate of 9.5 percent for a full forty years, a hot streak that the World Bank characterized as "the fastest sustained expansion by a major economy in history." Its gross domestic product increased by a factor of thirty-six, lifting more than eight hundred million people out of poverty along the way. It marked the single largest eradication of poverty in human history, probably the best demonstration of how economic liberalism outperforms socialism. China now boasts the second-largest economy in the world behind the United States.

When China began embracing freer market economics and Western technologies like the internet, many thought its citizens would soon begin clamoring for other features of Western society, like civil liberties and political freedom. Those predictions turned out to be wrong.

Most Chinese citizens do not view their newfound prosperity as a vindication of Western political and economic theory, but rather as a testament to the strength and wisdom of the government of the Chinese Communist Party. Though they acknowledge the merits of economic freedom, the majority of Chinese people think self-government is too messy. In their eyes, democracy leads to conflict and leaves societies vulnerable to violence and unrest, while politicians make promises they cannot keep. By comparison, the Chinese government has consistently delivered on the stability and economic prosperity it has promised its people for the last forty years. Most Chinese citizens would concede that the model is not perfect, but they still see it as a better alternative to the perceived chaos of Western democracy. This view is reinforced by the government, which uses state media to highlight turmoil in Western countries and downplay China's own problems. When citizens do cast doubt on the government, the party has plenty of ways to keep their ideas from spreading through its surveillance infrastructure.

Most citizens of the developed world would not tolerate this sort of government panopticon, but the people of mainland China have accepted it with little pushback. This is partly a product of history—given China's long track record of centralized state control, civil liberties and political freedom are not baked into the social fabric the way they are in western Europe or the United States. But a more significant reason is that the Chinese people see political control as a necessary cost of social stability. China tends to prioritize the harmony and cooperation of the collective over the freedom and liberty of the individual. If the price of peace is total surveillance, it is accepted. One Chinese national who has also spent years working in the United States explained to me that he feels unconflicted about living a more submissive life when he's in China and a more open life when abroad, pointing to how that duality has enabled his family to grow wealthy.

Political upheaval tends to come in times of turmoil and uncertainty, but the Chinese people entered the 2020s feeling more secure than ever. Most of the four hundred million members of the Chinese middle class grew up on less than two dollars per day. The entrepreneurs and executives who lead the country's business community are less than a generation removed from extreme poverty. Overbearing as it may be, the government has delivered well-being for the vast majority of the Chinese population.

This transaction—economic prosperity for political submission—is the core of the Chinese social contract. Instead of gaining the consent of the governed through the ballot box, the Chinese Communist Party did it through their wallets.

"China has five thousand years of centralized political history. It's not going to become democratic tomorrow," said geopolitical analyst Parag Khanna. "We thought that they could liberalize, democratize once they joined the World Trade Organization and became part of the global economy—we were wrong.

"The [Chinese Communist] Party has bought off the people through material welfare in exchange for political silence," he added.

Most recently, as the Chinese government encroached further into the physical and digital lives of its people, it also tightened its grip on the private sector. From the 1980s through the first decade of the 21st century, there was a boomtown energy in its market development, with corruption at its core. China's coastal cities became free markets where bribes and payouts were simply a cost of doing business. The more the country's economy grew, the richer government officials became. In the most recent count, at least 104 billionaires were members of the National People's Congress (China's parliament) or the Chinese People's Political Consultative Conference (Beijing's top advisory body). By contrast, though the 116th US Congress counted more than 250 millionaires, there was not a single billionaire on Capitol Hill. The British Parliament also has no billionaires.

Chinese companies work hand-in-glove with the government, leveraging public funding and state-sponsored intellectual property theft to gain an edge over their foreign competitors. There is little distinction between state and capital in China's industries of the future. The leaders of tech giants like Baidu, Huawei, Tencent, and Alibaba are as beholden to Beijing as the governors of the East India Company were to the British monarch. Still, China is by no means a state-run economy, according to Ian Bremmer, founder of the Eurasia Group.

"In China, there's a much more robust private sector than people appreciate. There's real competition . . . even among national champions and state-owned enterprises," Bremmer said. In other words, China remains a free market for those that play by Beijing's rules.

But the Chinese model is not bulletproof. The problems go beyond its lack of political freedom. The entire social contract is predicated on economic growth, and it seems unlikely that the Chinese government will be able to drive high growth numbers forever, given that there is no precedent in history for an economy to *never* falter. Every country has its ups and downs. If growth slows or the country falls into a recession, the goodwill that Chinese people feel toward Beijing may disappear. The Communist Party cannot afford the economic ebbs and flows that democratic countries regularly weather—this is part of the reason the government relies on central planning. The state offers little in the way of safety net programs, and independent trade unions are nonexistent. All organized labor is controlled by the Communist Party.

China's growth and stability have lent its model increasing appeal across much of Asia and Africa, especially when juxtaposed with the economic and political disorder that has more characterized the US and its allies in recent years. It is questionable, however, whether the Chinese model could ever be replicated by any nation that does not have the sheer size of China. And the trade-offs that a closed system requires may seem stabilizing in the short term, but if growth stalls or autocratic power stops benefiting the people without any outlet for reform, then history shows that the consequences will be terrible.

THE CONTEST BETWEEN CLOSED AND OPEN

The appeal of a controlled model like China is simple: stability. In a tumultuous world, many people will trade their freedom for security. It is easier to provide that sense of security when the social contract is closed off and determined from top down.

Over the last decade, we have seen a marked authoritarian turn around the world. For many well-meaning observers in long-standing democracies, it is tempting to reduce that trend to misinformation, irrationality, or a onetime backlash. But when you look closely at the appeal of the reigning closed models, you find they offer a very canny exchange with citizens. In China, citizens receive growth and a sense of solidarity for handing over their freedom to the state. In the Gulf kingdoms, absolute power is offset by generous benefits in some of the most generous welfare states in the world. The Saudi government sends monthly cash payments to about half its population. In Qatar, the state provides free water, electricity, and telephone lines. The United Arab Emirates and Kuwait furnish married couples with free plots of land and no-interest loans to build houses. Free health care and education are standard across the region. Nowhere in the Gulf States do citizens pay income taxes. In most countries, a substantial portion of the workforce is employed in government jobs. In Saudi Arabia, about two-thirds of all workers are employed by the government, where wages are 70 percent higher than in the private sector. A few years ago, a senior Saudi official revealed the scope of the average civil servant's daily workload: "The amount worked doesn't even exceed an hour—and that's based on studies."

In democratic countries that flirt with authoritarianism, the appeal of the authoritarian narrative is similar: for too long, establishment politicians have failed to make you wealthier or more secure; it's time to kick them out and let this strong new leader get out there and swing his fists on your behalf.

But in each of these closed models, the promise of stability and growth is a short-term gamble. It means imposing sharp limits on freedom. Minority groups are dealt with brutally; next-generation technology is channeled toward next-generation surveillance; citizens know there are harsh restrictions on what they can say or do. And countries like the United States, with its long history of racial strife and what Philip Roth called its "indigenous American berserk," are not immune from any of it.

The open model still leaves citizens with the ability to protest and work against injustice. The closed model leaves citizens without self-determination—at the mercy of state power or corporate power, or both, which is anathema to what a truly effective social contract can accomplish. The crowning achievement of history's strongest social contracts has been to create a sense of balance—where individuals have a meaningful say in the larger institutions and powers that direct their lives. As we have seen, that bold ideal has lost ground in recent decades. That is why closed models have resurged. But that is also why the path toward fixing the social contract for the 21st century lies beyond the closed models. Instead, it lies in the messier but democratic open models.

We have seen in each chapter of this book how the prevailing model in the US and major European countries has lost its way. But there are open models in the world today that have succeeded in adapting to the challenges we are facing now. In these countries, we can find useful lessons and examples for other countries around the world.

The prime example is the Nordic model. And to understand just how it has adapted to fill the gaps left lingering in the US-dominant social contract, we can find a clear contrast. Just look at how both handled the COVID-19 pandemic.

THE NORDIC MODEL

The way a society responds to a crisis reveals a lot about its social contract. As COVID-19 swept across the globe in March 2020, an economic downturn appeared imminent. To contain the damage, the United States created a patchwork of stimulus programs: directing loans, grants, and tax breaks to businesses while raising unemployment benefits and sending stimulus checks to citizens. It was a response that catered to capital over labor. The stimulus package kept the financial sector and large companies afloat by injecting liquidity into the market. But it also allowed a surge in unemployment and the widespread failure of small businesses. The stock market quickly rebounded from its crash, but more than ten million workers lost their jobs and more than a hundred thousand small businesses closed their doors. Many people were stuck waiting months to receive government benefits and stimulus payments with no stream of income. Markets recovered but people did not.

Now compare that to Denmark's pandemic response. After negotiating with employers and labor unions, the Danish government decided to effectively nationalize private-sector payrolls. For three months, the government paid 75–90 percent of the salaries of workers affected by the pandemic, as long as companies promised not to fire them. The government also deferred tax payments and covered costs like rent and employee sick leave, further reducing the financial toll on businesses hurt by the virus. The Danish relief program let companies of all sizes weather the pandemic without dipping too far into the red and allowed workers to shelter in place without losing too much of their income. It was a response that focused on labor over capital. Bankrolling the economy was expensive—the program cost an estimated $42 billion, 13 percent of the country's GDP—but in the eyes of the government, it was better to pay for people to keep their jobs than to bear the costs of mass unemployment.

"What we're trying to do is to freeze the economy," Danish Employment Minister Peter Hummelgaard said at the time. "It's about preserving 'Main Street' as much as we can. It's a radical plan. But radical times need radical responses."

In the first month of lockdown, the unemployment rate in Denmark rose just 1.3 percent, compared to 10.3 percent in the United States. Once the country reopened, companies did not need to waste time hiring new workers, nor did workers need to find new jobs. And, not for nothing, the Danish stock market fully recovered, too.

The United States and Denmark both devoted a significant amount of their GDP to pandemic response efforts, but the way each country targeted its resources revealed very different priorities. The US protected its biggest companies and investors, and Denmark protected its workforce and small businesses. If the US had made an equivalent investment in Main Street, the data would look much more Nordic.

Denmark and its Nordic neighbors—Sweden, Norway, Finland, and Iceland—have a long history of using the government to shield people from the more inhumane features of the free market. This includes pandemic-induced layoffs, but also more commonplace economic afflictions like health care costs and rent inflation. The Nordics have used democracy to build some of the world's strongest social safety nets. Under their social contract, the state and its institutions guarantee citizens a high quality of life from the cradle to the grave.

If you are born in a Nordic country, you enter the world in a government-funded hospital and receive free health care for your entire life. Your childcare is subsidized by the state. You can earn up to a bachelor's degree without paying a cent in tuition. When you rent or buy a home, you are eligible for government housing subsidies. When you have children, you are entitled to some of the world's most generous paid parental leave—more than nine months in Sweden, Norway, and Finland—as well as a government-funded allowance until your kids grow up. (All five Nordic countries offer paid leave to fathers as well as mothers.) If you lose your job, the government provides you generous unemployment benefits and helps you get back on your feet through effective job-retraining programs. Once you retire, the state supplies your pension. These benefits are available to everyone, not just people at the bottom of the income ladder. While welfare programs in the United States and other countries are viewed as government charity, Nordics see them simply as a benefit of citizenship.

This expansive welfare system is funded by some of the world's highest taxes. The top income tax bracket is 38.2 percent in Norway, 46.2 percent in Iceland, 51.1 percent in Finland, 55.9 percent in Denmark, and 57.2 percent in Sweden. But despite the popular perception within much of the political Left, these high taxes do not disproportionately target the wealthy. In Sweden, for instance, anyone earning more than 1.5 times the average income—the equivalent of about

$79,000 per year—qualifies for the upper bracket. By comparison, the top tax bracket in the United States kicks in only once someone earns 9.2 times the average national income. If the US adopted the Swedish tax structure, a person earning $87,000 per year would fall into the same tax bracket as someone earning $1 million per year. The Nordic ideals of fairness and equity extend to the wealthy—there is little desire to "eat the rich," at least in the tax code.

Nordic governments also generate a significant portion of their revenue through value-added taxes (or sales tax). VAT is what economists consider a *regressive* tax: it disproportionately targets people lower on the income ladder, who devote a greater portion of their income to living expenses. The corporate tax rate in each of the Nordic states is also slightly below average for developed countries, and the capital gains tax is below the top income bracket. In other words, the burden of funding the expansive Nordic welfare systems falls disproportionately on labor instead of capital, and particularly on low-, middle-, and upper-middle-income workers. It would be hard to imagine taxpayers in the United States or elsewhere supporting a system that overburdens the middle class.

However, Nordic people are generally happy to pay these high rates. Their societies enjoy relatively high levels of social cohesion and trust in government institutions. While American society's individualistic culture portrays taxes and government in a negative light, in Nordic countries there is a general sense that supporting the government promotes the common good. Scandinavians feel that the benefits they receive from state-funded programs outweigh the costs of high taxes, much as was the case in the United States in the years following World War II, when Americans paid much higher taxes during a time of massively increasing well-being across the country. The Nordic states also do a good job hiding their taxes from consumers, reducing the psychological costs people feel when parting with hard-earned money. Like other developed nations, the Nordics make it incredibly easy to file taxes. Tax forms arrive in the mail already filled out—all people need to do is review the documents and submit a digital signature. Instead of tax deductions, Nordic states tend to distribute welfare through direct cash payments. Ask any behavioral economist, and they will tell you that people generally feel better about receiving a payment than reducing a cost, even if the net result is the same.

The citizens of Nordic countries consistently rank among the happiest in the world despite living in a part of the world that can be dark and cold fifteen hours a day for months at a time. When asked, people often attribute their peace of mind to the welfare system. They know their basic necessities will be provided for and the safety net will catch them if they fall.

Your average Dane, Swede, Norwegian, Finn, and Icelander enjoy a higher standard of living than their counterparts in many other parts of the developed world. Poverty and unemployment rates are generally low. People are highly educated and have access to world-class health care. Gender inequality in the workplace is much lower than in other developed countries. Nordic countries are not plagued by the same broad economic inequality that we see in the United States and other parts of the world. The countries are not socialist utopias—today, there are more billionaires per capita in Iceland, Norway, and Sweden than in the United States—but they do ensure that even those on the bottom of the income ladder have their basic needs met. This is what a strong social contract looks like.

"What the northern Europeans have managed to do is to marry high taxes with a great deal of efficiency," political scientist Fareed Zakaria told me. "It's always more durable politically to have benefits that feel more universal."

Zakaria attributes the success of the Nordic model to the region's long history of egalitarianism: "These are societies that have always been less top-down, less hierarchical, and less authoritarian than others." Democracy in other parts of the West has generally manifested as a power struggle between the haves and the have-nots. But among the Nordics, it is used as a tool for building solidarity across class lines and leveling the playing field for all. They have developed "a really thoughtful understanding of what the purpose of the state is in society," said Zakaria.

Today, the state defends free trade and enacts policies to encourage entrepreneurship and private-sector growth. Policy makers shy away from antitrust enforcement and other government interference in the economy. Companies are permitted to hire and fire employees without getting bogged down in excessive regulation or legal battles (though Nordic workers still enjoy more protections than their American counterparts). As we previously discussed, the Nordic countries also have a strong, multitiered organized labor apparatus that negotiates fair pay and benefits for workers across the economy. Employees can also directly influence how businesses are run thanks to work councils and codetermination, in which managers and workers collaborate in decision-making.

To succeed in the technology-driven, knowledge-based economy of the 21st century, companies must be able to fail and scale quickly. They cannot waste too much time jumping through regulatory hoops. The comparatively light-touch labor laws in Nordic countries give companies certain advantages over their counterparts in other parts of Europe. They are the reason Helsinki, Stockholm, and Copenhagen boast some of the most vibrant start-up scenes in the world. In Mediterranean countries like Spain, France, and Italy, companies looking to hire and fire workers often find themselves bogged down in bureaucratic processes that make it difficult to impossible to do so. While these countries generally outperform Nordics in traditional industrial sectors, they are not effectively competing with them in high-tech industries and certainly not among start-ups. The kludgeocracy of Mediterranean governments makes it harder for start-ups to incorporate, acquire funding, and acquire and shed talent as needed.

The combination of labor flexibility and strong safety nets in the Nordics is known as flexicurity. People pay higher taxes in exchange for mobility and economic security.

The foundation of the Nordic social contract is collective action. Through high taxes, the Nordic people leverage their governments to build strong, comprehensive social safety nets for everyone. Through the democratic process, citizens foster an economic environment where human and financial capital can pool in the most innovative and efficient companies. Through organized labor, workers ensure they share in the gains created by the private sector. The Nordic social contract is agile, adaptable, and free, promoting individual autonomy and private competition while maintaining a high economic floor through which people rarely fall.

If there is a vulnerability, it is that the Nordic model depends on citizens' intrinsic willingness to work. Given the country's strong safety net, it would not be hard to survive as a free rider, reaping social benefits without holding down a job or otherwise contributing to the economy. If too many people picked the couch over the office, there would not be enough taxes to support the welfare state.

The model also relies on strong social cohesion. It is not hard to foster a general sense of cooperation and goodwill when almost everyone looks, speaks, worships, and lives the same way. But when you introduce new people into a homogenous population, even the most tight-knit societies can begin to fray.

Over the last two decades, the Nordic countries have seen a significant influx of immigrants, many of whom are fleeing violence in Africa and the Middle East. As their societies grow more ethnically and religiously diverse, the Nordic countries have seen a resurgence of nativism. Over the last decade, Far Right parties have increased their seats in the governments of Sweden, Norway, Finland, and Denmark. Across the region, you also see more people questioning the extent to which newcomers should benefit from their generous social welfare programs. Many migrants have comparatively little formal education and do not speak the native language, which makes it more difficult to hold down a job. Across the region, many people are beginning to balk at the idea of paying taxes to support those who are out of work, especially if those people look different from them.

"The kinds of benefits Nordic countries provide seem to have social support, political support, and durability when people think of them as being provided to a community that they identify with," said Fareed Zakaria. "When the community is one that they don't identify and attach with, they become much more American in their attitudes.

You're beginning to see this dilemma where basically you can have a homogenous society with strong social markets, or you can have a highly heterogeneous society with somewhat shallower benefits."

The key challenge for the Nordic social contract over the coming decade will be to determine if it can continue to provide a high-quality safety net as its population grows more diverse. Immigration and growing inequality rooted in a tax system that treats the very wealthy and workers the same will test the mettle of the Nordic social contract.

But ultimately, the Nordic model stands as an example for the rest of the world, and especially for democracies that are struggling to balance openness with stability. The Nordic countries have built an effectively egalitarian society for the 21st century. By combining free-market economics with an expansive safety net, their social contract guarantees a high quality of life for every citizen and fosters an environment where business can thrive. The private sector avoids the perils of shareholder capitalism because it has been compelled to pursue stakeholder capitalism—not so much by government mandate as by the collective influence of its workers, empowered by organized labor, work councils, and board-level representation. That makes for an effective balance of power: citizens, business, and government are each able to serve, and provide checks on, the next. As the world grows more connected and climate change spurs mass migration in the years ahead, the Nordic model will be put to the test. But when you spin the globe and look at all the social contracts in place, the Nordics have enacted the best set of solutions to address the forces that have shredded social contracts elsewhere.

MORE DEMOCRACIES, ESPECIALLY the United States, would benefit by drawing lessons from the Nordic model. But critics in the US often say that the Nordic approach would not be able to apply there, especially given the size and diversity of the United States. However, it is worth emphasizing just how much of an outlier the US social contract is among developed democratic states. It is even starkly different from countries with similar histories and makeups. In the bulk of these other Western countries, citizens rely on the government to construct strong, inclusive safety net programs largely independent of the private sector. Consider, for instance, Australia.

Australia and the United States have a lot in common. Both countries began as British colonies and both speak English; if you saw an American and an Australian at a dinner party, they would be indistinguishable but for their accents. However, if you examine their views on the responsibilities of government, they are very, very different.

Julia Gillard is a dynamo who served as Australia's first female prime minister while I was working at the US State Department, and we are now colleagues in a venture capital firm where we both serve as board partners. When I asked her how and why the United States and Australia take such a different approach to the role of government, she noted that Australia's tendency toward collectivism is rooted deep in its culture. She referenced historian Gavan Daws's account of Japanese prisoner of war camps during World War II. Even in "the depths of degradation," prisoners stayed true to their culture, she said. "The British still had their aristocratic structures, the Americans were the humorist individualists of the prison camps, and the Australians formed male-bonded welfare states to support each other.

"The Australian attitude is that the government should do things. To the extent they aren't doing things, that's because we've got a dumb mob of politicians, and you can always get another mob of politicians," Gillard told me. "If you're going to boil down the American attitude, it is that the government probably shouldn't be doing things, and to the extent it does things, you ought to be deeply suspicious of them."

In contrast to the United States, the Australian government provides all citizens with high-quality, universal health care, including free or heavily subsidized medical services. The state operates a universal pension system that is funded entirely by employers (workers also have the option to contribute). It supports a high-quality public education system, while also subsidizing private schools. In 1907, Australia became the second country, behind New Zealand, to create a national minimum wage, and today it boasts one of the highest wage floors in the world. As of August 2020, the lowest-paid Australian workers made $14.23 per hour, nearly double the earnings of their American counterparts.

Australians' proclivity for collective action extends to the workplace. While less than 15 percent of Australian workers belong to a labor union, about 60 percent of the workforce is covered by collective bargaining agreements. The country's labor markets are heavily regulated by the government, which reduces mobility but ensures a high standard of living for most Australians.

While safety net programs are a point of political contention in the United States, they receive near-universal support among Australian lawmakers, Gillard said. "Political parties contend on who is going to do better for Medicare and free public hospitals. No one contends on 'let's take that system away.'"

Australia is not unique in this regard. The citizens of New Zealand and Canada, both former British colonies, have also leveraged their democratic governments to build strong safety net programs. Even in the United Kingdom, which tends to behave more like the United States politically and economically, most politicians have thrown their support behind the government-funded health care system.

Because the state's safety net programs are so robust, the Australian business community is not expected to provide for their workforce in the same way as American companies are. They collaborate with the government on worker training programs and step in to support public welfare when compelled to do so by lawmakers. But for the most part, the companies "haven't historically conceived it to be their role to be big shapers of the social safety net," Gillard said.

The private sector's voice in Australian politics is also limited. While individual companies and industry groups may hire lobbyists, they aren't "dictating the play" in Canberra, Gillard noted. Election campaigns are financed by the government, and Australian candidates do not raise much from private donors. "Money speaks in our politics, but it doesn't speak as loudly as it does in the US," said Gillard.

At the core of the Australian model is the sense of collectivism. Using the levers of democracy, Australians and their counterparts in the other advanced Commonwealth countries have engineered a social contract in which the state provides basic necessities and keeps corporations from being the administrators of welfare programs. This has prepared them well for the 2020s, and as the United States eyes the future, it would do well to look not just to the Nordics but also to its peers in Australia, Canada, and New Zealand. Each offers a piece of the puzzle for balancing an open economy with the support citizens need to be able to take risks and thrive in an interconnected world.

THE CHOICES IN THE DEVELOPING WORLD

So far, we have looked at countries that have firmly chosen their approach to the 2020s. These nations have established 21st-century social contracts that will serve as models for the rest of the world. But scores of countries still stand at the crossroads, yet to determine their course through the decades ahead. They seek growth, stability, and a seat at the global table. But will they favor the controlled model presented by China, or the open model offered by the Nordics and Commonwealths, or something else entirely? This is still an open question for much of the world, and it is especially pressing for developing world countries throughout much of Latin America, Africa, and Asia, including India and its 1.3 billion people.

Over the last thirty years, the nations of Latin America have opened up their economies to the world and embraced more democratic forms of government. In 2001, the thirty-five countries of the Western Hemisphere came together to adopt the Inter-American Democratic Charter, which declared democracy to be the only legitimate form of government in the Western Hemisphere. On the whole, these reforms have been remarkably effective in fueling growth and self-government on the continent. As Tom Shannon, a former State Department leader on Latin America, put it, "We have in the Western Hemisphere a bunch of countries we can point to and say 'Hey, you can do this in forty years. You don't have to do it in three hundred years like us.'"

But the younger Latin American democracies tend to have a different flavor of democracy than the United States and Europeans. They are more rooted in results, according to Shannon. "For Latins, the measure of legitimacy of a democracy is going to be 'can it deliver the goods?' It isn't just about fair and free elections." The populace expects its government to provide the security, health care, and educational opportunities needed for citizens to achieve their rights. As the young Latin democracies run up against the shifting winds of the world economy, they will want to draw from Nordic models. Yet the United States is also a leader in the Western Hemisphere, and it is going to be crucial that the world's most powerful democracy reforms its own social contract as well if it wants to continue to be a beacon for democracy to the rest of the Americas. When democracies falter in Latin America, we've seen the authoritarian alternatives rush in. For the Latin American social contract to keep functioning, we need to see continued proof that democracies are able to "deliver the goods" in the 2020s and beyond.

Turning to Asia, we find one of the most striking examples of how a more open model can deliver—South Korea. In 1968, South Korea had a lower GDP per capita than Ghana, but fifty years later it ranks among the most modern, technologically developed countries in the world. Following the Korean War, which cemented the border between North and South Korea, the two new countries took widely divergent paths. North Korea implemented a medieval social contract in which the state controls almost every aspect of political, economic, and social life. South Korea opened its economy and fought to become a player on the world stage. For South Korea, its involvement in the world economy helped fuel its turn to democracy and more political openness. The military seized control of the country in 1961 and held on to power until civilian government was gradually restored in the 1980s. After watching Japan's rapid growth, South Korea's military government began directing loans and lucrative contracts to a handful of select companies that worked closely with the government. These conglomerates, called *chaebol*, helped jump-start South Korea's spectacular economic expansion, and they still control a large portion of the national economy—Samsung, the largest of these conglomerates, accounts for one-fifth of the country's gross domestic product.

But the country also now features a vibrant start-up scene that has pushed its economy to new heights year after year, and it has become a global cultural leader. In 2018, the K-pop group BTS became the first Korean act to reach the Number 1 spot on the Billboard Artist 100 chart. Korean director Bong Joon-ho's thriller *Parasite* became the first foreign film to win an Oscar for best picture in 2020. To other young democracies in Asia and around the world, South Korea serves as an example of the growth that's possible in an open model, while North Korea stands as a cautionary tale for a controlled model taken to extremes.

The inflection point for the two Korean states came half a century ago, but if there's any region of the world that's at a similarly high-stakes decision point right now it is sub-Saharan Africa. The fate of many African nations—and potentially their world power—will hinge on the decisions they make in the 2020s.

After the collapse of the Soviet Union, democracy spread across Africa. Socialist regimes and military dictatorships across the continent gave way to representative governments. Elections replaced military coups as the way for leaders to assume office. Those leaders established institutions to promote the health, security, and well-being of their citizens. While the push toward democracy was by no means universal, the early 21st century saw many African countries rebuilding a social contract that had been undone by centuries of colonization, war, and regime change. Those efforts also enjoyed the financial and political support of Western democracies fresh off a victory in the Cold War.

But over the last decade, a variety of familiar forces have chipped away at those reforms, destabilizing the continent's precarious democracies.

In many African countries, governments are reverting to old authoritarian tendencies. Leaders who came to power through the ballot box are exploiting their posts to remain in office. As of March 2020, seven of the world's eleven longest-serving non-royal heads of state hailed from Africa. All but one—President Isaias Afwerki of Eritrea—have retained power through general elections, though in most cases watchdogs questioned the legitimacy of the results.

Yet the biggest change facing Africa today is the makeup of society itself. Today, Africa is home to some 1.3 billion people, making it the world's second-most populous continent behind Asia. It's also the world's youngest continent. The median age is only twenty years old, which means children and teenagers make up more than half the population. As those young people start having children of their own, the continent is poised for a population boom unlike anything the world has ever seen.

Over the next three decades, the United Nations expects the population of Africa to nearly double, reaching 2.5 billion. By the turn of the next century, the population will surpass 4.3 billion. In the year 2100, about 40 percent of all humans will live in Africa. Meanwhile, the share of the population living in the thirty-six OECD member countries will shrink from 17.3 percent to 12.4 percent. African leaders need to figure out a way to provide basic necessities to a population that is expected to triple over the next eighty years.

If they fail to do so, the continent risks falling into chaos, and the world may follow. "If that youth bulge doesn't have a social contract with its government that allows for good education, good jobs, good housing, good infrastructure, and good health care, then things will start to fray at the edges," said Johnnie Carson, a former ambassador to Kenya, Uganda, and Zimbabwe, who coached me through all my diplomatic projects in Africa while we worked together at the State Department.

The population explosion is placing greater strain on the already rickety institutions established by African governments, exacerbating many of the problems countries are facing today. Terrorism and insurgency are on the rise in Africa, with extremist groups like Boko Haram and Al-Shabaab. High unemployment and weak social safety nets have proven the perfect recruitment tools for violent extremists, and when African governments are unable to provide their citizens with the basic necessities for a good life, people seek change not through ballot boxes but through bombs and the imposition of religious authoritarianism.

At the same time, climate change is reshaping the face of the continent. Already, people in the Sahel region of West Africa are fleeing the increasingly infertile lands for more lush coastal areas or immigrating to Europe. By 2050, the World Bank estimates some eighty-four million sub-Saharan Africans will be forced to migrate due to climate change.

The combination of explosive population growth, climate change, and weak social contracts could create a humanitarian crisis of massive proportions. In the first decades of the 21st century, the international community has struggled to handle the seventy million people displaced by conflict around the world. Imagine how countries would respond if the global refugee population grew tenfold.

Still, that future is not set in stone. A growing population could just as easily lead to prosperity as chaos. It just depends on how the society is structured. Today, the dilemma for many African nations mirrors the dilemma of the world at large. They are teetering between two very different visions of the future.

On one side of the spectrum, you have a handful of African nations that have embraced market democracy. In countries like Ghana, Senegal, Botswana, Mauritius, and Namibia, government institutions are mostly strong, and elected leaders tend to work to improve the lives of their citizens. Corruption is comparatively low, social programs are well funded, and there is mutual respect between government officials and citizens.

On the other side, a number of countries have reverted to a more authoritarian model. Though countries like Uganda, Cameroon, Zimbabwe, and Burundi are all democracies on paper, in practice they operate much more like autocracies. And as these notionally democratic governments become more authoritarian in practice, their actions are being reinforced by a powerful geopolitical ally: China.

Ambassador Carson sees the rise of China as one of the biggest threats to Africa's fledgling democratic institutions. Would-be authoritarians are "encouraged by the success of what they see in China and discouraged by what they see as a fraying of the social contract in some democratic societies," he told me.

Moreover, the success of China's "authoritarian capitalism" offers

African governments a blueprint for building an economically prosperous society while keeping citizens under tight control. And China is supplying leaders with the tools to do both.

Through the Belt and Road Initiative, China is investing tens of billions of dollars in building and refurbishing public infrastructure across Africa. State-of-the-art airport terminals funded by China have popped up, and Chinese companies are resurrecting dilapidated highways and railroads (some of which were laid more than a century ago by European colonists) to link rural outposts to seaports and metropolitan hubs. Even the headquarters of the African Union, a stunning glass-and-steel complex in the heart of Addis Ababa, was built through Chinese investment. As of September 2019, all but fourteen of Africa's fifty-four countries were participating in Belt and Road in some form.

"These are enormous infrastructure projects, things that they can't get the World Bank or the International Monetary Fund to finance," Ambassador Carson said. "They can't get the EU to do them and they can't get the US to do them, but they need them. And so they go to the Chinese."

The Belt and Road projects often come with strings attached. Much of the funding comes in the form of less-than-transparent loans, leaving African nations with bills they can't afford to pay. This "debt-trap diplomacy" gives China outsized influence over the policies of African countries, which the Chinese use to their benefit.

Sometimes these interests are economic. In 2017, the government of Guinea-Conakry granted China access to mineral reserves in exchange for a $20 billion loan to build roads, power lines, and a university. Chinese companies also flood Africa with inexpensive cell phones, cars, clothes, and other consumer goods, cornering a market largely ignored by Western retailers.

In other cases, the interests are strategic. China constructed its first overseas naval base in Djibouti after spending years supplying the country with new railways, telecommunications infrastructure, and ports. The African Union headquarters was completed after the Chinese government "donated" $200 million for its construction.

Employees later discovered the building's IT systems had been transmitting confidential data to Shanghai every night.

But while China has ramped up its investment in Africa, Western governments and companies have been more hesitant to do business on the continent. While the Americans and Europeans might balk at cutting a deal with an oppressive government, Carson said the Chinese have no such qualms. Additionally, US companies are forbidden from bribing foreign officials to further their business interests, but in certain parts of Africa payoffs are standard practice. Again, according to Ambassador Carson, the Chinese are happy to buy their way into a deal.

I recall being in Gabon for a summit of more than a dozen African heads of state and nine hundred African business leaders. I traveled there with a little group of economists and other thought leaders, and we were all being well paid to speak to the heads of state and business leaders. I came to realize that we were just a bit of side entertainment, like the soccer player hired to acrobatically juggle a soccer ball in front of the ballroom. The real business took place in hotel suites and the presidential palace, where a few dozen Chinese government and business representatives negotiated with the African leaders. When a deal was ready to be signed, a loud gong would indicate the beginning of a ceremony, complete with a light show, dramatic music, and foot-long ornamental pens with which the infrastructure deals were signed between the African governments and the Chinese representatives. When I asked one of the event organizers about it, he said the event organization itself obscured its real business, which was a cut of every deal that got signed. Since the business was incorporated in France, it was not subject to the Foreign Corrupt Practices Act.

China also does its part to help leaders maintain their grip on power. The governments of at least a dozen African countries—including Nigeria, Kenya, Zimbabwe, and South Africa—employ artificial intelligence tools built by the Chinese to conduct surveillance on their citizens. In some cases, these systems feed information back to China to help developers improve their own surveillance capabilities.

"The Chinese don't care whether they're dealing with a good government or bad government, they don't care whether the leader is a democrat or autocrat, they don't care whether he's got human rights violations," Ambassador Carson said. "We practice our political engagement, our diplomacy, with a higher degree of integrity and commitment to principles and values than they do."

As a result, many African countries looking to embrace democracy find themselves caught between a rock and a hard place. With little support from the West and faced with rapidly changing economic, social, and environmental tides, governments teetering between democracy and authoritarianism may have no choice but to work with China. And as those ties grow closer, their social contracts may follow suit.

Building a democratic Africa will require the US and other Western democracies to completely rethink their approach to the continent, Ambassador Carson said. Even if officials want to model their social contract after the United States or the Nordic countries, many still need help to build the trust and institutions that underlie an effective social contract. With sufficient support for democratic governments and social institutions, the forty-nine countries of sub-Saharan Africa could become important allies, lucrative trading partners, and proponents of human rights. Without it, African nations could fall under the Chinese sphere of influence and extend the reach of an authoritarian model of governance. Carson argues that Western democracies must recognize that investment in Africa isn't just "a humanitarian gesture . . . but a strategic investment to build stronger partnerships in the future."

This same principle applies across other regions of the world, including the United States. There are deep humanitarian reasons to identify the holes in our social contract and commit all the resources we have at our disposal to solve them. There are also simple strategic reasons. The next decade will be defined by the rivalry between Western democracy and Chinese authoritarianism. To keep alive the very basic idea of a social contract that serves and reflects the goals of real people, we need to embody what that looks like even as the world continues to change. That means not just learning from the nations that have proven what's possible, but also imagining new ways to combat the most vexing problems of the 2020s and beyond.

During the Engels' Pause in the 19th century, economic inequality and social unrest eventually gave rise to liberal democracy and a new social contract that lifted the economic prospects of the working class. It did so by introducing policy innovations like the minimum wage, child labor laws, the forty-hour workweek, pensions, and public education. As Western countries refine or rewrite their social contracts in the years ahead, they need to imagine similar innovations that will lead to a fairer future.

CONCLUSION

If nothing changes, rage will be the defining quality of the 2020s.

It does not have to be that way. But one way or the other, come 2030 the world will look very different from the one we know now.

Some things we know will happen regardless of our choices. Cities around the world will explode in population over the next decade. We will see spikes in migration as extreme storms and droughts become increasingly common. Artificial intelligence and surveillance technologies will grow more powerful. At work, either you will be telling a machine what to do or a machine will be telling you what to do.

But whether and how we respond to these changes is unknown. The future can still be molded to the benefit of most of us—or it can wind up serving only a select few. It's up to us what 2030 looks like.

Picture a young family in a rural part of the Philippines looking for a new home after buckling down through one too many typhoons. If trends continue as they have, by 2030 that family will face some nasty choices about where to go. They can stay in the Philippines and move to the capital, where there will be an average of ninety thousand people living per square kilometer and where the five-day workweek they spent farming becomes a six-day workweek doing whatever low-level labor has not yet been automated. There won't be any actual employers—or employer benefits—as the work will be managed through an app on whatever is the device of 2030.

Deciding instead to leave, the family looks east to the United States, northwest to China, south to Australia, and west to Europe.

If nothing changes, a move to the United States or Europe will not be as attractive or as easy as it was in prior generations. The rage and protest movements from both the political Right and Left will have grown larger, more violent, and more nativist. Because of continually more globalized capital, the race to the bottom on taxes will have all but eliminated corporate taxes and those for the very wealthy. This will have starved governments of the resources needed to rebuild infrastructure or strengthen safety nets. In order for Australia and the European countries to maintain the high level of social benefits they had at the beginning of the 2020s, they will have closed immigration to all but high-end knowledge workers. The US, by contrast, will have accelerated the individualization of its social contract and safety net, simultaneously surrendering to the logic of market forces and borrowing from China's tech-enabled social scoring system. People will compete for health care, training, and unemployment coverage, with benefits apportioned to those who have put in the most hours of work and received the best reviews from employers on the app that manages their work. The algorithms will be programmed to discount the benefits for immigrant workers.

But if we act to prevent this future, then 2030 could offer a very different reality. The automation made possible by AI and by-then 7G broadband networks will mean that we have enough wealth and well-being to share the benefits of the increased productivity broadly. Just as the six-day workweek of the agricultural age became a five-day workweek during the industrial age, the norm can evolve to a four-day workweek. Instead of competing for benefits in a sort of *Mad Max*–like competition, we could instead afford safety nets that are now more universally Nordic. This becomes possible, first and foremost, by a triumph of diplomacy—remaking the international system of taxation to rely on unitary taxation and formulary apportionment. This will ensure that every company and every person pays the taxes they ought to, which means that taxes for everyday workers will actually go down. At the same time, after decades of failing to live up to its promise, shareholder capitalism will have been relegated to the history books. Instead, governments will have enacted strong incentives—including in the tax system—for better wages, for employees to also be compensated in equity, and for stakeholders to be reflected in business's bottom line. There will be plenty of available cash for wages and stock for distribution because stock buybacks will be illegal. In this vision of 2030, that Filipino family won't find their options so stunted; they will be able to work hard and see that work amount to something. As a norm, compensation now comes with a small ownership stake in whichever company they are working for.

Imagining again what 2030 will look like if things do not change, we can anticipate the spread of the controlled political model of China, Russia, and the Gulf. As inequality grows even more entrenched, violent unrest is likely to become more frequent and ferocious, drawing more citizens and their governments toward controlled and authoritarian versions of the social contract rather than attempting the messiness of democracy. We will see a broader embrace of Chinese-style mass surveillance, firewall policies, and forceful crackdowns on any hint of protest. And more nations will rely on Chinese aid to put these policies in place, further increasing China's cultural and economic influence in the world while sidelining the United States and European democracies.

After that Filipino family looks to the United States and Europe, and finds the doors closed or closing, it is conceivable that they could choose to immigrate to China instead. There, under tight control of the state, the economy will have continued to produce growth and therefore will need low-cost labor like that of climate migrants. The family might not have a full path to citizenship in China and might get stuck in an underclass, but there is work in China's manufacturing hubs, education for their children, and security from the unrest in the messy, dysfunctional democracies. If they want just to work hard and keep their heads down, maybe China and the authoritarian dream are the way of the future.

But if things do change, the rights-respecting models of the democracies will continue to hold their appeal, as abuses made possible by powerful AI and surveillance technologies are regulated. A multistakeholder model can effectively balance the rights of citizens and the responsibilities of companies and countries to avoid a digital dystopia. Instead of allowing for a permanent underclass, upward economic and social mobility—the stuff of the American dream—will be renewed. A new wave of immigration from places navigating climate crises like the Philippines will be welcomed and well managed.

Scarred by the experience that prompted them to move in the first place, the Filipino family will likely want to move where they are less likely to encounter additional extreme weather events brought on by climate change. If nothing changes, this will mean that these safer places will become increasingly scarce and therefore increasingly expensive. The logic of market forces holds that as severe droughts and storms destroy the habitability of certain regions, both people and capital will flock to places that are more livable and safe. Simply stated, there may be another billion people on earth, but there will be fewer places for them to live, creating more megacities and slums.

The countermeasure to this possibility is an international push to address the climate crisis over the next decade. This is an all-hands-on-deck issue that requires public and private investment, so that the world can resoundingly move away from carbon combustion as a means to power our world. The combined efforts of leading nations and companies should fund a trillion-dollar Manhattan Project–style push for clean energy production and distribution that the whole world would benefit from. This sounds bold, and it is—but it is entirely possible and abundantly worth it, for elites, climate migrants, and everybody else.

In the background of these two visions of the future is the role of the world's elites. If nothing changes, the escalating rage will cause the world's most powerful people to consciously decouple from their home countries and move their money, their families, and their sense of citizenship away from anywhere there is trouble and toward the soft landings that await them in the financial and entertainment centers that have been built for them. Their ability to buy the public policies they want from government will have increased, so their winner-takes-all business models do not need to fear regulation or antitrust measures. Since they are the shareholders, they will be the sole winners of shareholder capitalism and their winnings will grow bigger, year in and year out. The problems back home and those faced by working-class or climate-vulnerable people like our Filipino family will grow more distant and abstract.

That does not need to happen either, though, and it ought not require any sort of moral or spiritual awakening. Our elites became elites in the first place because of capitalism, and the smartest among them recognize that in order to continue to live as well as they have in the past, more people need to live better; and that means repairing how capitalism works. This in turn means focusing more on the long term and less on the short term. When they and their companies pay taxes, it gives government the resources it needs to invest in the research and development that will save us from climate change calamity. It means that access to strong education, housing, and health care will be available to more people. This is ultimately in the self-interest of elites themselves, but it means optimizing for the long term, not the short term. Being elite in a world where there is more access to opportunity and greater well-being is better than being elite in a world burning around you.

We are currently edging toward the more frightening outcome, but the positive version of 2030 is not beyond our reach. We can change course over the next decade by enacting a series of interlocking reforms—reforms that will build a better contract for the whole planet. In short, these involve several key steps including replacing shareholder capitalism with stakeholder capitalism, reforming the international tax system, expanding safety nets that meet the reality of work in the 21st century, and pushing *now* for the transition to clean energy.

Each of the ideas works in concert. Each makes the next more attainable and likely. Killing off shareholder capitalism enables us to end tax havens, which gives governments the resources to fight climate change, which means less climate migration. Ending stock buybacks means companies have more money to pay workers in both cash and stock, which means less long-term dependency on safety net programs and greater worker well-being, which makes authoritarian control of society less appealing. The magic of these fixes is that they work together. None is unachievable, and progress toward one makes the others that much more possible.

Together, their impact will be enormous. What we need is to take our existing social contract—a threadbare remnant of the 19th and 20th centuries—and repair it to meet the 21st century. There are two potential paths ahead of us. One is easy to start—all we have to do is nothing—but it leads to hardship and more anger. The second requires bold action by citizens, companies, and governments alike. But it lets us look to the future with hope, and leaves rage to the past.

NOTES

INTRODUCTION

2 **government-funded university research:** "6. Bar Codes—Nifty 50," National Science Foundation, April 2000, https://www.nsf.gov/about/history/nifty50/barcodes.jsp.

4 **$49 billion on stock buybacks:** Philip van Doorn, "Opinion: Airlines and Boeing Want a Bailout—but Look How Much They've Spent on Stock Buybacks," Marketwatch, March 22, 2020, https://www.marketwatch.com/story/airlines-and-boeing-want-a-bailout-but-look-how-much-theyve-spent-on-stock-buybacks-2020-03-18.

6 **nearly 75 percent of Americans worked on farms:** Stanley Lebergott, "Labor Force and Employment, 1800–1960," in *Output, Employment, and Productivity in the United States after 1800*, ed. Dorothy S. Brady (National Bureau of Economic Research, 1966), 117–204, https://www.nber.org/system/files/chapters/c1567/c1567.pdf.

6 **about 17 percent of the population in England and Wales:** Christopher Watson, "Trends in World Urbanisation," in *Proceedings of the First International Conference on Urban Pests*, ed. K. B. Wildey and Wm. H. Robinson (1992), http://citeseerx.ist.psu.edu/viewdoc/download?doi=10.1.1.522.7409&rep=rep1&type=pdf.

8 **Over the last thirty years:** Matt Bruenig, "Top 1% up $21 Trillion. Bottom 50% down $900 Billion," People's Policy Project, June 14, 2019,

https://www.peoplespolicyproject.org/2019/06/14/top-1-up-21-trillion-bottom-50-down-900-billion/.

8 **If the level of inequality:** Carter C. Price and Kathryn A. Edwards, "Trends in Income from 1975 to 2018" (Working Paper WR-A516-1, RAND Corporation, Santa Monica, CA, 2020), https://doi.org/10.7249/WRA516-1.

1: SHAREHOLDER AND STAKEHOLDER CAPITALISM

13 **Like 1.6 million Americans:** "Statistics about Diabetes," American Diabetes Association, accessed June 4, 2020, https://www.diabetes.org/resources/statistics/statistics-about-diabetes.

13 **Nearly a century earlier:** "The History of a Wonderful Thing We Call Insulin," American Diabetes Association, July 1, 2019, https://www.diabetes.org/blog/history-wonderful-thing-we-call-insulin.

13 **Soon after, the trio visited:** "First Use of Insulin in Treatment of Diabetes on This Day in 1922," Diabetes UK, January 11, 2010, https://www.diabetes.org.uk/about_us/news_landing_page/first-use-of-insulin-in-treatment-of-diabetes-88-years-ago-today.

14 **Back then, most people with Type 1:** "First Use of Insulin in Treatment of Diabetes," https://www.diabetes.org.uk/about_us/news_landing_page/first-use-of-insulin-in-treatment-of-diabetes-88-years-ago-today.

14 **Realizing the implications:** Craig Idlebrook, "Selling a Lifetime of Insulin for $3," *Insulin Nation*, August 7, 2015, https://insulinnation.com/treatment/medicine-drugs/selling-lifetime-insulin/; "Inflation Calculator," Bank of Canada, accessed June 4, 2020, https://www.bankofcanada.ca/rates/related/inflation-calculator/; "CAD to USD Currency Converter," RBC Bank, accessed June 4, 2020, https://www.rbcbank.com/cgi-bin/tools/cadusd-foreign-exchange-calculator/start.cgi.

14 **The University of Toronto:** Idlebrook, "Selling a Lifetime of Insulin for $3," https://insulinnation.com/treatment/medicine-drugs/selling-lifetime-insulin/.

14 **Together, they make approximately $60,000:** Andrea Corley, interview with Amy Martyn, May 1, 2020.

15 **Then the Corleys discovered:** Andrea Corley, interview.

15 **Dozens of countries:** "The 2021 STC Health Index," GlobalResidenceIndex, accessed January 2, 2021, https://globalresidenceindex.com/hnwi-index/health-index/.

15 **Among the world's most developed countries:** *Health at a Glance 2019: OECD Indicators* (Paris: Organisation for Economic Co-operation and Development, 2020), figure 5.1, https://doi.org/10.1787/888934015619.

15 **Two countries:** *Health at a Glance 2019: OECD Indicators*, figure 5.1, https://doi.org/10.1787/888934015619; Aaron E. Carroll and Austin Frakt, "The Best Health Care System in the World: Which One Would

You Pick?" *New York Times*, September 18, 2017, https://www.nytimes.com/interactive/2017/09/18/upshot/best-health-care-system-country-bracket.html; Dylan Scott, "The Netherlands Has Universal Health Insurance—and It's All Private," *Vox*, January 17, 2020, https://www.vox.com/policy-and-politics/2020/1/17/21046874/netherlands-universal-health-insurance-private.

15 **In others, like Germany and Chile:** *Health at a Glance 2019: OECD Indicators*, figure 5.1, https://doi.org/10.1787/888934015619.

15 **Approximately three in five Americans:** Edward R. Berchick, Jessica C. Barnett, and Rachel D. Upton, *Health Insurance Coverage in the United States: 2018*, US Census Bureau, November 2019, p. 3, https://www.census.gov/content/dam/Census/library/publications/2019/demo/p60-267.pdf.

15 **Eventually, the Corley family:** Andrea Corley, interview.

16 **In 2017, Alec Smith:** Nicole Smith-Holt, interview with Amy Martyn, April 30, 2020.

16 **More than 90 percent:** Ryan Knox, "What Is Needed to Improve the Affordability of Insulin?," *T1International* (blog), December 16, 2015, https://www.t1international.com/blog/2015/12/16/how-do-we-improve-affordability-insulin/.

16 **On more than a dozen occasions:** Robert Langreth, "Hot Drugs Show Sharp Price Hikes in Shadow Market," *Bloomberg*, May 6, 2015, https://www.bloomberg.com/news/articles/2015-05-06/diabetes-drugs-compete-with-prices-that-rise-in-lockstep.

16 **In 2001, a vial of insulin:** Danielle K. Roberts, "The Deadly Cost of Insulin," *American Journal of Managed Care*, June 10, 2019, https://www.ajmc.com/contributor/danielle-roberts/2019/06/the-deadly-costs-of-insulin.

17 **A Yale University study:** Darby Herkert, Pavithra Vijayakumar, Jing Luo, et al., "Cost-Related Insulin Underuse among Patients with Diabetes," *JAMA Internal Medicine* 179, no. 1 (2019): 112–14, https://doi.org/10.1001/jamainternmed.2018.5008.

17 **Between 2017 and 2019:** "High Insulin Costs Are Killing Americans," Right Care Alliance, accessed April 30, 2020, https://rightcarealliance.org/actions/insulin/.

17 **Like Alec, Jesy Boyd:** Cindy Sherer Boyd, interview with Amy Martyn, May 2, 2020.

17 **But the following month:** Cindy Sherer Boyd, interview.

19 **In 1962, in his book:** Milton Friedman, "A Friedman Doctrine—The Social Responsibility of Business Is to Increase Its Profits," *New York Times*, September 13, 1970, https://www.nytimes.com/1970/09/13/archives/a-friedman-doctrine-the-social-responsibility-of-business-is-to.html.

21 **The United States had been the world leader:** Peri E. Arnold, "William Taft: Domestic Affairs," University of Virginia Miller Center, accessed July 20, 2020, https://millercenter.org/president/taft/domestic-affairs.

21 **In the aftermath of World War II:** Tim Wu, *The Curse of Bigness: Antitrust in the New Gilded Age* (New York: Columbia Global Reports, 2018), 79–80.

23 **In the United States:** Susan Lund, James Manyika, Liz Hilton Segel, André Dua, Bryan Hancock, Scott Rutherford, and Brent Macon, *The Future of Work in America: People and Places, Today and Tomorrow* (McKinsey Global Institute, July 11, 2019), https://www.mckinsey.com/featured-insights/future-of-work/the-future-of-work-in-america-people-and-places-today-and-tomorrow; Svet Smit, Tilman Tacke, Susan Lund, James Manyika, and Lea Thiel, *The Future of Work in Europe* (McKinsey Global Institute, June 10, 2020), https://www.mckinsey.com/featured-insights/future-of-work/the-future-of-work-in-europe.

23 **In 2019, the five hundred largest companies:** "Fortune 500," *Fortune*, accessed July 3, 2020, https://fortune.com/fortune500/.

23 **That year, the gross domestic product:** US Bureau of Economic Analysis, "Gross Domestic Product (GDP)," FRED, Federal Reserve Bank of St. Louis, accessed July 3, 2020, https://fred.stlouisfed.org/series/GDP.

24 **When the Fortune 500 list:** "Gross Domestic Product (GDP)," https://fred.stlouisfed.org/series/GDP; "Full List 1955," *Fortune*, accessed July 3, 2020, https://archive.fortune.com/magazines/fortune/fortune500_archive/full/1955/.

25 **Four airlines:** "Airline Domestic Market Share April 2019–March 2020," US Department of Transportation, Bureau of Transportation Statistics, accessed July 15, 2020, https://www.transtats.bts.gov/.

25 **This consolidation has reduced:** Jack Nicas, "Airline Consolidation Hits Smaller Cities Hardest," *Wall Street Journal*, September 10, 2015, https://www.wsj.com/articles/airline-consolidation-hits-smaller-cities-hardest-1441912457.

25 **provide cell service to nearly 70 percent:** "Wireless Subscriptions Market Share by Carrier in the U.S. from 1st Quarter 2011 to 3rd Quarter 2019," Statista, accessed July 6, 2020, https://www.statista.com/statistics/199359/market-share-of-wireless-carriers-in-the-us-by-subscriptions/.

25 **four in five American cable subscribers:** "2.5 Million Added Broadband in 2019," Leichtman Research Group, press release, March 5, 2020, https://www.leichtmanresearch.com/2-5-million-added-broadband-in-2019/.

25 **more than 70 percent of beer sales:** Wu, *The Curse of Bigness*, 117.

25 **more than 90 percent:** "Search Engine Market Share in 2020," Oberlo, accessed July 6, 2020, https://www.oberlo.com/statistics/search-engine-market-share.

25 **Matt Stoller's research has shown:** Matt Stoller, "A Land of Monopolists: From Portable Toilets to Mixed Martial Arts," *Big* (Substack), July 10, 2020, https://mattstoller.substack.com/p/a-land-of-monopolists-from

-portable; Matt Stoller, "Weird Monopolies and Roll-Ups: Horse Shows, School Spirit, Settlers of Catan, and Jigsaw Puzzles," *Big* (Substack), July 18, 2020, https://mattstoller.substack.com/p/weird-monopolies-and-roll-ups-horse.

26 **more than two hundred chickens:** Mark Eichmann, "Delaware's Growing Poultry Industry," WHYY, August 11, 2014, https://whyy.org/articles/delawares-growing-poultry-industry/.

26 **Drive around the peninsula:** Dave Layfield, interview with Jack Corrigan, July 17, 2020.

26 **In the aftermath of massive farm failures:** Sam Moore, "U.S. Farmers during the Great Depression," *Farm Collector*, November 2011, https://www.farmcollector.com/farm-life/u-s-farmers-during-great-depression; "Farming and Farm Income," US Department of Agriculture Economic Research Service, December 2, 2020, https://www.ers.usda.gov/data-products/ag-and-food-statistics-charting-the-essentials/farming-and-farm-income/.

26 **However, in the 1970s:** Bill Ganzel, "Farm Boom of the 1970s," Living History Farm, 2009, https://livinghistoryfarm.org/farminginthe70s/money_02.html.

27 **"Get big or get out":** Ganzel, "Farm Boom of the 1970s," https://livinghistoryfarm.org/farminginthe70s/money_02.html.

27 **At the time, Wisconsin senator:** B. Drummond Ayres Jr., "Rise of Corporate Farming a Worry to Rural America," *New York Times*, December 5, 1971, https://www.nytimes.com/1971/12/05/archives/rise-of-corporate-farming-a-worry-to-rural-america-rise-of-the.html.

27 **In 1979, the US:** Bill Ganzel, "Afghan Boycott," Living History Farm, 2009, https://livinghistoryfarm.org/farminginthe70s/money_06.html.

27 **By 1984, the total debt:** Kurt Lawton, "Taking a Look Back at the 1980s Farm Crisis and Its Impacts," *Farm Progress,* August 22, 2016, https://www.farmprogress.com/marketing/taking-look-back-1980s-farm-crisis-and-its-impacts.

27 **Thousands of small farmers:** Tom Philpott, "A Reflection on the Lasting Legacy of 1970s USDA Secretary Earl Butz," *Grist*, February 8, 2008, https://grist.org/article/the-butz-stops-here/.

27 **The consolidation continued:** Roberto Ferdman, "The Decline of the Small American Family Farm in One Chart," *Washington Post*, September 16, 2014, https://www.washingtonpost.com/news/wonk/wp/2014/09/16/the-decline-of-the-small-american-family-farm-in-one-chart/.

27 **The government does not:** "Animal Feeding Operations," US Department of Agriculture, accessed July 7, 2020, https://www.nrcs.usda.gov/wps/portal/nrcs/main/national/plantsanimals/livestock/afo/.

28 **Over the last sixty years:** "Per Capita Consumption of Poultry and Livestock, 1960 to Forecast 2021, in Pounds," National Chicken Council, June

2020, accessed July 19, 2020, https://www.nationalchickencouncil.org/about-the-industry/statistics/per-capita-consumption-of-poultry-and-livestock-1965-to-estimated-2012-in-pounds/.

28 **The Layfield family operated:** "Animal Feeding Operations," https://www.nrcs.usda.gov/wps/portal/nrcs/main/national/plantsanimals/livestock/afo/; Dave Layfield, interview.

29 **produced approximately half of the chicken:** Kim Souza, "Tyson Foods Maintains Its Top Ranking in Poultry Production," *Talk Business & Politics*, March 20, 2019, https://talkbusiness.net/2019/03/tyson-foods-maintains-its-top-ranking-in-poultry-production/.

30 **Under this model, the integrators:** Dave Layfield, interview.

30 **the integrators began:** Dave Layfield, interview.

31 **Then in 2019:** Dave Layfield, interview.

32 **In the 1950s, for every dollar:** Rhonda Skaggs, *The Future of Agriculture: Frequently Asked Questions* (Las Cruces: New Mexico State University, 2001), https://aces.nmsu.edu/pubs/research/economics/TR37/welcome.html; "Farmer's Share of the Food Dollar Falls to All-Time Low," National Farmers Union, press release, April 25, 2019, https://nfu.org/2019/04/25/farmers-share-of-the-food-dollar-falls-to-all-time-low/.

32 **Rural populations are shrinking:** Eduardo Porter, "The Hard Truths of Trying to 'Save' the Rural Economy," *New York Times*, December 14, 2018, https://www.nytimes.com/interactive/2018/12/14/opinion/rural-america-trump-decline.html; Brakkton Booker, "Report: Rural Poverty in America Is 'an Emergency,'" NPR, May 31, 2018, https://www.npr.org/2018/05/31/615578001/report-rural-poverty-in-america-is-an-emergency; "Americans in Rural Areas More Likely to Die by Suicide," *Centers for Disease Control and Prevention*, press release, October 5, 2017, https://www.cdc.gov/media/releases/2017/p1005-rural-suicide-rates.html.

32 **Senior executives saw their pay:** Brian Cheffins, "Stop Blaming Milton Friedman!," Harvard Law School Forum on Corporate Governance, April 16, 2020, https://corpgov.law.harvard.edu/2020/04/16/stop-blaming-milton-friedman/.

33 **between 1997 and 2014:** Gustavo Grullon, Yelena Larkin, and Roni Michaely, "Are US Industries Becoming More Concentrated?," *Review of Finance* 23, no. 4 (July 2019): 697–743, https://doi.org/10.1093/rof/rfz007.

33 **There were 66,847 corporate mergers:** "M&A in the United States," Thomson Financial, Institute for Mergers, Acquisitions and Alliances (IMAA) analysis, accessed July 2020, https://imaa-institute.org/m-and-a-us-united-states/#m-and-a-waves.

33 **In nearly every industry:** Jay Shambaugh, Ryan Nunn, Audrey Breitwieser, and Patrick Liu, "The State of Competition and Dynamism: Facts

about Concentration, Start-ups, and Related Policies," Brookings Institution, June 13, 2018, https://www.brookings.edu/research/the-state-of-competition-and-dynamism-facts-about-concentration-start-ups-and-related-policies/.

34 **The companies on the original Fortune 500:** "Full List 1955," *Fortune*, accessed July 3, 2020, https://archive.fortune.com/magazines/fortune/fortune500_archive/full/1955/; "CPI Inflation Calculator," US Bureau of Labor Statistics, accessed July 3, 2020, https://data.bls.gov/cgi-bin/cpicalc.pl?cost1=8265.7&year1=195512&year2=201912.

34 **$1.2 trillion in the black:** Shawn Tully, "Here's How Far Corporate Profits Could Tumble in 2020," *Fortune*, May 17, 2020, https://fortune.com/longform/corporate-profits-earnings-2020-outlook-fortune-500-companies-guidance/.

34 **In the United States, the top 1 percent:** "Compare Wealth Components across Groups," Board of Governors of the Federal Reserve System, accessed December 18, 2020, https://www.federalreserve.gov/releases/z1/dataviz/dfa/compare/chart/#quarter:124;series:Assets;demographic:networth;population:all;units:levels.

34 **Such price manipulation is legal:** Lenore Palladino, "The $1 Trillion Question: New Approaches to Regulating Stock Buybacks," *Yale Journal on Regulation*, November 8, 2019, https://www.yalejreg.com/bulletin/the-1-trillion-question-new-approaches-to-regulating-stock-buybacks-2/.

35 **$4.3 trillion on stock buybacks:** William Lazonick, Mustafa Erdem Sakinç, and Matt Hopkins, "Why Stock Buybacks Are Dangerous for the Economy," *Harvard Business Review*, January 7, 2020, https://hbr.org/2020/01/why-stock-buybacks-are-dangerous-for-the-economy.

35 **more than $49 billion in free cash flow:** van Doorn, "Opinion: Airlines and Boeing Want a Bailout," https://www.marketwatch.com/story/airlines-and-boeing-want-a-bailout-but-look-how-much-theyve-spent-on-stock-buybacks-2020-03-18.

36 **To put it bluntly:** Richard Feloni, "The Economist Joseph Stiglitz Explains Why He Thinks the Late Milton Friedman's Ideas Have Contributed to Rising Inequality in the US," *Business Insider*, March 13, 2018, https://www.businessinsider.com/joseph-stiglitz-milton-friedman-capitalism-theories-2018-3.

36 **In an interview with the *New York Times*:** "Greed Is Good. Except When It's Bad," *New York Times*, September 13, 2020, https://www.nytimes.com/2020/09/13/business/dealbook/milton-friedman-essay-anniversary.html.

36 **181 members of the Business Roundtable:** "Business Roundtable Redefines the Purpose of a Corporation to Promote 'An Economy That Serves All Americans,'" Business Roundtable, August 19, 2019, https://www.businessroundtable.org/business-roundtable-redefines-the-purpose-of-a-corporation-to-promote-an-economy-that-serves-all-americans.

37 **In January 2020, BlackRock committed:** Andrew Ross Sorkin, "BlackRock C.E.O. Larry Fink: Climate Crisis Will Reshape Finance," *New York Times*, January 14,2020,https://www.nytimes.com/2020/01/14/business/dealbook/larry-fink-blackrock-climate-change.html; Amy Harder, "JPMorgan Chase to Pull Support for Some Fossil Fuels," *Axios*, February 24, 2020, https://www.axios.com/jp-morgan-fossil-fuels-support-4b755a24-d57c-4d8b-8424-a401e994ec89.html.

37 **Hedge fund billionaire Daniel Loeb:** "Greed Is Good. Except When It's Bad," https://www.nytimes.com/2020/09/13/business/dealbook/milton-friedman-essay-anniversary.html.

38 **in the midst of the 2020 COVID-19 pandemic:** Carmen Reinicke, "Amazon Sees $83 billion in Market Cap Erased after Quarterly Profits Shrink," *Business Insider*, May 1, 2020, https://markets.businessinsider.com/news/stocks/amazon-stock-price-erasing-billions-market-value-post-earnings-coronavirus-2020-5-1029155310.

39 **CEOs are now speaking differently:** Sean Cao, Wei Jiang, Baozhong Yang, and Alan L. Zhang, "How to Talk When a Machine Is Listening: Corporate Disclosure in the Age of AI" (Working Paper 27950, National Bureau of Economic Research, Cambridge, MA, 2020), https://www.nber.org/system/files/working_papers/w27950/w27950.pdf.

40 **companies that are more rooted:** Hernando Cortina, *JUST Business, Better Margins* (New York: JUST Capital, June 2019), https://justcapital.com/wp-content/uploads/2019/06/JUSTCapital_JBBM_FullReport_06102019.pdf.

40 **If the US minimum wage:** Joe Sanberg (@JosephNSanberg), "It's Wednesday so you should know that if the minimum wage had increased at the rate of productivity since 1960, it would be $22.50. Instead, it's $7.25," Twitter, October 28, 2020, 8:26 a.m., https://twitter.com/JosephNSanberg/status/1321428054514626562.

41 **the global average temperature:** *WMO Statement on the State of the Global Climate in 2019* (Geneva: World Meteorological Organization, 2020), https://library.wmo.int/doc_num.php?explnum_id=10211.

41 **Absent "drastic action," the United Nations:** Brady Dennis, "In Bleak Report, U.N. Says Drastic Action Is Only Way to Avoid Worst Effects of Climate Change," *Washington Post*, November 26, 2019, https://www.washingtonpost.com/climate-environment/2019/11/26/bleak-report-un-says-drastic-action-is-only-way-avoid-worst-impacts-climate-change/.

42 **seven hundred thousand square miles of land:** Aristos Georgiou, "The Sea Is Rising at Such a Catastrophic Rate That We Could Lose 700,000 Square Miles of Land, Displacing 187 Million People," *Newsweek*, May 21, 2019, https://www.newsweek.com/sea-rising-700000-land-187-million-people-displaced-1431411.

42 **fashion is responsible for 10 percent:** "Putting the Brakes on Fast Fashion,"

United Nations Environment Programme, November 12, 2018, https://www.unenvironment.org/news-and-stories/story/putting-brakes-fast-fashion.

43 **It was the first "B Corp":** "B Lab," Patagonia, accessed June 3, 2020, https://www.patagonia.com/b-lab.html.

43 **eBay actually sued him:** eBay Domestic Holdings, Inc. v. Newmark et al., Civil Action No. 3705-CC (Del. Ch. Sept. 9, 2010).

43 **Chouinard and his comrades:** Cedar Wright, "The Wright Stuff: Dirtbagging Is Dead," *Climbing*, July 30, 2014, updated June 29, 2017, https://www.climbing.com/news/the-wright-stuff-dirtbagging-is-dead/.

43 **Chouinard started fashioning:** Nick Paumgarten, "Patagonia's Philosopher-King," *New Yorker*, September 12, 2016, https://www.newyorker.com/magazine/2016/09/19/patagonias-philosopher-king.

43 **He lived out of his car:** Paumgarten, "Patagonia's Philosopher-King," https://www.newyorker.com/magazine/2016/09/19/patagonias-philosopher-king.

44 **advises student entrepreneurs:** "CBEY Fellows, Business Leaders: Vincent Stanley," Yale Center for Business and the Environment, accessed June 3, 2020, https://cbey.yale.edu/our-community/vincent-stanley.

44 **In the early seventies:** Vincent Stanley, interview with Jack Corrigan, June 2, 2020.

44 **Chouinard discontinued his trademark pitons:** Paumgarten, "Patagonia's Philosopher-King," https://www.newyorker.com/magazine/2016/09/19/patagonias-philosopher-king.

44 **It was a risky move:** Stanley, interview.

44 **the company was selling chocks:** Matt Linderman, "On Writing: The 1972 Chouinard Catalog That Changed a Business—and Climbing—Forever," *Signalvnoise* (blog), February 15, 2011, https://signalvnoise.com/posts/2776-on-writing-the-1972-chouinard-catalog-that-changed-a-business-and-climbing-forever.

44 **Patagonia had opened a store:** Stanley, interview.

45 **require retooling Patagonia's whole supply chain:** Stanley, interview.

45 **In groups of forty:** Stanley, interview.

46 **As of June 2020:** Stanley, interview.

46 **During an interview around the launch:** Eun Kyung Kim, "Patagonia Founder to Shoppers: Don't Buy Clothes You Don't Need (Even Mine)," *Today*, April 21, 2015, https://www.today.com/news/patagonia-founder-refuse-buy-his-products-if-you-dont-need-t16491.

46 **when it sued the federal government:** Travis Andrews, "'The President Stole Your Land': Patagonia, REI Blast Trump on National Monument Rollbacks," *Washington Post*, December 5, 2017, https://www.washingtonpost.com/news/morning-mix/wp/2017/12/05/the-president-stole-your-land-patagonia-rei-blast-trump-on-national-monument-rollbacks/.

47 **In a LinkedIn post:** Rose Mercurio, "Our Urgent Gift to the Planet," LinkedIn, November 28, 2019, https://www.linkedin.com/pulse/our-urgent-gift-planet-rose-marcario/.

47 **Chouinard criticized his wealthy:** Paumgarten, "Patagonia's Philosopher-King," https://www.newyorker.com/magazine/2016/09/19/patagonias-philosopher-king.

47 **As of June 2020:** "R2 Fleece Jacket," Patagonia, accessed June 2020, https://www.patagonia.com/product/mens-r2-regulator-fleece-jacket/25139.html?dwvar_25139_color=RTSR&cgid=mens-fleece-technical.

47 **There is a reason that the company:** Paumgarten, "Patagonia's Philosopher-King," https://www.newyorker.com/magazine/2016/09/19/patagonias-philosopher-king.

47 **China is the world's largest:** "Prospects for the Textile and Clothing Industry in China, 2019 Market Report—ResearchAndMarkets.com," *Business Wire*, December 3, 2019, https://www.businesswire.com/news/home/20191203006080/en/Prospects-Textile-Clothing-Industry-China-2019-Market.

47 **A detailed investigation:** "Dirty Laundry," Greenpeace International, July 13, 2011, https://www.greenpeace.org/international/publication/7168/dirty-laundry/.

47 **six thousand environmental violations committed:** Susan Egan Keane, "How Clean Are Your Clothes? Pollution from China's Textile Industry," Natural Resources Defense Council, April 11, 2012, https://www.nrdc.org/experts/susan-egan-keane/how-clean-are-your-clothes-pollution-chinas-textile-industry.

48 **Their slogan, "Made in Earth":** "Sustainable Fashion Inspired by Millennia of Chinese Cultural History," *Euro News*, March 1, 2020, https://www.euronews.com/living/2020/03/01/sustainable-fashion-inspired-by-millenia-of-chinese-cultural-history.

48 **Icicle, along with its suppliers:** "Suppliers," Icicle, accessed June 2020, https://www.icicle.com.cn/en/suppliers/.

48 **That changed in 2019:** Anaïs Lerévérend, "Icicle to Open in Paris Its First Flagship Outside China," Fashion Network, April 19, 2019, https://ww.fashionnetwork.com/news/Icicle-to-open-in-paris-its-first-flagship-outside-china,1091104.html.

48 **According to a January 2020 report:** Nathalie Remy, Eveline Speelman, and Steven Swartz, "Style That's Sustainable: A New Fast-Fashion Formula," McKinsey & Company, October 20, 2016, https://www.mckinsey.com/business-functions/sustainability/our-insights/style-thats-sustainable-a-new-fast-fashion-formula.

48 **A 2017 study on consumer trends:** Ruonan Zheng, "How These Consumer Trends Will Affect Luxury Brands in China in 2018," *Jing Daily*,

November 1, 2017, https://jingdaily.com/consumer-trends-affect-luxury-brands-china-in-2018-mintel-report/.

49 **Walmart is the largest company:** "Global 500," *Fortune*, accessed June 30, 2020, https://fortune.com/global500/.

49 **With 2.1 million workers:** Kaityn Stimage, "The World's Largest Employers," WorldAtlas, February 15, 2018, https://www.worldatlas.com/articles/the-world-s-largest-employers.html.

49 **more than forty square miles:** "Walmart Inc. 2020 Annual Report," Walmart Inc., accessed June 30, 2020, https://s2.q4cdn.com/056532643/files/doc_financials/2020/ar/Walmart_2020_Annual_Report.pdf.

49 **If it were a country:** "Global 500," https://fortune.com/global500/; "GDP (current US$)," World Bank, accessed June 30, 2020, https://data.worldbank.org/indicator/NY.GDP.MKTP.CD?most_recent_value_desc=true.

49 **As Cory Doctorow wrote:** Cory Doctorow, "The People's Republic of Walmart: How Late-Stage Capitalism Gives Way to Early-Stage Fully Automated Luxury Communism," *BoingBoing*, March 5, 2019, https://boingboing.net/2019/03/05/walmart-without-capitalism.html.

50 **Walmart executives committed:** Marc Gunther, "The Green Machine," *Fortune*, July 31, 2006, https://archive.fortune.com/magazines/fortune/fortune_archive/2006/08/07/8382593/index.htm.

50 **Under the Toxic Substances Control Act:** Sheldon Krimsky, "The Unsteady State and Inertia of Chemical Regulation under the US Toxic Substances Control Act," *PLOS Biology* 15, no. 12 (2017), https://doi.org/10.1371/journal.pbio.2002404.

50 **In 2007, Walmart announced:** "Wal-Mart to Sell Only Concentrated Products in Liquid Laundry Detergent Category by May 2008," Walmart, September 26, 2007, https://corporate.walmart.com/newsroom/2007/09/26/wal-mart-to-sell-only-concentrated-products-in-liquid-laundry-detergent-category-by-may-2008.

50 **400 million gallons of water:** "Wal-Mart Completes Goal to Sell Only Concentrated Liquid Laundry Detergent," Walmart, May 29, 2008, https://corporate.walmart.com/newsroom/2008/05/29/wal-mart-completes-goal-to-sell-only-concentrated-liquid-laundry-detergent.

50 **Soon, the rest of the market:** Kerry Capell, "Unilever's Laundry Biz Is Greener, and Growing," *Bloomberg*, December 24, 2008, https://www.bloomberg.com/news/articles/2008-12-24/unilevers-laundry-biz-is-greener-and-growingbusinessweek-business-news-stock-market-and-financial-advice.

50 **In 2013, Walmart announced:** Randi Abrams-Caras, "Walmart: Two Steps Forward, One Step Back?," Safer Chemicals, Healthy Families, October 3, 2013, https://saferchemicals.org/2013/10/03/walmart-two-steps-forward-one-step-back/.

50 **In 2017, Walmart became:** Mike Schade, "Walmart Becomes First Retailer in Nation to Evaluate Its Chemical Footprint," Safer Chemicals, Healthy Families, August 2, 2017, https://saferchemicals.org/2017/08/02/walmart-becomes-first-retailer-to-evaluate-its-chemical-footprint/.

51 **The nonprofit group Safer Chemicals:** "New Report Reveals Top Retailers Making Major Chemical Safety Advances," Safer Chemicals, Healthy Families, November 19, 2019, https://saferchemicals.org/2019/11/19/new-report-reveals-top-retailers-making-major-chemical-safety-advances/.

51 **working with suppliers to reduce:** *2018 Global Responsibility Report*, Walmart, accessed June 30, 2020, https://corporate.walmart.com/media-library/document/2018-global-responsibility-report/_proxyDocument?id=00000170-ac54-d808-a9f1-ac7e9d160000.

51 **Walmart has also made notable strides:** Ian Graber-Stiehl, "Behind the Hype of Walmart's Sustainability Efforts," Gizmodo, October 23, 2018, https://earther.gizmodo.com/behind-the-hype-of-walmart-s-sustainability-efforts-1829931295; Andrew Spicer and David Graham Hyatt, "Walmart Tried to Make Sustainability Affordable. Here's What Happened," *Business Journals*, August 18, 2018, https://www.bizjournals.com/bizjournals/news/2018/08/13/walmart-tried-to-make-sustainability-affordable.html.

52 **Journalist Matt Taibbi famously:** Matt Taibbi, "The Great American Bubble Machine," *Rolling Stone*, April 5, 2010, https://www.rollingstone.com/politics/politics-news/the-great-american-bubble-machine-195229/.

52 **In 2018 and 2019, some sixty companies:** Claire Zillman, "The U.S. Doesn't Mandate Diverse Boardrooms—but Now Goldman Sachs Does," *Fortune*, January 23, 2020, https://fortune.com/2020/01/23/goldman-sachs-board-gender-quota-david-solomon/.

53 **Solomon fought to ensure:** Jena McGregor, "Goldman Sachs Says It Wants Half of Its Entry-Level Recruits to Be Women," *Washington Post*, March 18, 2019, https://www.washingtonpost.com/business/2019/03/18/goldman-sachs-says-it-wants-half-its-entry-level-recruits-be-women/.

53 **Certain energy companies:** Gregg Lemkau, interview with Alec Ross, June 2, 2020. All interviews not otherwise cited were conducted by Alec Ross in 2020.

54 **Women fill just 20 percent:** Subodh Mishra, "U.S. Board Diversity Trends in 2019," Harvard Law School Forum on Corporate Governance, June 18, 2019, https://corpgov.law.harvard.edu/2019/06/18/u-s-board-diversity-trends-in-2019/.

55 **In 2020, Jeff Bezos:** Karen Weise, "Jeff Bezos Commits $10 Billion to Address Climate Change," *New York Times*, February 17, 2020, https://www.nytimes.com/2020/02/17/technology/jeff-bezos-climate-change-earth-fund.html.

55 **Bill Gates has committed his fortune:** Matthew Brown, "Fact Check: Bill

Gates Has Given Over $50 Billion to Charitable Causes over Career," *USA Today*, June 11, 2020, https://www.usatoday.com/story/news/factcheck/2020/06/11/fact-check-bill-gates-has-given-over-50-billion-charitable-causes/3169864001/.

56 **One of the criticisms:** Steve Denning, "Why Stakeholder Capitalism Will Fail," *Forbes*, January 5, 2020, https://www.forbes.com/sites/stevedenning/2020/01/05/why-stakeholder-capitalism-will-fail/#36019f7b785a.

58 **Former Bank of England governor:** Kalyeena Makortoff, "Mark Carney Says Banks Should Link Executive Pay to Paris Climate Goals," *Guardian*, October 13, 2020, https://www.theguardian.com/business/2020/oct/13/mark-carney-says-banks-should-link-executive-pay-to-paris-climate-goals.

2: THE GOVERNMENT: BILLIONS OF PEOPLE ARE GOVERNED MORE BY COMPANIES THAN BY COUNTRIES

60 **With 150-mile-per-hour winds:** Robinson Meyer, "What's Happening with the Relief Effort in Puerto Rico?," *Atlantic*, October 4, 2017, https://www.theatlantic.com/science/archive/2017/10/what-happened-in-puerto-rico-a-timeline-of-hurricane-maria/541956/.

60 **The island's power grid and communication networks:** John Bacon, "Why Puerto Rico Faces a Monumental Recovery Effort," *USA Today*, September 26, 2017, https://www.usatoday.com/story/news/nation/2017/09/26/why-puerto-rico-faces-monumental-recovery-effort/703515001/#; Meyer, "What's Happening with the Relief Effort in Puerto Rico?," https://www.theatlantic.com/science/archive/2017/10/what-happened-in-puerto-rico-a-timeline-of-hurricane-maria/541956/; Brian Resnick, "Why Hurricane Maria Is Such a Nightmare for Puerto Rico," *Vox*, September 22, 2017, https://www.vox.com/science-and-health/2017/9/21/16345176/hurricane-maria-2017-puerto-rico-san-juan-meteorology-wind-rain-power.

60 **resulting in thousands:** Vann Newkirk II, "A Year after Hurricane Maria, Puerto Rico Finally Knows How Many People Died," *Atlantic*, August 28, 2018, https://www.theatlantic.com/politics/archive/2018/08/puerto-rico-death-toll-hurricane-maria/568822/.

61 **It took four days:** *2017 Hurricane Season FEMA After-Action Report*, US Federal Emergency Management Agency, July 12, 2018, https://www.fema.gov/sites/default/files/2020-08/fema_hurricane-season-after-action-report_2017.pdf.

61 **Senior government officials did not:** Abby Phillip, Ed O'Keefe, Nick Miroff, and Damian Paletta, "Lost Weekend: How Trump's Time at His Golf Club Hurt the Response to Maria," *Washington Post*, September 29, 2017, https://www.washingtonpost.com/politics/lost-weekend-how

-trumps-time-at-his-golf-club-hurt-the-response-to-maria/2017/09/29/ce92ed0a-a522-11e7-8c37-e1d99ad6aa22_story.html.

61 **It took eight days:** Alice Thomas, *Keeping Faith with Our Fellow Americans: Meeting the Urgent Needs of Hurricane Maria Survivors in Puerto Rico* (Washington, DC: Refugees International, 2017), https://static1.squarespace.com/static/506c8ea1e4b01d9450dd53f5/t/5a37d01bec212d3032461511/1513607203969/RI_Puerto+Rico_Advocacy+Report+R3.pdf; Meyer, "What's Happening with the Relief Effort in Puerto Rico?," https://www.theatlantic.com/science/archive/2017/10/what-happened-in-puerto-rico-a-timeline-of-hurricane-maria/541956/.

61 **The ship was equipped:** Frances Robles and Sheri Fink, "Amid Puerto Rico Disaster, Hospital Ship Admitted Just 6 Patients a Day," *New York Times*, December 6, 2017, https://www.nytimes.com/2017/12/06/us/puerto-rico-hurricane-maria-hospital-ship.html.

61 **By the two-week mark:** Meyer, "What's Happening with the Relief Effort in Puerto Rico?," https://www.theatlantic.com/science/archive/2017/10/what-happened-in-puerto-rico-a-timeline-of-hurricane-maria/541956/; Thomas, *Keeping Faith with Our Fellow Americans,* https://static1.squarespace.com/static/506c8ea1e4b01d9450dd53f5/t/5a37d01bec212d3032461511/1513607203969/RI_Puerto+Rico_Advocacy+Report+R3.pdf.

61 **The government was slow to clear:** José Andrés and Richard Wolffe, *We Fed an Island: The True Story of Rebuilding Puerto Rico, One Meal at a Time* (New York: HarperCollins, 2018).

61 **Weeks after the storm:** Meyer, "What's Happening with the Relief Effort in Puerto Rico?," https://www.theatlantic.com/science/archive/2017/10/what-happened-in-puerto-rico-a-timeline-of-hurricane-maria/541956/; Daniella Silva and Suzanne Gamboa, "Puerto Rico's Hospitals Still in Triage Mode, 2 Weeks after Maria," *NBC News*, October 4, 2017, https://www.nbcnews.com/storyline/puerto-rico-crisis/puerto-rico-s-hospitals-still-triage-mode-2-weeks-after-n807406.

61 **One cardiovascular surgeon in San Juan:** Andrés and Wolffe, *We Fed an Island*, 33.

61 **The island's power grid:** Francis Robles, "Puerto Rico Spent 11 Months Turning the Power Back On. They Finally Got to Her," *New York Times*, August 14, 2018, https://www.nytimes.com/2018/08/14/us/puerto-rico-electricity-power.html; Patricia Mazzei and Alejandra Rosa, "Hurricane Maria, 2 Years Later: 'We Want Another Puerto Rico,'" *New York Times*, September 20, 2019, https://www.nytimes.com/2019/09/20/us/puerto-rico-hurricane-maria.html.

62 **Some 3.2 million people:** "State Population Totals and Components of Change: 2010–2019," *US Census Bureau*, accessed June 16, 2020, https://www.census.gov/data/tables/time-series/demo/popest/2010s-state-total.html.

62 **almost half of all Americans:** Kyle Dropp and Brendan Nyhan, "Nearly Half of Americans Don't Know Puerto Ricans Are Fellow Citizens," *New York Times*, September 26, 2017, https://www.nytimes.com/2017/09/26/upshot/nearly-half-of-americans-dont-know-people-in-puerto-ricoans-are-fellow-citizens.html.

62 **Had Maria hit the mainland:** "Google Trends Data for the US: Which Hurricane Received the Most Attention?," Puerto Rico Data Lab, October 27, 2017, https://prdatalab.wordpress.com/2017/10/27/google-trends-data-for-the-us-which-hurricane-received-the-most-attention/; Danny Vinik, "How Trump Favored Texas over Puerto Rico," *Politico*, March 27, 2018, https://www.politico.com/story/2018/03/27/donald-trump-fema-hurricane-maria-response-480557.

62 **Beginning in the 1950s:** John Schoen, "Here's How an Obscure Tax Change Sank Puerto Rico's Economy," CNBC, September 26, 2017, https://www.cnbc.com/2017/09/26/heres-how-an-obscure-tax-change-sank-puerto-ricos-economy.html.

62 **after the tax break was repealed:** Laura Sullivan, "How Puerto Rico's Debt Created a Perfect Storm before the Storm," NPR, May 2, 2018, https://www.npr.org/2018/05/02/607032585/how-puerto-ricos-debt-created-a-perfect-storm-before-the-storm.

62 **They did not have enough personnel:** Francis Robles, "FEMA Was Sorely Unprepared for Puerto Rico Hurricane, Report Says," *New York Times*, July 12, 2018, https://www.nytimes.com/2018/07/12/us/fema-puerto-rico-maria.html.

63 **His plane was only the second:** Andrés and Wolffe, *We Fed an Island*, 11–20.

64 **After Hurricane Maria hit Puerto Rico:** Andrés and Wolffe, *We Fed an Island*, 23, 28.

64 **The next day, they prepared:** Andrés and Wolffe, *We Fed an Island*, 37.

64 **Within a week, he and his team:** Andrés and Wolffe, *We Fed an Island*, 91.

64 **The agency later admitted:** Adrian Carrasquillo, "Chef José Andrés and the Trump Administration Are Fighting over Puerto Rico," *Buzzfeed News*, November 6, 2017, https://www.buzzfeednews.com/article/adriancarrasquillo/chef-jose-andres-and-the-trump-administration-are-fighting.

64 **more than 146,000 meals per day:** Andrés and Wolffe, *We Fed an Island*, 218.

65 **a federal agency with a $20 billion:** *FEMA Human Capital Strategic Plan FY 2016–2020*, US Federal Emergency Management Agency, accessed June 16, 2020, https://www.fema.gov/media-library-data/1465232797001-0884912c49ec300ced75c391a0dc81dc/HumanCap_Final_Version.pdf.

65 **For nearly a year after Hurricane Maria:** Arelis R. Hernández and Laurie McGinley, "Harvard Study Estimates Thousands Died in Puerto Rico

because of Hurricane Maria," *Washington Post*, May 29, 2018, https://www.washingtonpost.com/national/harvard-study-estimates-thousands-died-in-puerto-rico-due-to-hurricane-maria/2018/05/29/1a82503a-6070-11e8-a4a4-c070ef53f315_story.html.

65 **on par with the 9/11 terrorist attacks:** Jason Silverstein, "Hurricane Maria Is Now One of the Deadliest Disasters in U.S. History," *CBS News*, August 28, 2018, https://www.cbsnews.com/news/puerto-rico-hurricane-maria-is-now-one-of-the-deadliest-disasters-in-u-s-history/; "Casualties and Damage after the 1906 Earthquake," US Geological Survey, accessed June 18, 2020, https://earthquake.usgs.gov/earthquakes/events/1906calif/18april/casualties.php.

65 **The vast majority of those deaths:** "Puerto Rico Increases Hurricane Maria Death Toll to 2,975," *BBC News*, August 29, 2018, https://www.bbc.com/news/world-us-canada-45338080.

65 **FEMA officials acknowledged:** Robles, "FEMA Was Sorely Unprepared for Puerto Rico Hurricane, Report Says," https://www.nytimes.com/2018/07/12/us/fema-puerto-rico-maria.html.

70 **Some experts think we need:** Jeff Lewis, "Polarization in Congress," Voteview, June 4, 2020, https://www.voteview.com/articles/party_polarization.

70 **As recently as the early 1990s:** Christopher Ingraham, "A Stunning Visualization of Our Divided Congress," *Washington Post*, April 23, 2015, https://www.washingtonpost.com/news/wonk/wp/2015/04/23/a-stunning-visualization-of-our-divided-congress/.

70 **both parties have become more evenly matched:** Ezra Klein, "The Political Scientist Donald Trump Should Read," *Vox*, January 24, 2019, https://www.vox.com/policy-and-politics/2019/1/24/18193523/donald-trump-wall-shutdown-congress-polarization-frances-lee.

71 **Republicans used their control to enact:** David Rogers, "Politico Analysis: At $2.3 Trillion Cost, Trump Tax Cuts Leave Big Gap," *Politico*, February 28, 2018, https://www.politico.com/story/2018/02/28/tax-cuts-trump-gop-analysis-430781.

71 **Not one of the 237 Democrats:** "Republicans Pass Historic Tax Cuts without a Single Democratic Vote," *Axios*, December 20, 2017, https://www.axios.com/republicans-pass-historic-tax-cuts-without-a-single-democratic-vote-1515110718-8cdf005c-c1c9-481a-975b-72336765ebe4.html.

71 **obstruct the other:** Ezra Klein, "Why We Can't Build," *Vox*, April 22, 2020, https://www.vox.com/2020/4/22/21228469/marc-andreessen-build-government-coronavirus.

71 **"The delegation of powers to different political actors":** Francis Fukuyama, "America in Decay," *Foreign Affairs*, Sept./Oct. 2014, http://cf.linnbenton

.edu/artcom/social_science/clarkd/upload/Fukuyama,%20America%20 in%20Decay.pdf.

72 **"For any particular problem we have":** Steven M. Teles, *Kludgeocracy: The American Way of Policy* (Washington, DC: New America Foundation, 2012), https://static.newamerica.org/attachments/4209-kludgeocracy-the-american-way-of-policy/Teles_Steven_Kludgeocracy_NAF_Dec2012.d8a805aa40e34bca9e2fecb018a3dcb0.pdf.

72 **Between 2010 and 2020:** Robert Frank, "How Congress Made It Easier to Avoid the IRS," CNBC, January 14, 2020, https://www.cnbc.com/2020/01/14/why-congress-made-it-easier-to-avoid-the-irs.html; Paul Kiel and Jesse Eisinger, "How the IRS Was Gutted," *ProPublica*, December 11, 2018, https://www.propublica.org/article/how-the-irs-was-gutted; *SOI Tax Stats—IRS Data Book*, Internal Revenue Service, May 20, 2019, https://www.irs.gov/pub/irs-pdf/p55b.pdf.

72 **Audit rates for individuals making:** Frank, "How Congress Made It Easier to Avoid the IRS," https://www.cnbc.com/2020/01/14/why-congress-made-it-easier-to-avoid-the-irs.htm; *SOI Tax Stats—IRS Data Book*, May 20, 2019, https://www.irs.gov/pub/irs-pdf/p55b.pdf.

72 **people making less than $20,000:** Paul Kiel, "It's Getting Worse: The IRS Now Audits Poor Americans at about the Same Rate as the Top 1%," *ProPublica*, May 30, 2019, https://www.propublica.org/article/irs-now-audits-poor-americans-at-about-the-same-rate-as-the-top-1-percent.

72 **the IRS performed annual audits:** Paul Kiel, "The IRS Decided to Get Tough against Microsoft. Microsoft Got Tougher," *ProPublica*, January 22, 2020, https://www.propublica.org/article/the-irs-decided-to-get-tough-against-microsoft-microsoft-got-tougher.

73 **The Environmental Protection Agency employed:** "EPA's Budget and Spending," US Environmental Protection Agency, accessed June 25, 2020, https://www.epa.gov/planandbudget/budget.

73 **The Federal Trade Commission, the US:** *Fiscal Year 2021 Congressional Budget Justification*, US Federal Trade Commission, accessed June 25, 2020, https://www.ftc.gov/system/files/documents/reports/fy-2021-congressional-budget-justification/fy_2021_cbj_final.pdf; *Fiscal Year 2011 Congressional Budget Justification Summary*, US Federal Trade Commission, accessed June 25, 2020, https://www.ftc.gov/sites/default/files/documents/reports_annual/fy-2011-congressional-budget-justification-summary/budgetsummary11_1.pdf; "CPI Inflation Calculator," US Bureau of Labor Statistics, accessed June 25, 2020, https://www.bls.gov/data/inflation_calculator.htm.

73 **The Erie Canal linked:** Tom Huntington, "America's Top 10 Public Works Projects," *Invention & Technology*, Winter 2009, https://www.inventionandtech.com/content/america%E2%80%99s-top-10-public

-works-projects-2; "About This Place—History," I&M Canal National Heritage Area, accessed June 29, 2020, https://iandmcanal.org/about-this-place-history/; "Transcontinental Railroad," History.com, September 11, 2019, https://www.history.com/topics/inventions/transcontinental-railroad.

75 **The presentation was led by Aaron Maniam:** "Aaron Maniam," University of Oxford, Blavatnik School of Government, accessed June 3, 2020, https://www.bsg.ox.ac.uk/people/aaron-maniam; "Aaron Maniam (b. 1979)," Poetry.sg, accessed June 3, 2020, http://www.poetry.sg/aaron-maniam-bio.

75 **The formula includes pay:** John Pennington, "Are Singapore's Civil Servants Overpaid and Overprotected," *ASEAN Today*, October 31, 2017, https://www.aseantoday.com/2017/10/are-singapores-civil-servants-overpaid-and-overprotected/; Joanne Poh, "Singapore Civil Service—The Ins and Outs of the Iron Rice Bowl," *MoneySmart* (blog), December 4, 2018, https://blog.moneysmart.sg/career/singapore-civil-service-iron-rice-bowl/.

75 **a compensated formula ensures:** *Salaries for a Capable and Committed Government*, Government of Singapore, December 30, 2011, https://www.psd.gov.sg/docs/default-source/default-document-library/white-paper---salaries-for-a-capable-and-committed-govt.pdf; Martino Tan and Sulaiman Daud, "Breakdown of Entry-Level S'pore Ministerial Salaries: 13 (fixed) + 3 + 3 + 1 Month Bonus = S$1.1m," Mothership.sg, October 1, 2018, https://mothership.sg/2018/10/minister-salary-parliament/.

76 **This dynamic is especially pronounced:** *The Hill Staffer's Reality*, Congressional Management Foundation, 2015, accessed June 3, 2020, https://www.apaservices.org/practice/advocacy/state/leadership/hill-staffers-reality.pdf; *House of Representatives Compensation and Diversity Study Report: Member, Committee, and Leadership Offices*, US House of Representatives, 2019, accessed June 3, 2020, https://www.house.gov/sites/default/files/uploads/documents/2019_house_compdiversitystudy_finalreport_membcommlead.pdf.

77 **The term—and practice of:** "A Lobbyist by Any Other Name?," NPR, January 22, 2016, https://www.npr.org/templates/story/story.php?storyId=5167187.

77 **the industry grew more prominent and professionalized:** "Lobbyists" (US Senate, in print in Robert C. Byrd, *The Senate, 1789–1989*, vol. 2, pp. 491–508), accessed June 26, 2020, https://www.senate.gov/legislative/common/briefing/Byrd_History_Lobbying.htm.

78 **During the mid-20th century:** Phillip Wallach, "America's Lobbying Addiction," Brookings Institution, April 13, 2015, https://www.brookings.edu/blog/fixgov/2015/04/13/americas-lobbying-addiction/.

78 **future Supreme Court Justice Lewis Powell Jr. noted:** Lee Drutman, "How

Corporate Lobbyists Conquered American Democracy," *Atlantic*, April 20, 2015, https://www.theatlantic.com/business/archive/2015/04/how-corporate-lobbyists-conquered-american-democracy/390822/.

78 **In 1972, two anti-labor groups:** Jerome L. Himmelstein, *To the Right: The Transformation of American Conservatism* (Berkeley: University of California Press, 1990), 140, https://publishing.cdlib.org/ucpressebooks/view?docId=ft5h4nb372&chunk.id=d0e2257&toc.depth=100&toc.id=d0e2246&brand=ucpress.

78 **The group worked alongside a growing army:** Drutman, "How Corporate Lobbyists Conquered American Democracy," https://www.theatlantic.com/business/archive/2015/04/how-corporate-lobbyists-conquered-american-democracy/390822/.

78 **After logging a few early victories:** Wallach, "America's Lobbying Addiction," https://www.brookings.edu/blog/fixgov/2015/04/13/americas-lobbying-addiction/.

78 **In 1975, federal lobbyists collectively:** "Lobbying Data Summary," Center for Responsive Politics, accessed May 31, 2020, https://www.opensecrets.org/federal-lobbying/summary?inflate=Y; Robert Kaiser, "Citizen K Street," *Washington Post*, accessed May 31, 2020, https://web.archive.org/web/20120524031659/http://blog.washingtonpost.com/citizen-k-street/chapters/introduction/.

79 **Approximately a quarter of the lawmakers:** "Revolving Door," Center for Responsive Politics, accessed June 26, 2020, https://www.opensecrets.org/revolving/.

79 **For every dollar that public interest groups:** "Business, Labor & Ideological Split in Lobbying Data," Center for Responsive Politics, accessed June 28, 2020, https://www.opensecrets.org/federal-lobbying/business-labor-ideological.

79 **Reporters found that seventy of the eighty-five lines:** Erika Eichelberger, "House Passes Bill Written by Citigroup Lobbyists," *Mother Jones*, October 31, 2013, https://www.motherjones.com/politics/2013/10/citigroup-bill-passes-house/.

79 **more than 2,100 state laws:** Rob O'Dell and Nick Penzenstadler, "You Elected Them to Write New Laws. They're Letting Corporations Do It Instead," Center for Public Integrity, April 4, 2019, https://publicintegrity.org/politics/state-politics/copy-paste-legislate/you-elected-them-to-write-new-laws-theyre-letting-corporations-do-it-instead/.

80 **With more than eighty clients:** "Top Lobbyists," Center for Responsive Politics, accessed June 28, 2020, https://www.opensecrets.org/federal-lobbying/top-lobbyists.

80 **the number of registered lobbyists in Washington:** "Lobbying Data Summary," https://www.opensecrets.org/federal-lobbying/summary?inflate=Y.

81 **Outside groups spent a total of $680 million:** "Total Outside Spending

by Election Cycle, Excluding Party Committees," Center for Responsive Politics, accessed May 31, 2020, https://www.opensecrets.org/outsidespending/cycle_tots.php?cycle=2020&view=A&chart=N#summ.

82 **Dark money groups spent nearly $1 billion:** Anna Massoglia, "'Dark Money' Groups Steering Millions to Super PACs in 2020 Elections," Center for Responsive Politics, February 7, 2020, https://www.opensecrets.org/news/2020/02/dark-money-steers-millions-to-super-pacs-2020/.

82 **83 percent of Senate races and 89 percent of House races:** "Did Money Win?," Center for Responsive Politics, accessed June 28, 2020, https://www.opensecrets.org/elections-overview/winning-vs-spending?chamber=S&cycle=2018.

83 **In 2018, just 225,000:** "Donor Demographics," Center for Responsive Politics, accessed June 28, 2020, https://www.opensecrets.org/elections-overview/donor-demographics?cycle=2018&display=A; "Cost of Election," Center for Responsive Politics, accessed June 28, 2020, https://www.opensecrets.org/elections-overview/cost-of-election.

83 **After comparing public opinion and public policy:** Martin Gilens and Benjamin I. Page, "Testing Theories of American Politics: Elites, Interest Groups, and Average Citizens," *Perspectives on Politics* 12, no. 3 (2014): 564–81, https://doi.org/10.1017/S1537592714001595.

85 **The Roman Empire ran a pension program:** *Encyclopaedia Britannica Online*, s.v. "Aerarium," by E. Badian, accessed July 14, 2020, https://www.britannica.com/topic/aerarium.

85 **During the Tang dynasty:** Sheng Hui-lian, *Pension Schemes during Tang and Five Dynasties in Ancient China* (Beijing: Beijing Institute of Cultural Relics, January 2012), http://en.cnki.com.cn/Article_en/CJFDTotal-ZSDB201201006.htm.

85 **These programs were so successful:** "[Archive] When Islam eradicated Poverty: Umar b. Abdul Aziz & Zakat," National Zakat Foundation, accessed July 14, 2020, https://nzf.org.uk/news/when-islam-eradicated-poverty-umar-b-abdul-aziz-zakat/.

86 **Unlike many other developed countries:** Ganesh Sitaraman and Anne L. Alstott, *The Public Option: How to Expand Freedom, Increase Opportunity, and Promote Equality* (Cambridge, MA: Harvard University Press, 2019), 12.

86 **The private model emerged out of a quirk:** Aaron E. Carroll, "The Real Reason the U.S. Has Employer-Sponsored Health Insurance," *New York Times*, September 5, 2017, https://www.nytimes.com/2017/09/05/upshot/the-real-reason-the-us-has-employer-sponsored-health-insurance.html.

86 **Between 2002 and 2018:** James Manyika, Anu Madgavkar, Tilman Tacke, Jonathan Woetzel, Sven Smit, and Abdulla Abdulaal, *The Social Contract in the 21st Century: Outcomes So Far for Workers, Consumers, and*

Savers in Advanced Economies, McKinsey Global Institute, February 2020, https://www.mckinsey.com/~/media/McKinsey/Industries/Social Sector/Our Insights/The social contract in the 21st century/MGI-The-social-contract-in-the-21st-century-Full-report-final.pdf.

86 **These growing expenses disproportionately:** Bourree Lam, "The Surging Cost of Basic Needs," *Atlantic*, June 2, 2016, https://www.theatlantic.com/business/archive/2016/06/household-basic-spending/485330/.

86 **researchers found that 40 percent of American households:** Natasha Bach, "Millions of Americans Are One Missed Paycheck away from Poverty, Report Says," *Fortune*, January 29, 2019, https://fortune.com/2019/01/29/americans-liquid-asset-poor-propserity-now-report/; "A Profile of the Working Poor, 2017," US Bureau of Labor Statistics, April 2019, https://www.bls.gov/opub/reports/working-poor/2017/home.htm.

87 **Workers who received welfare payments:** Henry Aaron, "The Social Safety Net: The Gaps That COVID-19 Spotlights," Brookings Institution, June 23, 2020, https://www.brookings.edu/blog/up-front/2020/06/23/the-social-safety-net-the-gaps-that-covid-19-spotlights/.

88 **transformed China from an agrarian state:** "Poverty Headcount Ratio at $1.90 a Day (2011 PPP) (% of Population)—World, China," World Bank Group, accessed July 20, 2020, https://data.worldbank.org/indicator/SI.POV.DDAY?end=2015&locations=1W-CN&start=1981&view=chart.

3: THE WORKERS

90 **On Wednesday, December 30, 1936:** Timothy P. Lynch, "How Did Workers Win the Right to Form a Union and Go on Strike?," History News Network, George Washington University, September 3, 2017, https://historynewsnetwork.org/article/166796; "Sit-Down Strike Begins in Flint," This Day in History: December 30, 1936, History.com, December 27, 2019, https://www.history.com/this-day-in-history/sit-down-strike-begins-in-flint; Erik de Gier, "Paradise Lost Revisited: GM and the UAW in Historical Perspective" (working paper, Cornell University, ILR School, 2010), http://digitalcommons.ilr.cornell.edu/intlvf/30.

90 **Surrounded by the half-built bodies:** Erin Blakemore, "The 1936 Strike That Brought America's Most Powerful Automaker to Its Knees," History.com, September 17, 2019, https://www.history.com/news/flint-sit-down-strike-general-motors-uaw; David D. Jackson, "The Fisher Body Flint, MI Plant #1 in World War Two," The American Automobile History in World War Two, November 7, 2019, http://usautoindustryworldwartwo.com/Fisher%20Body/fisherbodyflintone.htm; "The GM Strike That Changed the U.S. Workplace," *Detroit News*, July 14, 2018, https://www.detroitnews.com/picture-gallery/news/local/michigan-history/2018/07/14/the-gm-strike-that-changed-the-us-workplace/36797583/.

91 **GM got a court order:** Blakemore, "The 1936 Strike That Brought America's Most Powerful Automaker to Its Knees," https://www.history.com/news/flint-sit-down-strike-general-motors-uaw.

91 **The heat shuddered off on January 11:** Vivian Baulch and Patricia Zacharias, "The Historic 1936–37 Flint Auto Plant Strikes," *Detroit News*, June 23, 1997, https://wayback.archive-it.org/all/20120726124441/http://apps.detnews.com/apps/history/index.php?id=115.

91 **After the clash, Michigan's governor deployed:** Blakemore, "The 1936 Strike That Brought America's Most Powerful Automaker to Its Knees," https://www.history.com/news/flint-sit-down-strike-general-motors-uaw.

91 **After some 136,000 GM employees:** Blakemore, "The 1936 Strike That Brought America's Most Powerful Automaker to Its Knees," https://www.history.com/news/flint-sit-down-strike-general-motors-uaw.

91 **The GM sit-down strike was called:** Sidney Fine, *Sit-Down: The General Motors Strike of 1936–1937* (Ann Arbor: University of Michigan Press, 1969), 341.

91 **workers in Detroit launched eighty-seven sit-down strikes:** Ertan Tuncer, "The Flint, Michigan, Sit-Down Strike (1936–37)," Library of Congress, July 2012, https://www.loc.gov/rr/business/businesshistory/February/flint.html.

91 **Between 1934 and 1943, the proportion of the US workforce:** Gerald Mayer, *Union Membership Trends in the United States* (Washington, DC: Congressional Research Service, 2004), https://core.ac.uk/download/pdf/144981482.pdf.

92 **After signing the law, President Franklin D. Roosevelt:** Leroy Chatfield, "How to Start a Union When You Don't Have the Right," *Yes! Magazine*, December 26, 2019, https://www.yesmagazine.org/economy/2019/12/26/union-farmer-how-to/.

95 **FBI statistics for the years 2017 through 2019:** William Finnegan, "How Police Unions Fight Reform," *New Yorker*, July 27, 2020, https://www.newyorker.com/magazine/2020/08/03/how-police-unions-fight-reform.

95 **Organized labor in the United States peaked:** "Union Members Summary," US Bureau of Labor Statistics, January 22, 2020, https://www.bls.gov/news.release/union2.nr0.htm; Mayer, *Union Membership Trends in the United States,* https://core.ac.uk/download/pdf/144981482.pdf.

96 **Both trends are the direct result:** Anna Stansbury and Lawrence Summers, "Declining Worker Power and American Economic Performance," BPEA Conference Draft, Spring 2020.

98 **The writer Upton Sinclair summarized:** Upton Sinclair, *The Jungle* (New York: Doubleday, Page & Co., 1906), chap. 10.

98 **An estimated one million rounds of ammunition:** Evan Andrews, "The

Battle of Blair Mountain," History.com, September 1, 2018, https://www.history.com/news/americas-largest-labor-uprising-the-battle-of-blair-mountain.

99 **spent $1 million:** Lynch, "How Did Workers Win the Right to Form a Union and Go on Strike?," https://historynewsnetwork.org/article/166796; "CPI Inflation Calculator," US Bureau of Labor Statistics, accessed July 2020, https://www.bls.gov/data/inflation_calculator.htm.

99 **In the early 20th century, the American labor movement:** *Encyclopaedia Britannica Online*, s.v. "Samuel Gompers," accessed May 7, 2020, https://www.britannica.com/biography/Samuel-Gompers.

99 **In the first two decades after the war:** Caleb Crain, "State of the Unions," *New Yorker*, August 19, 2019, https://www.newyorker.com/magazine/2019/08/26/state-of-the-unions.

99 **As Dr. Martin Luther King Jr. accurately put it:** Peter Dreier, "This Labor Day, Remember That Martin Luther King's Last Campaign Was for Workers' Rights," *Huffington Post*, September 4, 2017, https://www.huffpost.com/entry/this-labor-day-remember-that-martin-luther-kings_b_59ab51d4e4b0d0c16bb525a9.

99 **the proportion of income that went to the top 1 percent:** "Top 1% National Income Share, USA, 1913–2018," World Inequality Database, accessed May 2020, https://wid.world/country/usa/.

99 **corporate CEOs earned approximately $30:** Lawrence Mishel and Julia Wolfe, "CEO Compensation Has Grown 940% since 1978," Economic Policy Institute, August 14, 2019, https://www.epi.org/publication/ceo-compensation-2018/.

100 **union members earn 15–25 percent:** Henry S. Farber, Daniel Herbst, Ilyana Kuziemko, and Suresh Naidu, "Unions and Inequality over the Twentieth Century: New Evidence from Survey Data" (Working Paper 24587, National Bureau of Economic Research, Cambridge, MA, May 2018), https://www.nber.org/papers/w24587.pdf.

100 **When a quarter or more of an industry:** Jake Rosenfeld, Patrick Denice, and Jennifer Laird, "Union Decline Lowers Wages of Nonunion Workers," Economic Policy Institute, August 30, 2016, https://www.epi.org/publication/union-decline-lowers-wages-of-nonunion-workers-the-overlooked-reason-why-wages-are-stuck-and-inequality-is-growing/.

100 **as union membership in the United States has declined:** Rosenfeld, Denice, and Laird, "Union Decline Lowers Wages of Nonunion Workers," https://www.epi.org/publication/union-decline-lowers-wages-of-nonunion-workers-the-overlooked-reason-why-wages-are-stuck-and-inequality-is-growing/.

100 **In the summer of 1981:** Andrew Glass, "Reagan Fires 11,000 Striking Air Traffic Controllers, Aug. 5, 1981," *Politico*, August 5, 2017, https://www

.politico.com/story/2017/08/05/reagan-fires-11-000-striking-air-traffic-controllers-aug-5-1981-241252.

100 **company management started simply replacing:** Kathleen Schalch, "1981 Strike Leaves Legacy for American Workers," NPR, August 3, 2006, https://www.npr.org/2006/08/03/5604656/1981-strike-leaves-legacy-for-american-workers.

100 **There were 234 strikes:** "Work Stoppages Involving 1,000 or More Workers, 1947–2017," US Bureau of Labor Statistics, February 9, 2018, https://www.bls.gov/news.release/wkstp.t01.htm.

101 **An early blow came in 1957:** Crain, "State of the Unions," https://www.newyorker.com/magazine/2019/08/26/state-of-the-unions.

103 **More than two-thirds of the job creation:** Manyika et al., *The Social Contract in the 21st Century*, https://www.mckinsey.com/~/media/McKinsey/Industries/Social Sector/Our Insights/The social contract in the 21st century/MGI-The-social-contract-in-the-21st-century-Full-report-final.pdf.

103 **A 2020 study by former Treasury secretary Larry Summers:** Stansbury and Summers, "Declining Worker Power and American Economic Performance."

104 **workers received an estimated eleven cents of every dollar:** Stansbury and Summers, "Declining Worker Power and American Economic Performance."

104 **only the United States experienced:** Stansbury and Summers, "Declining Worker Power and American Economic Performance."

105 **In September 2019, members of the United Auto Workers:** Alexia Fernández Campbell, "The GM Strike Has Officially Ended. Here's What Workers Won and Lost," *Vox*, October 25, 2019, https://www.vox.com/identities/2019/10/25/20930350/gm-workers-vote-end-strike.

105 **only 57 percent voted to approve the contract:** Eli Rosenberg, "UAW Members Approve New Contract with GM, Ending One of the Largest Strikes in Years," *Washington Post*, October 25, 2019, https://www.washingtonpost.com/business/2019/10/25/gm-strike-is-nearly-over-workers-are-voting-contract/.

105 **UAW president Gary Jones resigned:** Rosenberg, "UAW Members Approve New Contract with GM," https://www.washingtonpost.com/business/2019/10/25/gm-strike-is-nearly-over-workers-are-voting-contract/; Clifford Atiyeh, "Former UAW President Gary Jones Charged in Union Embezzlement Scandal," *Car and Driver*, March 6, 2020, https://www.caranddriver.com/news/a31253503/uaw-embezzlement-scandal-gary-jones-arrest/.

106 **Just two months later, his predecessor:** Michael Wayland, "Second Ex–United Auto Workers President Charged with Embezzling Union Funds,"

CNBC, August 27, 2020, https://www.cnbc.com/2020/08/27/second-ex-uaw-president-charged-with-embezzling-union-funds.html.

106 **earned a nearly $400,000 salary:** "Salary Report—The $150K Club," Teamsters for a Democratic Union, October 24, 2019, https://www.tdu.org/teamster_officer_salaries.

106 **Today, the AFL-CIO represents 12.7 million workers:** "About Us," AFL-CIO, 2020, accessed May 7, 2020, https://aflcio.org/about-us; "Our Unions and Allies," AFL-CIO, 2020, accessed May 7, 2020, https://aflcio.org/about-us/our-unions-and-allies; "Union Members Summary," https://www.bls.gov/news.release/union2.nr0.htm.

107 **a seventeen-foot-tall, fifty-one-foot-wide:** Michael Padwee, "Architectural Murals of Lumen Martin Winter," *Tiles in New York* (blog), October 1, 2016, https://tilesinnewyork.blogspot.com/2016/10/architectural-murals-of-lumen-martin.html.

107 **where he worked through college:** Daniel Malloy, "Trumka Puts AFL-CIO in Middle of Every Issue," *Pittsburgh Post-Gazette*, October 24, 2010, https://www.post-gazette.com/news/nation/2010/10/24/Trumka-puts-AFL-CIO-in-middle-of-every-issue/stories/201010240203.

108 **pending legislation that would strengthen:** Eli Rosenberg, "House Passes Bill to Rewrite Labor Laws and Strengthen Unions," *Washington Post*, February 6, 2020, https://www.washingtonpost.com/business/2020/02/06/house-passes-bill-rewrite-labor-laws-strengthen-unions/.

109 **by 2028, researchers estimate:** *2018 Skills Gap and Future of Work Study*, Deloitte Insights and the Manufacturing Institute, accessed May 2020, https://operationalsolutions.nam.org/mi-skills-gap-study-18/.

110 **Today only 14 percent of British:** Carl Roper, "Trade Union Membership Is Growing, but There's Still Work to Do," Trades Union Congress, May 31, 2018, https://www.tuc.org.uk/blogs/trade-union-membership-growing-there%E2%80%99s-still-work-do.

111 **These "alternative work arrangements" offer workers:** David Weil and Tanya Goldman, "Labor Standards, the Fissured Workplace, and the On-Demand Economy," *Perspectives on Work* 20 (2016), http://www.fissuredworkplace.net/assets/Weil_Goldman.pdf.

111 **They include nearly all the baggage handlers:** Robert Silk, "Labor Unrest Grows as Airlines Outsource Jobs to Contractors," *Travel Weekly*, July 15, 2019, https://www.travelweekly.com/Travel-News/Airline-News/Labor-unrest-grows-as-airlines-outsource-jobs-to-contractors; "Contingent and Alternative Employment Arrangements Summary," table 8, US Bureau of Labor Statistics, June 7, 2018, https://www.bls.gov/news.release/conemp.nr0.htm; Mark Bergen and Josh Eidelson, "Inside Google's Shadow Workforce," *Bloomberg*, July 25, 2018, https://www.bloomberg.com/news/articles/2018-07-25/inside-google-s-shadow-workforce.

111 **The US Department of Labor reports:** "Contingent and Alternative Employment Arrangements Summary," https://www.bls.gov/news.release/conemp.nr0.htm.

111 **less than 2 percent of the US labor force:** "Electronically Mediated Work: New Questions in the Contingent Worker Supplement," *Monthly Labor Review*, US Bureau of Labor Statistics, September 2018, https://www.bls.gov/opub/mlr/2018/article/electronically-mediated-work-new-questions-in-the-contingent-worker-supplement.htm; "How Many Gig Workers Are There?," Gig Economy Data Hub, Aspen Institute Future of Work Initiative and Cornell University ILR School, https://www.gigeconomydata.org/basics/how-many-gig-workers-are-there.

112 **On August 22, 2017, more than one hundred:** Marie Targonski-O'Brien, "Uber, Lyft Drivers Crowd LAX, Protest Low Pay," KCET, August 22, 2017, https://www.kcet.org/shows/socal-connected/uber-lyft-drivers-crowd-lax-protest-low-pay.

112 **Between 2013 and 2017:** "The Online Platform Economy in 2018: Drivers, Workers, Sellers, and Lessors," JPMorgan Chase & Co. Institute, April 2019, https://institute.jpmorganchase.com/institute/research/labor-markets/report-ope-2018.htm.

112 **"Most of us as drivers":** Targonski-O'Brien, "Uber, Lyft Drivers Crowd LAX, Protest Low Pay," https://www.kcet.org/shows/socal-connected/uber-lyft-drivers-crowd-lax-protest-low-pay.

112 **Like many other grassroots initiatives:** Brian Dolber, interview with Jack Corrigan, May 25, 2020; Brian Dolber, interview with Will Peischel, May 15, 2020.

112 **With the help of a freelance developer:** Noam Schreiber and Kate Conger, "Uber and Lyft Drivers Gain Labor Clout, with Help from an App," *New York Times*, September 20, 2019, https://www.nytimes.com/2019/09/20/business/uber-lyft-drivers.html.

113 **Most adjunct faculty:** "Average Adjunct Professor Salary," PayScale, accessed May 20, 2020, https://www.payscale.com/research/US/Job=Adjunct_Professor/Salary.

113 **about five hundred of the estimated three hundred thousand rideshare drivers:** Brian Dolber, interview with Will Peischel, May 15, 2020; "About Us," Rideshare Drivers United, accessed May 21, 2020, https://drivers-united.org/about.

113 **the group had recruited most of its members:** Brian Dolber, *From Independent Contractors to an Independent Union: Building Solidarity through Rideshare Drivers United's Digital Organizing Strategy* (Philadelphia, PA: Media, Inequality & Change Center, October 2019), 9, https://mic.asc.upenn.edu/wp-content/uploads/2020/07/Dolber_final1.pdf.

113 **Armed with an academic grant:** Dolber, *From Independent Contractors to*

an Independent Union, 9, https://mic.asc.upenn.edu/wp-content/uploads/2020/07/Dolber_final1.pdf.

113 **The strategy was simple:** Brian Dolber, interview with Will Peischel, May 15, 2020.

114 **Between October 2018 and January 2019:** Dolber, *From Independent Contractors to an Independent Union*, 9, https://mic.asc.upenn.edu/wp-content/uploads/2020/07/Dolber_final1.pdf.

114 **while technology can enable an organization:** Brian Dolber, interview with Jack Corrigan, May 25, 2020.

114 **By March 25, 2019, Rideshare Drivers United:** Alexia Fernández Campbell, "Thousands of Uber Drivers Are Striking in Los Angeles," *Vox*, March 25, 2019, https://www.vox.com/2019/3/25/18280718/uber-lyft-drivers-strike-la-los-angeles; Bryce Covert, "'It's Not Right': Why Uber and Lyft Drivers Went on Strike," *Vox*, May 9, 2019, https://www.vox.com/the-goods/2019/5/9/18538206/uber-lyft-strike-demands-ipo.

114 **On May 8, 2019, days before Uber:** Covert, "Why Uber and Lyft Drivers Went on Strike," https://www.vox.com/the-goods/2019/5/9/18538206/uber-lyft-strike-demands-ipo; Ben Chapman, "Uber Drivers in UK Cities Go on Strike in Protest over Pay and Workers' Rights," *Independent*, May 7, 2019, https://www.independent.co.uk/news/business/news/uber-drivers-strike-london-birmingham-glasgow-nottingham-pay-rights-a8898791.html.

115 **On May 10, its first day:** Lucinda Shen, "Uber Is One of the Worst Performing IPOs Ever," *Fortune*, May 10, 2019, https://fortune.com/2019/05/10/uber-ipo-worst-performing-percentage/; Danielle Abril, "Lyft Stock Tumbles Two Days after Its IPO," *Fortune*, April 1, 2019, https://fortune.com/2019/04/01/lyft-stock-drops-after-ipo/.

115 **There are real changes that can be enacted:** Rideshare Drivers United homepage, accessed May 21, 2020, https://drivers-united.org/.

116 **Uber has more than 3.9 million drivers:** "Company Info," Uber, accessed May 21, 2020, https://www.uber.com/newsroom/company-info/; Steve Minter, "Who Are the World's Biggest Employers?" *IndustryWeek*, June 24, 2015, https://www.industryweek.com/talent/article/21965429/who-are-the-worlds-biggest-employers.

117 **"There has to be":** Dara Khosrowshahi, "I Am the C.E.O. of Uber. Gig Workers Deserve Better," *New York Times*, August 10, 2020, https://www.nytimes.com/2020/08/10/opinion/uber-ceo-dara-khosrowshahi-gig-workers-deserve-better.html%20?.

118 **Organized labor is in Sara Horowitz's blood:** David Gelles, "To Guide the Labor Movement's Future, She Looks to Its Past," *New York Times*, January 9, 2020, https://www.nytimes.com/2020/01/09/business/sara-horowitz-trupo-corner-office.html; Tejal Rao, "A Decade On, Freelancers

Union Founder Sara Horowitz Takes Her Fight Mainstream," *Village Voice*, February 13, 2013, https://www.villagevoice.com/2013/02/13/a-decade-on-freelancers-union-founder-sara-horowitz-takes-her-fight-mainstream/.

119 **Thirty years ago, more than half:** "National Compensation Survey," US Department of Labor.

121 **In Denmark, Finland, Norway, and Sweden:** "Denmark," European Trade Union Institute, accessed May 2020, https://www.worker-participation.eu/National-Industrial-Relations/Countries/Denmark; "Finland," European Trade Union Institute, accessed May 2020, https://www.worker-participation.eu/National-Industrial-Relations/Countries/Finland; "Norway," European Trade Union Institute, accessed May 2020, https://www.worker-participation.eu/National-Industrial-Relations/Countries/Norway; "Sweden," European Trade Union Institute, accessed May 2020, https://www.worker-participation.eu/National-Industrial-Relations/Countries/Sweden.

121 **In Denmark, Sweden, and Finland:** Dylan Matthews, "The Emerging Plan to Save the American Labor Movement," *Vox*, September 3, 2018, https://www.vox.com/policy-and-politics/2018/4/9/17205064/union-labor-movement-collective-wage-boards-bargaining.

121 **Finland's prime minister has called for:** Anne Kauranen, "Finland's PM Calls for Shortening Working Hours," Reuters, August 24, 2020, https://www.reuters.com/article/us-finland-politics/finlands-pm-calls-for-shortening-working-hours-idUSKBN25K1M1.

121 **where 70 percent of the workforce is unionized:** "Trade Unions," European Trade Union Institute, accessed May 2020, https://www.worker-participation.eu/National-Industrial-Relations/Countries/Sweden/Trade-Unions.

122 **In Denmark, workers at companies:** "Denmark: Board-Level Representation," European Trade Union Institute, accessed May 2020, https://www.worker-participation.eu/National-Industrial-Relations/Countries/Denmark/Board-level-Representation; "Netherlands: Board-Level Representation," European Trade Union Institute, accessed May 2020, https://www.worker-participation.eu/National-Industrial-Relations/Countries/Netherlands/Board-level-Representation; "Germany: Board-Level Representation," European Trade Union Institute, accessed May 2020, https://www.worker-participation.eu/National-Industrial-Relations/Countries/Germany/Board-level-Representation.

122 **The data support his claim:** Nir Kaissar, "To Help Improve U.S. Wages, Check Out Germany," *Bloomberg*, March 29, 2020, https://www.bloomberg.com/opinion/articles/2019-03-29/to-help-improve-u-s-wages-check-out-germany; Aleksandra Gregorič and Marc Steffen Rapp, "Board-Level Employee Representation and Firms' Responses to Crisis," *Industrial Relations* 58, no. 3 (2019), 376–422; Fernando Duarte, "It

Takes a CEO Just Days to Earn Your Annual Wage," *BBC News*, January 9, 2019, https://www.bbc.com/worklife/article/20190108-how-long-it-takes-a-ceo-to-earn-more-than-you-do-in-a-year.

123 **Businesses in Denmark, Sweden, Germany, and Austria:** "How Much Does Your Country Invest in R&D?," UNESCO Institute for Statistics, accessed May 30, 2020, http://uis.unesco.org/apps/visualisations/research-and-development-spending/.

123 **Between 1998 and 2014:** Alberto Manconi, Urs Peyer, and Theo Vermaelen, *Buybacks around the World*, INSEAD, September 2015, accessed May 2020, https://knowledge.insead.edu/sites/www.insead.edu/files/images/1bb_around_the_world_revised_-_september_8_2015–2.pdf.

123 **dozens of studies have found no clear evidence:** Aline Conchon, *Board-Level Employee Representation Rights in Europe: Facts and Trends* (Brussels: European Trade Union Institute, 2011), https://www.etui.org/Publications2/Reports/Board-level-employee-representation-rights-in-Europe.

123 **councils have the right to veto:** "Germany: Workplace Representation," European Trade Union Institute, accessed May 2020, https://www.worker-participation.eu/National-Industrial-Relations/Countries/Germany/Workplace-Representation.

123 **Larger companies have larger work councils:** "Germany: Workplace Representation," https://www.worker-participation.eu/National-Industrial-Relations/Countries/Germany/Workplace-Representation.

130 **more than $32,000 spent per person:** "Annual Determination of Average Cost of Incarceration: A Notice by the Prisons Bureau," *Federal Register*, April 30, 2018, https://www.federalregister.gov/documents/2018/04/30/2018-09062/annual-determination-of-average-cost-of-incarceration; Nicole Lewis and Beatrix Lockwood, "The Hidden Cost of Incarceration," Marshall Project, December 17, 2019, https://www.themarshallproject.org/2019/12/17/the-hidden-cost-of-incarceration.

132 **In 1945, members of the United Auto Workers:** Merrie Najimy and Joseph McCartin, "The Origins and Urgency of Bargaining for the Common Good," *The Forge*, March 31, 2020, https://forgeorganizing.org/article/origins-and-urgency-bargaining-common-good.

132 **The company resisted the union's demands:** Stephen Lerner, interview with Jack Corrigan, June 1, 2020.

133 **In December 2019, the organization published:** "Concrete Examples of Bargaining for the Common Good," Bargaining for the Common Good, December 20, 2019, https://smlr.rutgers.edu/sites/default/files/ciwo_bcg-memo.pdf; Stephen Lerner, "What Is Not to Be Done," *American Prospect*, April 29, 2020, https://prospect.org/labor/what-is-not-to-be-done/.

4: TAXES AND THE WORMHOLE IN THE GLOBAL ECONOMY

135 **No less than Albert Einstein said:** "Tax Quotes," US Internal Revenue Service, June 5, 2020, https://www.irs.gov/newsroom/tax-quotes.

138 **the billions of ads Google serves:** Elisa Gabbert, "25 Fast Facts about Google Ads," *WordStream* (blog), November 14, 2018, https://www.wordstream.com/blog/ws/2012/08/13/google-adwords-facts.

138 **Economists estimate that governments:** Nicholas Shaxson, "Tackling Tax Havens," *Finance & Development* 56, no. 3 (September 2019), International Monetary Fund, https://www.imf.org/external/pubs/ft/fandd/2019/09/tackling-global-tax-havens-shaxon.htm.

138 **FedEx pays less money in federal taxes:** Matthew Gardner, Lorena Roque, and Steve Wamhoff, *Corporate Tax Avoidance in the First Year of the Trump Tax Law* (Institute on Taxation and Economic Policy, December 16, 2019), https://itep.org/corporate-tax-avoidance-in-the-first-year-of-the-trump-tax-law/.

140 **The merchants of ancient Sumer:** "Taxes in the Ancient World," *University of Pennsylvania Almanac* 48, no. 28 (April 2002), https://almanac.upenn.edu/archive/v48/n28/AncientTaxes.html.

140 **In medieval Japan, landowners lobbied:** *Encyclopaedia Britannica Online*, s.v. "Japan," by Marius B. Jansen and Kitajima Masamoto, March 19, 2020, https://www.britannica.com/place/Japan/The-Heian-period-794–1185; Amanda Foreman, "Tax Evasion's Bite, from the Ancient World to Modern Days," *Wall Street Journal*, September 23, 2015, https://www.wsj.com/articles/tax-evasions-bite-from-the-ancient-world-to-modern-days-1443028212.

140 **They proliferated after World War I:** Nicholas Shaxson, *Treasure Islands: Uncovering the Damage of Offshore Banking and Tax Havens* (New York: St. Martin's Publishing Group, 2011), 26–27; John Christensen, email to Jack Corrigan, July 10, 2020.

142 **about one-third of all international trade:** Nick Shaxson, "Over a Third of World Trade Happens inside Multinational Corporations," Tax Justice Network, April 9, 2019, https://www.taxjustice.net/2019/04/09/over-a-third-or-more-of-world-trade-happens-inside-multinational-corporations/.

142 **In 2019, American corporations reported:** Analysis of Bureau of Economic Analysis data (via Haver Analytics), by Brad Setser and Cole Frank of the Council on Foreign Relations, accessed March 18, 2020.

144 **Between 2004 and 2019, Google used:** Edward Helmore, "Google Says It Will No Longer Use 'Double Irish, Dutch Sandwich' Tax Loophole," *Guardian*, January 1, 2020, https://www.theguardian.com/technology/2020/jan/01/google-says-it-will-no-longer-use-double-irish-dutch-sandwich-tax-loophole.

145 **Google was forced to abandon:** Toby Sterling, "Google to End 'Double Irish, Dutch Sandwich' Tax Scheme," Reuters, December 31, 2019, https://www.reuters.com/article/us-google-taxes-netherlands-idUSKBN1YZ10Z; Jeremy Kahn, "Google's 'Dutch Sandwich' Shielded 16 Billion Euros from Tax," *Bloomberg*, January 2, 2018, https://www.bloomberg.com/news/articles/2018-01-02/google-s-dutch-sandwich-shielded-16-billion-euros-from-tax.

145 **Created in 2003, this Irish company:** "Google Ireland Ltd.," *Bloomberg*, March 16, 2020, https://www.bloomberg.com/profile/company/0202877D:ID.

145 **Google maintains corporate offices in dozens:** Giovanni Legorano, "Google Reaches $333 Million Tax Settlement in Italy," *Wall Street Journal*, May 4, 2017, https://www.wsj.com/articles/google-agrees-306-million-tax-settlement-in-italy-1493901007.

145 **The surrounding neighborhood:** Art Patnaude, "Tech Workers Flock to Dublin's Silicon Docks," *Wall Street Journal*, May 28, 2015, https://www.wsj.com/articles/tech-workers-flock-to-dublins-silicon-docks-1432822827; Fiona Reddan, "Top 1000: Apple Overtakes CRH to Become Ireland's Largest Firm," *Irish Times*, May 10, 2018, https://www.irishtimes.com/business/top-1000-apple-overtakes-crh-to-become-ireland-s-largest-firm-1.3488309.

145 **the country's 24 percent corporate tax rate:** "Corporate Tax Rates Table," KPMG, https://home.kpmg/xx/en/home/services/tax/tax-tools-and-resources/tax-rates-online/corporate-tax-rates-table.html.

146 **In 2018, Google's Italian subsidiary:** Google Italy Srl, "Google Italy Srl con Socio Unico: Financial Statements to 31-12-2018," 4, accessed April 2020.

146 **In 2018, Google Ireland Limited generated:** Google Ireland Limited, *Directors' Report and Financial Statements for the Year Ended 31 December 2018*, 12, accessed April 2020.

146 **a €16.1 billion royalty payment:** Google Netherlands Holdings B.V., *Annual Accounts for Publication Purposes 2018 of Google Netherlands Holdings B.V.*, 11, accessed April 2020.

147 **In 2018, Google Netherlands Holdings B.V. did not employ:** Sony Kassam, "Google Cuts Taxes by Shifting Billions to Bermuda—Again," *Bloomberg Tax*, January 3, 2019, https://news.bloombergtax.com/transfer-pricing/google-cuts-taxes-by-shifting-billions-to-bermuda-again; Google Netherlands Holdings B.V., *Annual Accounts for Publication Purposes 2018*, 4.

147 **Where did it receive that license?:** Gabriel Zucman, "How Corporations and the Wealthy Avoid Taxes (and How to Stop Them)," *New York Times*, November 10, 2017, https://www.nytimes.com/interactive/2017/11/10/opinion/gabriel-zucman-paradise-papers-tax-evasion.html.

147 **where the corporate tax rate is 0 percent:** "Corporate Tax Rates Table,"

https://home.kpmg/xx/en/home/services/tax/tax-tools-and-resources/tax-rates-online/corporate-tax-rates-table.html.

147 **In 2018, Google Netherlands Holdings B.V. paid:** Google Netherlands Holdings B.V., *Annual Accounts for Publication Purposes 2018*, 11.

147 **The Netherlands did not tax:** Isabel Gottlieb and Ruben Munsterman, "Netherlands to Impose Withholding Tax on Royalties, Interest (1)," *Bloomberg Tax,* September 17, 2019, https://news.bloombergtax.com/daily-tax-report-international/netherlands-to-impose-withholding-tax-on-royalties-interest.

147 **Like its Dutch counterpart:** "Google Ireland Holdings Unlimited Company," CRIF Vision-net, February 1, 2020, https://www.vision-net.ie/Company-Info/Google-Ireland-Holdings-Unlimited-Company-369511.

147 **Yet in 2018, Google Ireland Holdings took in:** Google Ireland Holdings Unlimited Company, *Directors' Report and Financial Statements for the Year Ended 31 December 2018*, 10, accessed April 2020.

148 **Through an agreement with Alphabet:** George Turner, "Why the End of Google's 'Double Irish' Tax Avoidance Will Come with a Nasty Hangover," *New Statesman*, January 3, 2020, https://www.newstatesman.com/politics/economy/2020/01/why-end-google-s-double-irish-tax-avoidance-will-come-nasty-hangover.

148 **the company's only physical presence on the island:** Tim Sculthorpe, "The Post Box in Bermuda Numbered 666 Which Receives Google Profits Worth £8BILLION a Year," *Daily Mail*, January 31, 2016, https://www.dailymail.co.uk/news/article-3425097/Don-t-evil-Google-sends-profits-worth-8BILLION-year-post-box-number-666-tax-haven-island-Bermuda.html.

149 **Eric Schmidt, CEO of Google at the time:** Sissi Cao, "Ex-Google CEO Eric Schmidt Defends Tax Dodging, Monopoly in New Hardball Interview," *Observer*, May 15, 2019, https://observer.com/2019/05/ex-google-ceo-eric-schmidt-defends-tax-dodging-monopoly-bbc-interview/; Eric Schmidt, interview by Max Bergami, "QuaranTalks 40: Eric Schmidt," Bologna Business School, May 13, 2020, *YouTube* video, 50:34, https://youtu.be/FmS0XuzVmms.

150 **Many times, corporate tax avoidance schemes:** John Christensen, email to Jack Corrigan, July 10, 2020.

151 **"Companies and capital migrate":** Shaxson, *Treasure Islands*, 16.

151 **But looking at the data, researchers estimate:** Shaxson, "Tackling Tax Havens," https://www.imf.org/external/pubs/ft/fandd/2019/09/tackling-global-tax-havens-shaxon.htm.

151 **The United States and European Union each lose:** Niall McCarthy, "Tax Avoidance Costs the U.S. Nearly $200 Billion Every Year [Infographic]," *Forbes*, March 23, 2017, https://www.forbes.com/sites/niallmccarthy/2017/03/23/tax-avoidance-costs-the-u-s-nearly-200-billion-every-year

-infographic/; Marcin Goclowski, "Tax Avoidance, Evasion Costs EU 170 Billion Euros a Year, Says Poland," Reuters, January 22, 2020, https://www.reuters.com/article/us-davos-meeting-eu-tax-idUSKBN1ZL1H4; Shaxson, "Tackling Tax Havens," https://www.imf.org/external/pubs/ft/fandd/2019/09/tackling-global-tax-havens-shaxon.htm.

151 **Developing countries in Latin America, South Asia, and Africa:** Shane Darcy, "'The Elephant in the Room': Corporate Tax Avoidance & Business and Human Rights," *Business and Human Rights Journal* 2, no. 1 (January 2017): 1–30, https://doi.org/10.1017/bhj.2016.23.

152 **developing countries in 2008 lost:** Shaxson, *Treasure Islands*.

152 **In 2014, under heavy pressure from the EU:** Sam Schechner, "Ireland to Close 'Double Irish' Tax Loophole," *Wall Street Journal*, October 14, 2014, https://www.wsj.com/articles/ireland-to-close-double-irish-tax-loophole-1413295755; Toby Sterling, "Google to End 'Double Irish, Dutch Sandwich' Tax Scheme," Reuters, December 31, 2019, https://www.reuters.com/article/us-google-taxes-netherlands-idUSKBN1YZ10Z.

152 **Italy and France both implemented:** Eric Sylvers and Sam Schechner, "Italy Follows France in Levying a Digital Tax," *Wall Street Journal*, December 24, 2019, https://www.wsj.com/articles/italy-follows-france-in-levying-a-digital-tax-11577209660.

152 **The two countries also launched tax fraud:** Mark Scott, "Google Agrees to Pay Italy $334 Million in Back Taxes," *New York Times*, May 4, 2017, https://www.nytimes.com/2017/05/04/technology/google-italy-tax.html; Romain Dillet, "Google to Pay $549 Million Fine and $510 Million in Back Taxes in France," TechCrunch, September 12, 2019, http://social.techcrunch.com/2019/09/12/google-to-pay-549-million-fine-and-510-million-in-back-taxes-in-france/.

153 **The Netherlands also introduced:** Isabel Gottlieb, "Dutch Closing Door on Popular Corporate Tax Breaks (Corrected)," *Bloomberg Tax*, September 18, 2019, https://news.bloombergtax.com/daily-tax-report-international/Netherlands-Closes-Door-on-Popular-Corporate-Tax-Breaks.

153 **When one Irish lawmaker:** "Dáil Éireann debate—Thursday, 23 Nov 2017," vol. 962, no. 2, Houses of the Oireachtas, https://www.oireachtas.ie/en/debates/debate/dail/2017-11-23/18/.

153 **For years, Apple saved billions:** Charles Duhigg and David Kocieniewski, "How Apple Sidesteps Billions in Taxes," *New York Times*, April 28, 2012, https://www.nytimes.com/2012/04/29/business/apples-tax-strategy-aims-at-low-tax-states-and-nations.html.

153 **Other offshore affiliates were so well disguised:** Nelson D. Schwartz and Charles Duhigg, "Apple's Web of Tax Shelters Saved It Billions, Panel Finds," *New York Times*, May 20, 2013, https://www.nytimes.com/2013/05/21/business/apple-avoided-billions-in-taxes-congressional-panel-says.html; Ivana Kottasova, "How Apple Paid Just 0.005% Tax on Its

Global Profits," *CNN Business*, August 31, 2016, https://money.cnn.com/2016/08/30/technology/apple-tax-ruling-numbers/.

154 **After reaching out to lawyers:** Simon Bowers, "Leaked Documents Expose Secret Tale of Apple's Offshore Island Hop," International Consortium of Investigative Journalists, November 6, 2019, https://www.icij.org/investigations/paradise-papers/apples-secret-offshore-island-hop-revealed-by-paradise-papers-leak-icij/; "Financial Secrecy Index 2020: Narrative Report on Jersey," Tax Justice Network, February 18, 2020, https://fsi.taxjustice.net/PDF/Jersey.pdf.

154 **In late 2014, Apple had two:** Bowers, "Leaked Documents Expose Secret Tale of Apple's Offshore Island Hop," https://www.icij.org/investigations/paradise-papers/apples-secret-offshore-island-hop-revealed-by-paradise-papers-leak-icij/.

154 **Upon organizing its corporate structure:** Cole Frank, "Tax Avoidance and the Irish Balance of Payments," *Follow the Money* (blog), Council on Foreign Relations, April 25, 2018, https://www.cfr.org/blog/tax-avoidance-and-irish-balance-payments.

155 **it is gaining popularity among companies:** Emma Clancy, "Apple, Ireland and the New Green Jersey Tax Avoidance Technique," *Social Europe*, July 4, 2018, https://www.socialeurope.eu/apple-ireland-and-the-new-green-jersey-tax-avoidance-technique.

156 **Fair Tax Mark estimated:** *The Silicon Six and Their $100 Billion Global Tax Gap* (Fair Tax Mark, December 2019), https://fairtaxmark.net/wp-content/uploads/2019/12/Silicon-Six-Report-5-12-19.pdf.

156 **In 2017, the Institute on Taxation and Economic Policy:** Richard Phillips, Matt Gardner, Alexandria Robins, and Michelle Surka, *Offshore Shell Games 2017: The Use of Offshore Tax Havens by Fortune 500 Companies* (U.S. PIRG Education Fund & the Institute on Taxation and Economic Policy, October 17, 2017), https://uspirgedfund.org/sites/pirg/files/reports/USP%20ShellGames%20Oct17%201.2.pdf.

157 **The European Commission launched an investigation:** Foo Yun Chee, "IKEA to Face EU Order to Pay Dutch Back Taxes: Sources," Reuters, October 7, 2019, https://www.reuters.com/article/us-eu-ikea-ab-taxavoidance-exclusive/ikea-to-face-eu-order-to-pay-dutch-back-taxes-sources-idUSKBN1WM0PP; Simon Hage, Martin Hesse, and Blaz Zgaga, "The Lure of Luxembourg: A Peek behind the VW Tax Haven Curtain," *Der Spiegel*, October 28, 2017, https://www.spiegel.de/international/europe/volkswagen-relies-on-luxembourg-to-save-on-taxes-a-1175060.html.

157 **America's largest banks and investment banks:** Phillips, Gardner, Robins, and Surka, *Offshore Shell Games 2017*, https://uspirgedfund.org/sites/pirg/files/reports/USP%20ShellGames%20Oct17%201.2.pdf.

157 **The four largest pharmaceutical companies:** Phillips, Gardner, Robins, and

Surka, *Offshore Shell Games 2017*, https://uspirgedfund.org/sites/pirg/files/reports/USP%20ShellGames%20Oct17%201.2.pdf.

157 **Even companies that are inextricably linked:** Phillips, Gardner, Robins, and Surka, *Offshore Shell Games 2017*, https://uspirgedfund.org/sites/pirg/files/reports/USP%20ShellGames%20Oct17%201.2.pdf.

158 **If a local coffee roaster is forced:** Gardner, Roque, and Wamhoff, *Corporate Tax Avoidance in the First Year of the Trump Tax Law*, https://itep.org/corporate-tax-avoidance-in-the-first-year-of-the-trump-tax-law/.

159 **The City of London has a peculiar history:** "The City's Government," The City of London, 2020, accessed April 17, 2020, https://www.cityoflondon.gov.uk/about-the-city/history/Pages/city-government.aspx; Shaxson, *Treasure Islands*, 74.

160 **The official responsibility of the city's top executive:** "The Lord Mayor," The City of London, 2020, https://www.cityoflondon.gov.uk/about-the-city/the-lord-mayor/Pages/default.aspx; "About," TheCityUK, accessed April 21, 2020, https://www.thecityuk.com/about-us/.

160 **Reuters called TheCityUK:** Andy MacAskill, "Britain's Finance Industry Warns of Threat from Brexit Law Changes," Reuters, June 23, 2017, https://uk.reuters.com/article/uk-britain-eu-lawmaking/britains-finance-industry-warns-of-threat-from-brexit-law-changes-idUKKBN19E0UV; "About," https://www.thecityuk.com/about-us/.

160 **The City of London Corporation also appoints:** "Key City Officers," The City of London, 2020, https://www.cityoflondon.gov.uk/about-the-city/about-us/Pages/key-officers.aspx; Ros Wynne Jones, "Kick Privileged Bankers' Man the Remembrancer out of Parliament," *The Mirror*, May 8, 2013, https://www.mirror.co.uk/news/uk-news/kick-bankers-man-remembrancer-out-1874811; John Christensen, interview with Jack Corrigan, April 9, 2020.

160 **In municipal elections, the City's eight thousand human residents:** Nicholas Shaxson, "The Tax Haven in the Heart of Britain," *New Statesman*, February 24, 2011, https://www.newstatesman.com/economy/2011/02/london-corporation-city; "About the City Corporation," The City of London, 2020, https://www.cityoflondon.gov.uk/about-the-city/about-us/Pages/default.aspx.

161 **Shaxson calls it a lobbying organization:** Shaxson, *Treasure Islands*, 70.

161 **One of the major contributors to the City's:** "The London Charter of Liberties,"The City of London, August 22, 2018, accessed April 20, 2020, https://www.cityoflondon.gov.uk/things-to-do/london-metropolitan-archives/the-collections/Pages/london-charter-of-liberties.aspx.

162 **The British banking sector began courting:** Shaxson, *Treasure Islands*, 69, 75, 78–79.

162 **Fewer than 6,500 people:** "History of the Cayman Islands," ExploreCayman,

accessed February 1, 2021, https://www.explorecayman.com/about-cayman/history-of-the-cayman-islands; Shaxson, *Treasure Islands*, 90.

162 **Some officials back in London objected:** Shaxson, *Treasure Islands*, 92.

163 **Eventually the Cayman Islands adopted:** Shaxson, *Treasure Islands*, 92–93.

163 **There are now thirteen jurisdictions:** Elke Asen, "Corporate Tax Rates around the World, 2019," Tax Foundation, December 10, 2019, https://taxfoundation.org/publications/corporate-tax-rates-around-the-world/.

165 **When Christensen served in the Jersey government:** Michael Sesit, "A Fund's Suspicious Losses Draw Minimal Scrutiny," *Wall Street Journal*, September 17, 1996, https://www.wsj.com/articles/SB842911743535012500.

165 **Both the senators implicated:** Sesit, "A Fund's Suspicious Losses Draw Minimal Scrutiny," https://www.wsj.com/articles/SB842911743535012500.

168 **The United States loses at least $225 billion:** Niall McCarthy, "Tax Avoidance Costs the U.S. Nearly $200 Billion Every Year [Infographic]," *Forbes*, March 23, 2017, https://www.forbes.com/sites/niallmccarthy/2017/03/23/tax-avoidance-costs-the-u-s-nearly-200-billion-every-year-infographic/; Gabriel Zucman, *The Hidden Wealth of Nations: The Scourge of Tax Havens* (Chicago: University of Chicago Press, 2015), 53, digamo.free.fr/zucman152.pdf.

168 **In its 2020 financial secrecy index:** *Financial Secrecy Index 2020: Narrative Report on United States of America* (Tax Justice Network, February 18, 2020), https://fsi.taxjustice.net/PDF/UnitedStates.pdf.

168 **In 1961, President John F. Kennedy:** "Full Text: President John F. Kennedy's Special Message to the Congress on Taxation, April 20th, 1961," Tax History Project, accessed April 1, 2020, http://www.taxhistory.org/thp/readings.nsf/ArtWeb/2B727964C0A28BE5852571690051FD23?OpenDocument.

168 **But as the expanding offshore markets:** Shaxson, *Treasure Islands*, 109–15.

169 **It wants to fight non-American tax havens:** *Financial Secrecy Index 2020: Narrative Report on United States of America*, https://fsi.taxjustice.net/PDF/UnitedStates.pdf.

169 **In 1952, corporate taxes accounted for:** "Historical Tables: Table 2.1—Receipts by Source: 1934–2025," Office of Management and Budget, accessed June 1, 2020, https://www.whitehouse.gov/omb/historical-tables/; "CPI Inflation Calculator," US Bureau of Labor Statistics, accessed June 1, 2020, https://data.bls.gov/cgi-bin/cpicalc.pl.

170 **As a result, between 1980 and 2019:** Asen, "Corporate Tax Rates around the World, 2019," https://taxfoundation.org/publications/corporate-tax-rates-around-the-world/.

171 **The funds that reinvest this hidden wealth:** Zucman, *The Hidden Wealth of Nations*, digamo.free.fr/zucman152.pdf; *Financial Secrecy Index 2020:*

Narrative Report on United States of America, https://fsi.taxjustice.net/PDF/UnitedStates.pdf.

172 **After federal authorities locked up Chicago gangster:** Shaxson, *Treasure Islands*, 88.

172 **The effort was orchestrated by Meyer Lansky:** Shaxson, *Treasure Islands*, 88.

172 **In the 1960s, Finance Minister Stafford Sands:** Banks and Trust Companies Regulation, Statute Law of the Bahamas, chap. 316, 2010; Shaxson, *Treasure Islands*, 89.

172 **By the 1980s, Latin American drug traffickers:** Zucman, *The Hidden Wealth of Nations*, 25, digamo.free.fr/zucman152.pdf; Shaxson, *Treasure Islands*, 85.

172 **about $7.6 trillion in private assets:** Zucman, *The Hidden Wealth of Nations*, 35, 47, digamo.free.fr/zucman152.pdf.

173 **more than €10 trillion:** "International Community Continues Making Progress against Offshore Tax Evasion," Organisation for Economic Co-operation and Development, June 30, 2020, https://www.oecd.org/ctp/exchange-of-tax-information/international-community-continues-making-progress-against-offshore-tax-evasion.htm; Alex Cobham, "It's Got to Be Automatic: Trillions of Dollars Offshore Revealed by Tax Justice Network Policy Success," Tax Justice Network, July 3, 2020, https://www.taxjustice.net/2020/07/03/its-got-to-be-automatic-trillions-of-dollars-offshore-revealed-by-tax-justice-network-policy-success/; Clare Coffey, Patricia Espinoza Revollo, Rowan Harvey, Max Lawson, Anam Parvez Butt, Kim Piaget, Diana Sarosi, and Julie Thekkudan, *Time to Care: Unpaid and Underpaid Care Work and the Global Inequality Crisis* (briefing paper, Oxfam International, January 2020), https://oxfamilibrary.openrepository.com/bitstream/handle/10546/620928/bp-time-to-care-inequality-200120-en.pdf.

173 **According to Zucman's estimates:** Zucman, *The Hidden Wealth of Nations*, 53, digamo.free.fr/zucman152.pdf.

173 **it is the developing world that suffers the most:** Zucman, *The Hidden Wealth of Nations*, 53, digamo.free.fr/zucman152.pdf.

173 **In Africa alone, a High Level Panel:** Darcy, "'The Elephant in the Room': Corporate Tax Avoidance & Business and Human Rights," https://doi.org/10.1017/bhj.2016.23.

174 **Oil accounts for more than 90 percent:** "Africa: Angola," World Factbook, Central Intelligence Agency, April 6, 2020, https://www.cia.gov/library/publications/resources/the-world-factbook/geos/ao.html; "Monetary Poverty Rate Rises to 41 Percent in Angola," *Agência Angola Press*, December 6, 2019, http://www.angop.ao/angola/en_us/noticias/economia/2019/11/49/Monetary-poverty-rate-rises-percent-Angola,c96d1f24-0361-42d3-b661-d30aefd0bb23.html.

174 **With his government under an international arms embargo:** Emily Crowley, "'Angolagate' Revisited," Financial Transparency Coalition, April 7, 2010, https://financialtransparency.org/angolagate-revisited/.

175 **José Filomeno dos Santos, the president's son:** "José Filomeno dos Santos: Son of Angola's Ex-Leader in 'Extraordinary' Trial," *BBC News*, December 9, 2019, https://www.bbc.com/news/world-africa-50712492.

175 **In 2020, Isabel dos Santos:** Michael Forsythe, Gilberto Neto, and Megan Specia, "Africa's Richest Woman Set to Face Charges in Angola over Embezzlement," *New York Times*, January 23, 2020, https://www.nytimes.com/2020/01/23/world/africa/angola-santos-embezzlement.html.

175 **In 2012, Sodiam and dos Santos's husband:** Hilary Osborne and Caelainn Barr, "The Diamond Deal That Rocked Angola," *Guardian*, January 19, 2020, https://www.theguardian.com/world/2020/jan/19/diamond-deal-that-rocked-angola-de-grisogono-luanda-leaks.

175 **an estimated $2 billion in assets:** Sydney P. Freedberg, Scilla Alecci, Will Fitzgibbon, Douglas Dalby, and Delphine Reuter, "How Africa's Richest Woman Exploited Family Ties, Shell Companies and Inside Deals to Build an Empire,"International Consortium of Investigative Journalists, January 19, 2020, https://www.icij.org/investigations/luanda-leaks/how-africas-richest-woman-exploited-family-ties-shell-companies-and-inside-deals-to-build-an-empire/.

176 **Researchers at the University of Massachusetts Amherst:** Leonce Ndikumana and James K. Boyce, *Capital Flight from Africa: Updated Methodology and New Estimates* (research report, Political Economy Research Institute, University of Massachusetts Amherst, June 1, 2018), https://www.peri.umass.edu/publication/item/1083-capital-flight-from-africa-updated-methodology-and-new-estimates.

177 **By 2019, the program had helped:** "Four Years On and Half a Billion Dollars Later—Tax Inspectors Without Borders," Organisation for Economic Co-operation and Development, September 25, 2019, https://www.oecd.org/ctp/four-years-on-and-half-a-billion-dollars-later-tax-inspectors-without-borders.htm.

177 **countries participating in the program:** John Christensen, email to Jack Corrigan, July 10, 2020.

180 **the fifty states use formulary apportionment:** Scott Drenkard, "A Very Short Primer on Tax Nexus, Apportionment, and Throwback Rule," Tax Foundation, March 28, 2016, https://taxfoundation.org/very-short-primer-tax-nexus-apportionment-and-throwback-rule/.

181 **earn more than €750 million per year:** *Action 13: Country-by-Country Reporting Implementation Package* (OECD/G20 Base Erosion and Profit Shifting Project, 2015), accessed April 2020, https://www.oecd.org/tax/beps/beps-action-13-on-country-by-country-reporting-peer-review-documents.pdf.

181 **Though every country loses revenue to tax avoidance:** *Measuring and Monitoring BEPS, Action 11—2015 Final Report* (OECD/G20 Base Erosion and Profit Shifting Project, Paris, 2015), 80, accessed April 2020, https://www.oecd.org/tax/measuring-and-monitoring-beps-action-11–2015-final-report-9789264241343-en.htm.

183 **If the profits were made in Hungary:** "Corporate Tax Rates Table," https://home.kpmg/xx/en/home/services/tax/tax-tools-and-resources/tax-rates-online/corporate-tax-rates-table.html.

185 **Both the OECD and the United Nations endorse:** "Tax Transparency," Organisation for Economic Co-operation and Development, 2019, https://www.oecd.org/tax/beps/tax-transparency/; "International Tax Cooperation: International Efforts to Combat Tax Avoidance and Evasion," United Nations Inter-Agency Task Force on Financing for Development, accessed April 2020, https://developmentfinance.un.org/international-efforts-combat-tax-avoidance-and-evasion.

185 **As of November 2019, nearly one hundred jurisdictions:** *The 2019 AEOI Implementation Report* (Global Forum on Transparency and Exchange of Information for Tax Purposes, Organisation for Economic Co-operation and Development, November 24, 2019), https://www.oecd.org/tax/transparency/AEOI-implementation-report-2019.pdf.

186 **By combining these disparate logs:** Zucman, *The Hidden Wealth of Nations*, 92, digamo.free.fr/zucman152.pdf.

188 **The company has been sued:** Mark Scott, "Google Agrees to Pay Italy $334 Million in Back Taxes," *New York Times*, May 4, 2017, https://www.nytimes.com/2017/05/04/technology/google-italy-tax.html; Simon Carraud and Mathieu Rosemain, "Google to Pay $1 Billion in France to Settle Fiscal Fraud Probe," Reuters, September 12, 2019, https://www.reuters.com/article/us-france-tech-google-tax/google-agrees-to-550-million-fine-in-france-to-settle-fiscal-fraud-probe-idUSKCN1VX1SM.

188 **After the French court's decision:** Carraud and Rosemain, "Google to Pay $1 Billion in France to Settle Fiscal Fraud Probe," https://www.reuters.com/article/us-france-tech-google-tax/google-agrees-to-550-million-fine-in-france-to-settle-fiscal-fraud-probe-idUSKCN1VX1SM.

5: FOREIGN POLICY: DOES EVERY COMPANY NEED ITS OWN STATE DEPARTMENT, PENTAGON, AND CIA?

191 **The Syrian government developed Android apps:** Shannon Vavra, "Syrian Government Surveillance Campaign Turns to Spreading Malware in Coronavirus Apps," Cyberscoop, April 16, 2020, https://www.cyberscoop.com/coronavirus-syria-surveillance-apps-lookout/.

193 **In the United States, General Motors:** A. J. Baime, "U.S. Auto Industry Came to the Rescue during WWII," *Car and Driver*, March 31, 2020,

https://www.caranddriver.com/news/a31994388/us-auto-industry-medical-war-production-history/; David Vergun, "During WWII, Industries Transitioned from Peacetime to Wartime Production," US Department of Defense, March 27, 2020, https://www.defense.gov/Explore/Features/story/Article/2128446/during-wwii-industries-transitioned-from-peacetime-to-wartime-production/.

193 **It was at the dawn of this era:** Ellen Terrell, "When a Quote Is Not (Exactly) a Quote: General Motors," *Inside Adams* (blog), Library of Congress, April 22, 2016, https://blogs.loc.gov/inside_adams/2016/04/when-a-quote-is-not-exactly-a-quote-general-motors/.

194 **The number of multinational companies:** Pankaj Ghemawat and Niccolò Pisani, "Are Multinationals Becoming Less Global?," *Harvard Business Review*, October 28, 2013, https://hbr.org/2013/10/are-multinationals-becoming-less-global; United Nations Conference on Trade and Development, *The Universe of the Largest Transnational Corporations* (New York and Geneva: United Nations, 2007), https://unctad.org/en/Docs/iteiia20072_en.pdf; United Nations Conference on Trade and Development, *World Investment Report 2010: Investing in a Low-Carbon Economy* (New York and Geneva: United Nations, 2010), https://unctad.org/en/Docs/wir2010_en.pdf.

196 **That year, the White House had launched:** Robinson Meyer, "The Secret Startup That Saved the Worst Website in America," *Atlantic*, July 9, 2015, https://www.theatlantic.com/technology/archive/2015/07/the-secret-startup-saved-healthcare-gov-the-worst-website-in-america/397784/.

198 **The same year Facebook released software:** Jack Clark, "Why 2015 Was a Breakthrough Year in Artificial Intelligence," *Bloomberg*, December 8, 2015, https://www.bloomberg.com/news/articles/2015-12-08/why-2015-was-a-breakthrough-year-in-artificial-intelligence.

201 **the International Traffic in Arms Regulations:** Jeff Petters, "What Is ITAR Compliance? Definition and Regulations," *Inside Out Security Blog*, Varonis, March 29, 2020, https://www.varonis.com/blog/itar-compliance/; "Part 121—The United States Munitions List," *Electronic Code of Federal Regulations*, US Government Publishing Office, accessed August 10, 2020, https://www.ecfr.gov/cgi-bin/text-idx?node=pt22.1.121.

203 **In January 2020, the US Commerce Department:** "Addition of Software Specially Designed to Automate the Analysis of Geospatial Imagery to the Export Control Classification Number 0Y521 Series," *Federal Register*, January 6, 2020, https://www.federalregister.gov/documents/2020/01/06/2019-27649/addition-of-software-specially-designed-to-automate-the-analysis-of-geospatial-imagery-to-the-export.

203 **Geospatial technology was already highly regulated:** "Part 121—The

United States Munitions List," https://www.ecfr.gov/cgi-bin/text-idx?node =pt22.1.121.

203 **US military leaders have begun to stress:** "DOD Adopts Ethical Principles for Artificial Intelligence," Department of Defense, news release, February 24, 2020, https://www.defense.gov/Newsroom/Releases /Release/Article/2091996/dod-adopts-ethical-principles-for-artificial -intelligence/.

205 **Within months, Google employees began protesting:** Scott Shane and Daisuke Wakabayashi, "'The Business of War': Google Employees Protest Work for the Pentagon," *New York Times*, April 4, 2018, https://www .nytimes.com/2018/04/04/technology/google-letter-ceo-pentagon-project .html.

206 **Anduril was contracted to build:** Lee Fang, "Defense Tech Startup Founded by Trump's Most Prominent Silicon Valley Supporters Wins Secretive Military AI Contract," *Intercept*, March 9, 2019, https://theintercept.com /2019/03/09/anduril-industries-project-maven-palmer-luckey/.

206 **The company went on to build:** Steven Levy, "Inside Palmer Luckey's Bid to Build a Border Wall," *Wired*, June 11, 2018, https://www.wired.com /story/palmer-luckey-anduril-border-wall/.

207 **Russian president Vladimir Putin remarked:** Radina Gigova, "Who Vladimir Putin Thinks Will Rule the World," CNN, September 2, 2017, https://www.cnn.com/2017/09/01/world/putin-artificial-intelligence-will -rule-world/index.html.

208 **In 2020, the number of companies:** Alan Murray and David Meyer, "The Fortune Global 500 Is Now More Chinese Than American," *Fortune*, August 10, 2020, https://fortune.com/2020/08/10/fortune-global-500 -china-rise-ceo-daily/.

209 **Between 2007 and 2017, the government:** Ross Davies, "High-Speed Rail: Should the World Be Following China's Example?,"RailwayTechnology, September 24, 2019, https://www.railway-technology.com/features/high -speed-rail-in-china/.

209 **In 2017, President Xi Jinping unveiled:** Paul Mozur, "Beijing Wants A.I. to Be Made in China by 2030," *New York Times*, July 20, 2017, https:// www.nytimes.com/2017/07/20/business/china-artificial-intelligence .html; *Notice of the State Council Issuing the New Generation of Artificial Intelligence Development Plan*, State Council Document No. 35 (China, July 8, 2017; trans. Flora Sapio, Weiming Chen, and Adrian Lo, Foundation for Law and International Affairs), https://flia.org/wp -content/uploads/2017/07/A-New-Generation-of-Artificial-Intelligence -Development-Plan-1.pdf.

210 **Local governments started pouring funds:** Nicholas Thompson and Ian Bremmer, "The AI Cold War That Threatens Us All," *Wired*, October 23,

2018, https://www.wired.com/story/ai-cold-war-china-could-doom-us-all/.

210 **The following month, the government drafted:** Benjamin Larsen, "Drafting China's National AI Team for Governance," *New America*, November 18, 2019, https://www.newamerica.org/cybersecurity-initiative/digichina/blog/drafting-chinas-national-ai-team-governance/.

210 **China's foray into artificial intelligence:** Sean O'Connor, "How Chinese Companies Facilitate Technology Transfer from the United States" (staff research report, U.S.-China Economic and Security Review Commission, May 6, 2019), https://www.uscc.gov/sites/default/files/Research/How%20Chinese%20Companies%20Facilitate%20Tech%20Transfer%20from%20the%20US.pdf.

210 **Foreign companies that want to do business:** Sean O'Connor, "How Chinese Companies Facilitate Technology Transfer from the United States," https://www.uscc.gov/sites/default/files/Research/How%20Chinese%20Companies%20Facilitate%20Tech%20Transfer%20from%20the%20US.pdf.

211 **when Uber launched in China:** Leslie Hook, "Uber's Battle for China," *Financial Times Weekend Magazine*, June 2016, https://ig.ft.com/sites/uber-in-china/.

211 **He made frequent visits to the country:** Leslie Hook, "Uber's Battle for China," https://ig.ft.com/sites/uber-in-china/; Ben Chiang, "Baidu Partners with Uber," Uber, December 17, 2014, https://www.uber.com/en-CN/newsroom/%e7%99%be%e5%ba%a6%e3%80%81uber%e5%90%88%e4%bd%9c-baidu-partners-with-uber; William C. Kirby, "The Real Reason Uber Is Giving Up in China," *Harvard Business Review*, August 2, 2016, https://hbr.org/2016/08/the-real-reason-uber-is-giving-up-in-china.

211 **"Travis structured something that worked":** Shervin Pishevar, interview with Alec Ross and Jack Corrigan, April 30, 2020.

211 **The two companies entered "a massive war":** Shervin Pishevar, interview.

211 **By 2016, Uber China had expanded:** Zheping Huang, "China Finally Made Ride-Hailing Legal, in a Way That Could Destroy Uber's Business Model," *Quartz*, July 29, 2016, https://qz.com/745337/china-finally-made-ride-hailing-legal-in-a-way-that-could-destroy-ubers-business-model/.

211 **The company received billions of dollars:** Heather Timmons, "All the Things That Went Wrong for Uber in China," *Quartz*, August 1, 2016, https://qz.com/746990/all-the-things-that-went-wrong-for-uber-in-china/.

212 **In July 2016, the Chinese government:** Kirby, "The Real Reason Uber Is Giving Up in China," https://hbr.org/2016/08/the-real-reason-uber-is-giving-up-in-china.

212 **Uber China was sold to Didi:** Alyssa Abkowitz and Rick Carew, "Uber Sells China Operations to Didi Chuxing," *Wall Street Journal*, August 1, 2016, https://www.wsj.com/articles/china-s-didi-chuxing-to-acquire-rival-uber-s-chinese-operations-1470024403.

212 **After beating out Uber:** Sarah Dai, "'China's Uber' Ramps Up AI Arms Race, Says It Will Open Third Deep Learning Research Lab," *South China Morning Post*, January 26, 2018, https://www.scmp.com/tech/start-ups/article/2130793/didi-chuxing-ramps-artificial-intelligence-arms-race-says-it-will; Jonathan Cheng, "China's Ride-Hailing Giant Didi to Test Beijing's New Digital Currency," *Wall Street Journal*, July 8, 2020, https://www.wsj.com/articles/chinas-ride-hailing-giant-didi-to-test-beijings-new-digital-currency-11594206564.

213 **As of 2019, China has deployed approximately one:** Thomas Ricker, "The US, Like China, Has about One Surveillance Camera for Every Four People, Says Report," *The Verge*, December 9, 2019, https://www.theverge.com/2019/12/9/21002515/surveillance-cameras-globally-us-china-amount-citizens; Charlie Campbell, "'The Entire System Is Designed to Suppress Us.' What the Chinese Surveillance State Means for the Rest of the World," *Time*, November 21, 2019, https://time.com/5735411/china-surveillance-privacy-issues/.

213 **The CEO of the Chinese computer vision company SenseTime:** Ross Andersen, "The Panopticon Is Already Here," *Atlantic*, September 2020, https://www.theatlantic.com/magazine/archive/2020/09/china-ai-surveillance/614197/.

214 **But less than six months later:** Amy Hawkins, "Beijing's Big Brother Tech Needs More African Faces," *Foreign Policy*, July 24, 2018, https://foreignpolicy.com/2018/07/24/beijings-big-brother-tech-needs-african-faces/; Kudzai Chimhangwa, "How Zimbabwe's Biometric ID Scheme—and China's AI Aspirations—Threw a Wrench in Elections," GlobalVoices, January 30, 2020, https://globalvoices.org/2020/01/30/how-zimbabwes-biometric-id-scheme-and-chinas-ai-aspirations-threw-a-wrench-into-the-2018-election/.

215 **China has engaged in similar partnerships:** Andersen, "The Panopticon Is Already Here," https://www.theatlantic.com/magazine/archive/2020/09/china-ai-surveillance/614197/.

216 **The United States is beginning to recognize:** Lucy Fisher, "CIA Warning over Huawei," *The Times* (London), April 20, 2019, https://www.thetimes.co.uk/edition/news/cia-warning-over-huawei-rz6xc8kzk; Edward Wong and Julian E. Barnes, "U.S. to Expel Chinese Graduate Students with Ties to China's Military Schools," *New York Times*, May 28, 2020, https://www.nytimes.com/2020/05/28/us/politics/china-hong-kong-trump-student-visas.html.

216 **In 2016, a Chinese gaming company:** Georgia Wells, "Grindr Sells Majority Stake to Chinese Gaming Company," *Digits* (blog), *Wall Street Journal*, January 11, 2016, https://blogs.wsj.com/digits/2016/01/11/grindr-sells-majority-stake-to-chinese-gaming-company/?mod=article_inline; Georgia Wells and Kate O'Keeffe, "U.S. Orders Chinese Firm to Sell Dating App Grindr over Blackmail Risk," *Wall Street Journal*, March 27, 2019, https://www.wsj.com/articles/u-s-orders-chinese-company-to-sell-grindr-app-11553717942.

218 **Eric Schmidt, the former chairman:** Eric Schmidt, "Eric Schmidt: I Used to Run Google. Silicon Valley Could Lose to China," *New York Times*, February 27, 2020, https://www.nytimes.com/2020/02/27/opinion/eric-schmidt-ai-china.html.

6: THE GEOGRAPHY OF CHANGE: THE CONTEST FOR POWER BETWEEN CLOSED AND OPEN SYSTEMS

225 **A strong central government has ruled:** Geremie Barmé, *The Forbidden City* (Cambridge, MA: Harvard University Press, 2008), 594.

225 **Its 1.4 billion people remain subject:** "China's Mainland Population Crosses 1.4 Billion," *China Daily*, January 17, 2020, https://www.chinadaily.com.cn/a/202001/17/WS5e211902a310128217271a51.html.

226 **an economy slightly smaller than that of the Netherlands:** "Comparison: Annual GDP 1978," Countryeconomy, accessed July 23, 2020, https://countryeconomy.com/gdp?year=1978; "China—Population," Countryeconomy, accessed July 23, 2020, https://countryeconomy.com/demography/population/china; "Netherlands—Population," Countryeconomy, accessed July 23, 2020, https://countryeconomy.com/demography/population/netherlands; Max Roser and Esteban Ortiz-Ospina, "Global Extreme Poverty: How Much Does the Reduction of Falling Poverty in China Matter for the Reduction of Global Poverty?," Our World in Data, accessed July 23, 2020, https://ourworldindata.org/extreme-poverty.

226 **The state loosened its grip:** Wayne Morrison, *China's Economic Rise: History, Trends, Challenges, and Implications for the United States* (US Congressional Research Service, June 25, 2019), https://fas.org/sgp/crs/row/RL33534.pdf; Raghuram Rajan, *The Third Pillar: How Markets and the State Leave the Community Behind* (New York: HarperCollins Publishers, 2019), 247.

226 **The country sustained an average annual growth rate:** Morrison, *China's Economic Rise*, https://fas.org/sgp/crs/row/RL33534.pdf; "GDP (constant 2010 US$)—China," World Bank, accessed July 23, 2020, https://data.worldbank.org/indicator/NY.GDP.MKTP.KD?locations=CN.

226 **China now boasts:** "GDP (current US$)," World Bank, accessed July 23,

2020, https://data.worldbank.org/indicator/NY.GDP.MKTP.CD?most_recent_value_desc=true.

227 **This view is reinforced by the government:** Li Yuan, "With Selective Coronavirus Coverage, China Builds a Culture of Hate," *New York Times*, April 22, 2020, https://www.nytimes.com/2020/04/22/business/china-coronavirus-propaganda.html.

228 **Most of the four hundred million members:** Melissa Cyrill, "China's Middle Class in 5 Simple Questions," *China Briefing*, February 13, 2019, https://www.china-briefing.com/news/chinas-middle-class-5-questions-answered/; Roser and Ortiz-Ospina, "Global Extreme Poverty: How Much Does the Reduction of Falling Poverty in China Matter for the Reduction of Global Poverty?," https://ourworldindata.org/extreme-poverty.

228 **at least 104 billionaires:** Tara Francis Chan, "Communist China Has 104 Billionaires Leading the Country while Xi Jinping Promises to Lift Millions out of Poverty," *Business Insider*, March 2, 2018, https://www.businessinsider.com/billionaires-in-china-xi-jinping-parliament-income-inequality-2018-3; Karl Evers-Hillstrom, "Majority of Lawmakers in 116th Congress Are Millionaires," Center for Responsive Politics, April 23, 2020, https://www.opensecrets.org/news/2020/04/majority-of-lawmakers-millionaires/; Adela Whittingham, "Britain's Richest MP Worth £110 Million Banned from Roads after Being Caught Texting in His BMW," *The Mirror*, December 20, 2017, https://www.mirror.co.uk/news/uk-news/britains-richest-mp-worth-110million-11729352.

229 **The state offers little in the way:** Nicholas R. Lardy and Tianlei Huang, "China's Weak Social Safety Net Will Dampen Its Economic Recovery," Peterson Institute for International Economics, May 4, 2020, https://www.piie.com/blogs/china-economic-watch/chinas-weak-social-safety-net-will-dampen-its-economic-recovery; "Workers' Rights and Labour Relations in China," *China Labour Bulletin*, June 22, 2020, https://clb.org.hk/content/workers%E2%80%99-rights-and-labour-relations-china.

230 **In the Gulf kingdoms, absolute power is offset:** Aya Batrawy, "Half the Saudi Population Receiving Welfare in New System," *Seattle Times*, December 21, 2017, https://www.seattletimes.com/business/half-the-saudi-population-receiving-welfare-in-new-system/; Robin Vinod, "Cost of Living in Doha Qatar," *Expat Life* (blog), OnlineQatar, March 20, 2019, http://www.onlineqatar.com/living/expat-life/cost-of-living-in-doha-qatar; Doug Bandow, "Kuwait Needs Economic Reform, but Opponents Dominated National Assembly Election," *Forbes*, January 9, 2017, https://www.forbes.com/sites/dougbandow/2017/01/09/kuwait-needs-economic-reform-but-opponents-dominated-national-assembly-election/#ca68f257c8df; "Housing Authorities and Programs," United Arab Emirates, accessed July 29, 2020, https://u.ae/en/information-and-services

/housing/housing-authorities-and-programmes; "Individual Income Tax Rates," KPMG, accessed July 29, 2020, https://home.kpmg/xx/en/home/services/tax/tax-tools-and-resources/tax-rates-online/individual-income-tax-rates-table.html.

230 **In Saudi Arabia, about two-thirds of all workers:** Elizabeth Dickinson, "Can Saudi Arabia's Young Prince Wean the Welfare State?," *Foreign Policy*, June 5, 2017, https://foreignpolicy.com/2017/06/05/is-saudi-arabias-massive-economy-reform-coming-off-the-rails-mohammed-bin-salman/; Zahraa Alkhalisi, "How Many Saudis Are Only Working One Hour a Day?," *CNN Money*, October 20, 2016, https://money.cnn.com/2016/10/20/news/saudi-government-workers-productivity/index.html.

232 **The stock market quickly rebounded:** "Civilian Unemployment Rate," US Bureau of Labor Statistics, accessed July 20, 2020, https://www.bls.gov/charts/employment-situation/civilian-unemployment.htm; Heather Long, "Small Business Used to Define America's Economy. The Pandemic Could Change That Forever," *Washington Post*, May 12, 2020, https://www.washingtonpost.com/business/2020/05/12/small-business-used-define-americas-economy-pandemic-could-end-that-forever/; Aimee Picchi, "As Many as 35 Million People May Still Be Waiting for Their Stimulus Checks," *CBS News*, June 9, 2020, https://www.cbsnews.com/news/stimulus-checks-as-many-as-35-million-people-may-still-be-waiting/.

232 **After negotiating with employers and labor unions:** Peter S. Goodman, "The Nordic Way to Economic Recovery," *New York Times*, April 2, 2020, https://www.nytimes.com/2020/03/28/business/nordic-way-economic-rescue-virus.html.

232 **the program cost an estimated $42 billion:** Ulrik Boesen, "Denmark Unplugs the Economy," *Tax Foundation*, March 26, 2020, https://taxfoundation.org/denmark-coronavirus-relief-plan/; Matt Apuzzo and Monika Pronczuk, "Covid-19's Economic Pain Is Universal. But Relief? Depends on Where You Live," *New York Times*, April 5, 2020, https://www.nytimes.com/2020/03/23/world/europe/coronavirus-economic-relief-wages.html.

232 **"What we're trying to do":** Derek Thompson, "'Do More—Fast. Don't Wait,'" *Atlantic*, March 24, 2020, https://www.theatlantic.com/ideas/archive/2020/03/denmark-has-a-message-for-america-do-more-fast/608629/.

232 **In the first month of lockdown:** "Denmark Unemployment Rate," Trading Economics, accessed July 20, 2020, https://tradingeconomics.com/denmark/unemployment-rate; "Civilian Unemployment Rate," US Bureau of Labor Statistics, accessed July 20, 2020, https://www.bls.gov/charts/employment-situation/civilian-unemployment-rate.htm.

233 **Your childcare is subsidized:** Gretchen Livingston and Deja Thomas,

"Among 41 Countries, Only U.S. Lacks Paid Parental Leave," Pew Research Center, December 16, 2019, https://www.pewresearch.org/fact-tank/2019/12/16/u-s-lacks-mandated-paid-parental-leave/; Christine Ro, "Parental Leave: How Rich Countries Compare," *BBC News*, June 14, 2019, https://www.bbc.com/worklife/article/20190615-parental-leave-how-rich-countries-compare; Peter S. Goodman, "The Nordic Model May Be the Best Cushion against Capitalism: Can It Survive Immigration?," *New York Times*, July 11, 2019, https://www.nytimes.com/2019/07/11/business/sweden-economy-immigration.html.

233 **The top income tax bracket:** "Table I.7. Top Statutory Personal Income Tax Rates," Organisation for Economic Co-operation and Development, accessed July 21, 2020, https://stats.oecd.org/Index.aspx?DataSetCode=TABLE_I7.

234 **Nordic governments also generate:** Elke Asen, "Insights into the Tax Systems of Scandinavian Countries," Tax Foundation, February 24, 2020, https://taxfoundation.org/bernie-sanders-scandinavian-countries-taxes/.

234 **The corporate tax rate in each of the Nordic states:** "Corporate Tax Rates Table," https://home.kpmg/xx/en/home/services/tax/tax-tools-and-resources/tax-rates-online/corporate-tax-rates-table.html; Asen, "Corporate Tax Rates around the World, 2019," https://taxfoundation.org/publications/corporate-tax-rates-around-the-world/.

234 **Tax forms arrive in the mail:** Tom Heberlein, "I'm an American Living in Sweden. Here's Why I Came to Embrace the Higher Taxes," *Vox*, April 17, 2017, https://www.vox.com/2016/4/8/11380356/swedish-taxes-love.

234 **Instead of tax deductions:** Tom Heberlein, "I'm an American Living in Sweden," https://www.vox.com/2016/4/8/11380356/swedish-taxes-love; Joel Michael, *Tax Expenditures vs. Direct Expenditures: A Primer* (St. Paul, MN: Minnesota House Research, December 2018), https://www.house.leg.state.mn.us/hrd/pubs/taxvexp.pdf.

235 **The citizens of Nordic countries consistently rank:** Katia Hetter, "During a Pandemic, What Does Being the World's Happiest Country Mean?," CNN, March 20, 2020, https://www.cnn.com/travel/article/worlds-happiest-country-wellness-2020/index.html.

235 **Your average Dane, Swede, Norwegian, Finn, and Icelander:** "Poverty Rate," Organisation for Economic Co-operation and Development, accessed July 21, 2020, https://data.oecd.org/inequality/poverty-rate.htm; Bill Hussar, Jijun Zhang, Sarah Hein, Ke Wang, Ashley Roberts, Jiashan Cui, Mary Smith, Farrah Bullock Mann, Amy Barmar, and Rita Dilig, "International Educational Attainment" (Indicator 4.5), *The Condition of Education 2020* (NCES 2020-144, U.S. Department of Education, Washington, DC: National Center for Education Statistics, 2020), https://nces.ed.gov/pubs2020/2020144.pdf; Sintia Radu, "Countries with the Most Well-Developed Public Health Care Systems," *U.S. News*

and World Report, January 21, 2019, https://www.usnews.com/news/best-countries/slideshows/countries-with-the-most-well-developed-public-health-care-system; *Is the Last Mile the Longest?: Economic Gains from Gender Equality in Nordic Countries* (summary brief, Paris: Organisation for Economic Co-operation and Development, May 2018), https://www.oecd.org/els/emp/last-mile-longest-gender-nordic-countries-brief.pdf; "Income Inequality," Organisation for Economic Co-operation and Development, accessed July 21, 2020, https://data.oecd.org/inequality/income-inequality.htm#indicator-chart; Jacob Funk Kirkegaard, "Which Places Have the Highest Concentration of Billionaires?," Peterson Institute for International Economics, June 29, 2018, https://www.piie.com/research/piie-charts/which-places-have-highest-concentration-billionaires.

235 **Today, the state defends free trade:** Michael Cembalest, "Lost in Space: The Search for Democratic Socialism in the Real World, and How I Ended Up Halfway around the Globe from Where I Began," J.P. Morgan, June 24, 2019, https://privatebank.jpmorgan.com/content/dam/jpm-wm-aem/global/pb/en/insights/eye-on-the-market/lost-in-space-the-search-for-democratic-socialism-in-the-real-world-and-how-i-ended-up-halfway-around-the-globe-from-where-i-began.pdf.

236 **Companies are permitted to hire and fire:** Fareed Zakaria, "Bernie Sanders's Scandinavian Fantasy," *Washington Post*, February 27, 2020, https://www.washingtonpost.com/opinions/bernie-sanderss-scandinavian-fantasy/2020/02/27/ee894d6e-599f-11ea-9b35-def5a027d470_story.html; Matt Bruenig, "Fareed Zakaria Is Completely Ignorant about the Nordics," People's Policy Project, March 2, 2020, httxtps://www.peoplespolicyproject.org/2020/03/02/fareed-zakaria-is-completely-ignorant-about-the-nordics/.

236 **They are the reason Helsinki, Stockholm, and Copenhagen:** Anna Thorsen, "50 Best Startup Cities in 2019," *Valuer* (blog), February 5, 2019, https://www.valuer.ai/blog/top-50-best-startup-cities.

237 **As their societies grow more ethnically and religiously diverse:** Anders Widfeldt, *The Growth of the Radical Right in Nordic Countries: Observations from the Past 20 Years* (Washington, DC: Migration Policy Institute, 2018), https://www.migrationpolicy.org/research/growth-radical-right-nordic-countries.

237 **Across the region, many people are beginning to balk:** Goodman, "The Nordic Model May Be the Best Cushion against Capitalism. Can It Survive Immigration?," https://www.nytimes.com/2019/07/11/business/sweden-economy-immigration.html.

239 **In contrast to the United States:** "The Australian Health System," Australian Government Department of Health, accessed August 14, 2020, https://www.health.gov.au/about-us/the-australian-health-system; "Your Superannuation Basics," Australian Government Australian Taxation Office,

accessed August 14, 2020, https://www.ato.gov.au/General/Other-languages/In-detail/Information-in-other-languages/Your-superannuation-basics/?page=1#How_is_money_paid_into_my_super_; "Best Countries for Education," *U.S. News and World Report*, accessed August 14, 2020, https://www.usnews.com/news/best-countries/best-education; Julia Gillard, interview with Alec Ross and Jack Corrigan, August 10, 2020; Luke Ryan, "Australia Shows Why Raising the Minimum Wage Doesn't Always Fix Poverty," *Quartz*, August 1, 2016, https://qz.com/747814/other-countries-have-sorted-out-their-minimum-wage-woes-why-not-america/; "Australia Has the World's Highest Minimum Wage," *Economist*, July 20, 2019, https://www.economist.com/asia/2019/07/20/australia-has-the-worlds-highest-minimum-wage; "Minimum Wages," Australian Government Fair Work Ombudsman, accessed August 14, 2020, https://www.fairwork.gov.au/how-we-will-help/templates-and-guides/fact-sheets/minimum-workplace-entitlements/minimum-wages; "Currency Converter," Transferwise, accessed August 14, 2020, https://transferwise.com/us/currency-converter/aud-to-usd-rate?amount=1000.

240 **While less than 15 percent of Australian workers:** "Collective Bargaining Coverage," Organisation for Economic Co-operation and Development, accessed August 14, 2020, https://stats.oecd.org/Index.aspx?DataSetCode=CBC.

240 **Even in the United Kingdom:** "Strengthening Our NHS," Conservative Party, accessed August 14, 2020, https://www.conservatives.com/our-priorities/nhs.

242 **In 1968, South Korea had a lower GDP:** "GDP per Capita (Current US$)—Korea, Rep., Ghana, Japan, United States," World Bank, accessed July 27, 2020, https://data.worldbank.org/indicator/NY.GDP.PCAP.CD?end=2019&locations=KR-GH-JP-US&start=1960&view=chart.

242 **The military seized control of the country:** "South Korea—Timeline," *BBC News*, May 1, 2018, https://www.bbc.com/news/world-asia-pacific-15292674.

242 **After watching Japan's rapid growth:** Peter Pae, "South Korea's Chaebol," *Bloomberg*, August 29, 2019, https://www.bloomberg.com/quicktake/republic-samsung.

242 **Samsung, the largest of these conglomerates:** Will Kenton, "Chaebol Structure," Investopedia, September 29, 2019, https://www.investopedia.com/terms/c/chaebol-structure.asp.

243 **In 2018, the K-pop group BTS:** Xander Zellner, "BTS Becomes First K-Pop Act to Hit No. 1 on Billboard Artist 100 Chart," *Billboard*, May 20, 2018, https://www.billboard.com/articles/columns/chart-beat/8458534/bts-first-k-pop-act-hit-no-1-artist-100-chart.

243 **seven of the world's eleven longest-serving:** Dave Lawler, "How the World's Longest-Serving Leaders Keep Power, and Hand It Over," *Axios*, March

21, 2019, https://www.axios.com/worlds-longest-serving-leaders-africa-putin-8046c3c0-3cef-4166-bd1a-46533f1b46a4.html.

244 **The median age is only twenty years old:** Jacob Ausubel, "Populations Skew Older in Some of the Countries Hit Hard by COVID-19," Pew Research Center, April 22, 2020, https://www.pewresearch.org/fact-tank/2020/04/22/populations-skew-older-in-some-of-the-countries-hit-hard-by-covid-19/.

244 **Over the next three decades:** "World Population Prospects 2019," United Nations Department of Economic and Social Affairs, accessed January 3, 2020, https://population.un.org/wpp/Graphs/Probabilistic/POP/TOT/903.

245 **Already, people in the Sahel region:** Ahmadou Aly Mbaye, "Africa's Climate Crisis, Conflict, and Migration Challenges," *Africa in Focus* (blog), Brookings Institution, September 20, 2019, https://www.brookings.edu/blog/africa-in-focus/2019/09/20/africas-climate-crisis-conflict-and-migration-challenges/; Kanta Kumari Rigaud, Alex de Sherbinin, Bryan Jones, Jonas Bergmann, Viviane Clement, Kayly Ober, Jacob Schewe, Susana Adamo, Brent McCusker, Silke Heuser, and Amelia Midgley, *Groundswell: Preparing for Internal Climate Migration* (Washington, DC: World Bank, 2018), https://openknowledge.worldbank.org/handle/10986/29461.

245 **seventy million people displaced:** "More Than 70 Million Displaced World wide, Says UNHCR," *BBC News*, June 19, 2019, https://www.bbc.com/news/world-48682783.

246 **all but fourteen of Africa's fifty-four countries:** Abdi Latif Dahir, "These Are the African Countries Not Signed to China's Belt and Road Project," *Quartz*, September 30, 2019, https://qz.com/africa/1718826/the-african-countries-not-signed-to-chinas-belt-and-road-plan/.

246 **The Belt and Road projects often come with strings attached:** Mark Green, "China's Debt Diplomacy," *Foreign Policy*, April 25, 2019, https://foreignpolicy.com/2019/04/25/chinas-debt-diplomacy/.

246 **In 2017, the government of Guinea-Conakry:** Saliou Samb, "China to Loan Guinea $20 Billion to Secure Aluminum Ore," Reuters, September 6, 2017, https://www.reuters.com/article/us-guinea-mining-china/china-to-loan-guinea-20-billion-to-secure-aluminum-ore-idUSKCN1BH1YT.

246 **China constructed its first overseas naval base:** Max Bearak, "In Strategic Djibouti, a Microcosm of China's Growing Foothold in Africa," *Washington Post*, December 30, 2019, https://www.washingtonpost.com/world/africa/in-strategic-djibouti-a-microcosm-of-chinas-growing-foothold-in-africa/2019/12/29/a6e664ea-beab-11e9-a8b0-7ed8a0d5dc5d_story.html; Mailyn Fidler, "African Union Bugged by China: Cyber Espionage as Evidence of Strategic Shifts," *Net Politics* (blog), Council on Foreign

Relations, March 7, 2018, https://www.cfr.org/blog/african-union-bugged-china-cyber-espionage-evidence-strategic-shifts.

247 **The governments of at least a dozen African countries:** Steven Feldstein, *The Global Expansion of AI Surveillance* (Washington, DC: Carnegie Endowment for International Peace, September 17, 2019), https://carnegieendowment.org/2019/09/17/global-expansion-of-ai-surveillance-pub-79847.

ACKNOWLEDGMENTS

I relied on a group of essential family, friends, and advisers who offered wisdom, judgment, and support throughout the writing process. Foremost among the many are my wife, Felicity, and brother, Steve. Nothing is more important to me than family, and Felicity and Steve protected and sustained our family as the 2020s began to rage.

I must also single out Max Bergami, Robert Bole, Jared Cohen, Ben Scott, Sheel Tyle, and Ari Wallach. Without their friendship and support on things big and small I would not have made it through these last several years in one piece. They are indispensable friends and partners.

I am profoundly grateful to UTA's Pilar Queen and Holt's Serena Jones. Pilar has fought for me and for this book since I introduced the idea of it to her. She is a savvy, passionate advocate for her authors and I am lucky to be among them. Serena was the perfect editor. She gave me the freedom and encouragement I needed to produce a manuscript along with the guidance and expertise to make it a much better, more disciplined work. She brought just the right combination of head and heart to our book. Among Serena's colleagues at Henry

Holt and Company, I am especially grateful to Amy Einhorn, Maggie Richards, Marian Brown, Caitlin O'Shaughnessy, Sarah Crichton, Pat Eisemann, Anita Sheih, Devon Mazzone, and Maia Sacca-Schaeffer.

Jack Corrigan and Jonathan Cox worked with me from what was just the beginning of an idea and turned it into this book. Jack brought passion, persistence, a perpetually positive attitude, and journalistic excellence to the project. He is the latest of Northwestern University's stars of journalism. Jonathan Cox immersed himself in my vision, intent, and content and then understood better than me what it would take to produce a great book. He is a master of understanding a book's architecture and how to construct something with both a foundation and flourish.

I drew on the skills of a great many researchers to help turn ideas into thoroughly researched prose. They include Amy Martyn, Leigh Giangreco, Matthew Spector, and Will Peischel.

I completed this book while serving as a distinguished visiting professor at the business school of the University of Bologna, the world's oldest university, founded by students in the year 1088. The dean of Bologna Business School, Max Bergami, is an inspirational leader and friend. He has built a remarkable institution with a team I am blessed to be a part of, and I offer special thanks to those who have been so helpful to me, including Emanuele Bajo, Giulia Beltramelli, Barbara Biondi, Anna Pia Chiarandini, Michele Ferrari, Riccardo Fini, Roberto Grandi, Ludovia Leone, Andrea Lipparini, Ilaria Manghi, Alfredo Montanari, Gabriele Morandin, Eloisa Palacio, Francesco Porro, Giorgio Prodi, Marcello Russo, Massimo Sideri, Maurizio Sobrero, Augusto Valeriani, and Alessandra Zammit.

Also from my life in Italy I must offer special thanks for the friendship and guidance of Enzo, Domitilla, and Lorenzo Benigni; Riccardo Busi; Marco Checchi; Max Ciociola; Gianluca D'Agostino; Paolo Dalla Mora; Luca della Godenza; Valerio De Molli; Gabriele and Giovanni Domenichini; Michelangelo Fasoli; Carlo Feltrinelli; Karin Fischer; Giuseppe Fontana; Rosanna Gaja; Marco Lombardo; Monica Maggioni; Paola Manes; Maurizio Molinari; Alessandro Monti; Bruno and Matteo Riffeser Monti; Mattia Mor; Giulio Napolitano;

Giovanna Pancheri; Giacomo Pescatore; Andrea Petremoli; Romano Prodi; Massimo Redaelli; Gianni Riotta; Sara Roversi; Germano Scarpa; Filippo Sensi; Jack Sintini; Maurizio Tamagnini; Massimiliano Tarantino; Francesco Ubertini; Armando Varricchio; and Dario Zanotti.

Thank you for the continued partnership from the team representing me at United Talent Agency, including Don Epstein, Kristen Sena, Evan Martino, Michael Steele, Jennifer Peykar, David Buchalter, Charlotte Perman, and Mike D'Andrea.

Thank you to Bobby Duffy and his colleagues at the Policy Institute of King's College London for access to your tremendous research resources and expertise.

I must acknowledge one of the spiritual fathers of the words in this book: Brunello Cucinelli. Brunello has built a multibillion-dollar business while demonstrating that it can be done in service to the broadest possible stakeholder community. I appreciate his friendship and guidance and that of his colleagues and family members, including Camilla and Carolina Cucinelli, Riccardo Stefanelli, Alessio Piastrelli, Francesco Tomassini, and Francesco Bottigliero.

And a final, heartfelt thank-you to the nearly one hundred people who sat for interviews, offered analysis of our complicated world, and reviewed my text for accuracy and completeness. Any credit is shared with them and any shortcomings or errors are my own.

INDEX

ABOUT THE AUTHOR

A *New York Times* bestselling author and a distinguished visiting professor at the University of Bologna Business School, ALEC ROSS is one of the world's leading experts on innovation. He served as Senior Advisor for Innovation to the Secretary of State to help modernize the practice of diplomacy and advance America's foreign policy interests. He began his career as a sixth-grade teacher in Baltimore.